ESAR'S COMIC DICTIONARY

ESAR'S
COMIC
DICTIONARY

By Evan Esar

HARVEST HOUSE, Publishers

NEW YORK

*Published by Harvest House, 363 Broadway, New York 13.
Manufactured in the United States of America.*

FIRST EDITION

FOREWORD

The reader must be forewarned at the outset that this Foreword is not a facetious introduction. It is intended to present concisely the background and nature of this work, and therefore must be on the serious, rather than on the amusing side. It does not undertake, however, to analyze the wit and humor of the contents—the usual invitation to boredom.

This dictionary is the outgrowth of a private collection of original comic definitions and epigrams which comprised a small "comictionary." It was but one step from this to the development of a full-length dictionary containing the best jests from available printed sources. During the preparation of this work, a comprehensive survey was made of the publications in this and related fields. It revealed the existence of many pamphlets and booklets containing humorous sayings and definitions, and several jokebooks which included small sections devoted to this type of material. All these were hardly more than lists, inadequate in size and impractical in use, and characterized by the complete absence of any dictionary plan. In other words, no considered attempt has ever before been made to compile a comic dictionary.

The present publication is thus a pioneer effort. It is the first attempt to organize a large body of the shorter forms of wit and humor for reference as well as for reading purposes. As such, it may be worthwhile to summarize here the fundamental principles which underlie its form and function. These cover its system, or the lexicographical arrangement; its field, or the particular types of wit and humor to which this work is limited; and its selectivity, or the base lines which have determined the choice of contents.

The lexicographical arrangement of this book makes it a function of the contents it covers. It is based on modern dictionary techniques and index methods, and the writer has tried to make it as self-explanatory as the book is self-contained. There are three types of entries: (1) major entries, under which most of the items are listed; (2) minor entries, under which no items are listed but which are cross-referenced to other entries; and (3) sub-entries, which are listed under major and minor entries. The entries themselves are alphabetically arranged and, wherever possible, consist of (a) definitions, ·(b) illustrative sentences, and (c) cross-references. Definitions generally omit the entry word, whereas the illustrative sentences generally contain it. Whenever two or more of these items are listed under a single entry, they are numbered to facilitate cross-reference. Cross-references are always introduced by "See," and each carries a superior figure whenever it is directed to a numbered definition or illustrative sentence.

The special nature of this work has compelled several important departures from standard dictionary practice. Particular prominence has been given to sub-entries and cross-references. Idiomatic and common phrases have been listed under subject rather than spelling. Cross-references have been directed to words rather than ideas. These and other less conspicuous deviations have been instituted to make this work more serviceable as a reference tool.

The field of this work is inherently circumscribed by its dictionary form. Since the contents must be restricted to words, phrases and sentences, all types of wit and humor within these verbal limits have been included. All types beyond single-sentence length, like the anecdotal joke or comic dialogue, have necessarily been excluded. Some particular types, like boners and howlers, whose provinces of pleasantry are narrowly confined, are represented very slightly. Other broader classes, like comic proverbs, whose domain of drollery contains different particular types, are given greater representation. The more general classes of wit and humor, like puns, which have no fixed boundaries but spill over into many particular types, are given considerable representation. This is not the place to list the multitudinous short types of the comic which abound in English for, being as yet unnamed, they require explanation and exemplification. But it may properly be stated that more than a score of such distinct types, as opposed to the vague categories known as epigrams, wisecracks, witticisms, etc., have gone into the compilation of this book.

If both the system and the field of this work follow closely-defined principles, the same cannot be said for the contents. Since each of us is as individual as his sense of humor, it would be altogether unwarranted to establish a personal test for inclusion or exclusion. Thus, it has been found desirable to give this dictionary a fairly low floor of humor and a rather high ceiling, on the comparable theory that language dictionaries include words which are both inside and outside the reader's vocabulary range. Naturally, since one man's pun is another man's groan, every reader is sure to find the floor too low or the ceiling too high. But the items he finds unfunny will evoke laughter in other readers.

A few of the policies which have determined the choice of contents merit a passing explanation. The writer has been guided in matters of taste by the forthright freedom of our literature and stage and not by the prudery of our movies and radio. The timeless subjects of wit and humor are all included here, but ephemeral phases have been excluded whenever dated or likely soon to be. As to language, since most of the contemporary comic is expressed in informal speech, it will be found here in close succession. Slang has been employed with less frequency, and only the type of slang which has become colloquial or familiar.

The wit and humor which constitute the contents of this dictionary are of popular origin and therefore unattributed. They stem, in the main, not from professional humorists or celebrated wits but rather from the world of anonymity, from unknown persons in all walks of life and departments of activity. Many of these items, to be sure, are to be found elsewhere with various credits, for anonymous wit and humor is frequently assigned to famous persons who give them wide quotation. Now more than ever is it a wise crack that knows its own father, for the general practice of apocryphal ascription has been aggravated by the rise of radio. The latter has virtually revolutionized the whole field of wit and humor, chiefly its shorter forms, and has made it doubly difficult to authenticate sources, especially items of contemporary origin. Some of the unattributed items in this work doubtless derive from present-day humorists and men of letters, and for their inadvertent inclusion the writer wishes to apologize in advance.

The indirect significance of this dictionary as a sociological document deserves a word of parenthetical comment. It is axiomatic that the wit and humor of a nation is an unerring index of its spirit and civilization. Because this work is more comprehensive in subject coverage than other books of humor, and because its contents are the briefer, more satiric types of wit, it furnishes an unusually clear mirror of contemporary manners and morals. Excluding its verbalisms and wordplay, which have no sub-surface connotation, this dictionary is a genuine *vox populi*. Here indeed is what the

Foreword

average man thinks about society, about its activities and relations, and about the types of individuals that comprise it.

Some day, when psychology gets around to it, it will probably evolve a "comic quotient," and measure the humor of humans. In the meantime, everyone of us believes he has a sense of humor, no matter how humorless he may be. And so everyone of us will discover in this book his own level of the comic, dismissing what is above and below that level as so much unfunny surplusage. Apart from this aspect of entertaining reading, it seems hardly necessary to point out the different practical uses of this book for different readers. As Shakespeare said of himself, so may it be said of this book: "I am not only witty in myself, but the cause that wit is in other men."

I must here acknowledge my debt to my wife, Patsy, who has assisted me throughout the preparation of this dictionary. In resolving numerous problems, her counsel has led to the adoption of features which have enhanced its utility considerably. And by the elimination of the less satisfactory items which had received my original approval, her judgment has heightened its comic character. In other respects also this work owes much to her co-operation and criticism.

The first edition of a pioneer work of this kind cannot escape imperfections which arise out of its very nature—the imprisonment of vagrant humor in a lexicographical mold. The writer is aware that, in addition to these innate shortcomings, this work suffers from defects of judgment and errors of omission which impair its efficiency and completeness. Some of these he hopes to correct after obtaining an outside slant on the book through the means of cold print and the passage of time, but the solution of other moot points may require the opinions of critical readers. The writer therefore will be grateful to readers who will send any suggestions or additional comic items to him, in care of the publishers, for inclusion in a revised edition.

EVAN ESAR.

A

aardvark.   Aan aanimal that resembles the aanteater.

abbreviation.   A word that's not an abbreviation.
See B.A.; B.C.; M.A.; Mrs.; P.S.; skirt[1].

A B C.   A series of letters which are often written but never sent.
See alphabet.

abdomen.   A bowl-shaped cavity containing the organs of indigestion.
See organ: abdominal organ.

abet.   A term which sometimes means to aid but more often to gamble.

ability.   1. The trouble with college is that the professors don't recognize ability and the students don't possess it.   2. Time was when to get on the stage all a girl had to show was ability.
See lawyer[6]; personality[1].

> **executive ability.**   The art of convincing your wife that you hired your pretty stenographer on account of her experience.

abroad.   See ambassador; monologue[4].

absence.   Absence conquers love, but not when money is the thing that's absent.
See church[2]; fond; present[2, 3].

absinthe.   Absinthe makes the heart grow fonder.

abuse.   What to try when argument fails.
See plaintiff.

accelerator.   Men still die with their boots on, but usually one boot is on the accelerator.

accept.   See propose[1].

accident.   Where presence of mind is good but absence of body is better.
See curve[2]; driver: bad driver[1]; rehearse; traffic: traffic jam; wheel.

> **auto accidents.**   1. They are less often caused by tires that are loose than by drivers that are tight.   2. They occur when the man at the wheel refuses to release his clutch.   3. Car, caress,

3

careless, carless.   4. Most auto accidents occur on Saturday
and Sunday; it's a great life if you don't weekend.

accordion.   An instrument invented by the man who couldn't
decide how big the fish was that got away.
See fold.

account.   Many a wife who cares nothing for her husband, lives
on his account.
See bank: bank account; check: returned check; reducing.

joint checking account.   Where the husband puts the money
in and the wife takes it out.
See commonwealth.

ace.   See reform[3].

ache.   See corn[2].

acquaintance.   A person we know well enough to borrow from
but not well enough to lend to.
See fault: woman's faults; politician[7].

acquaintanceship.   A degree of friendship called slight when its
object is poor or obscure, and intimate when he is rich or famous.
See politician[7].

acquiesce.   Acqui-yes.
See Hollywood[1].

acquit.   In murder trials, whom the juries would acquit they first
make mad.

acrobat.   The only person who can do what everybody else would
like to do: pat himself on the back.

act.   See bachelor[12]; intelligence: human intelligence; kiss: before
& after; manage[1]; play; white[2].

action.   A husband's actions are generally right, but his reasons
seldom are.
See kiss[4].

actor.   1. The only honest hypocrite.   2. A man who tries to be
everything but himself.   3. One who plays when he works and
works when he plays.   4. One who believes that a small role is
better than a long loaf.
See center; ham; movies[5]; performance; pool; publicity[3]; stage.

amateur actor.   A hamateur or dramateur.

ham actor.   The drama critic's meat.

Adam.   The first great benefactor of the human race; he brought
death into the world.

See adamant; apple; evolution[3]; joke[2]; mother-in-law[6]; operation: surgical operation; radio[2]; rib.

Adam & Eve. 1. They were the first bookkeepers; they invented the loose-leaf system. 2. The time of day when Adam was born was a little before Eve. 3. The time of day that Adam liked best was when Eve was falling. 4. Adam & Eve in the Garden of Eden couldn't complain how much better things were in the good old days.

See B.C.; teethe.

adamant. Adam should have been adamant.

add. See secretary: pretty secretary.

adherent. A follower who has not yet gotten all he expects.

adjust. See girdle.

admiration. Our feeling of delight that another person resembles us.

See conceit[3]; dog[3]; fool[1]; virtue[2].

admit. There's only one thing a wife will admit she doesn't know, and that is, why she married her husband.

See courage[3]; old[6]; old-fashioned: old-fashioned girl[2]; self-made: self-made man[11].

adolescence. 1. The age between puberty and adultery. 2. The age when a girl's voice changes from no to yes.

adolescent. A person in his early nicoteens.

adult. 1. One who has stopped growing vertically and has begun to grow horizontally. 2. A person who has stopped growing at both ends and has started growing in the middle.

See adultery[1].

adultery. 1. The adulteration of marriage by an adult. 2. A new sport created by the marriage system.

See adolescence[1].

advance. You often hear of a man in advance of his age, but never of a woman in that condition.

See age: old age[1]; pawnbroker[6]; resist.

advances. Many a girl who receives advances from a young man has a father who has more need for them.

advancement. The disadvantage of being president of a company is that you have no chance for advancement.

advantage. 1. There's one advantage the horse had over the car: it had enough horse sense to be afraid of a train. 2. Some people never take advantage of their friends because they never have any.

See friend[4]; successful: successful people; teethe; telephone[4]; walk: walk on air.

adversity. A condition often caused by perversity.

See friend[5].

advertise. Early to bed and early to rise won't help you much if you don't advertise.

See air: air travel; diplomacy: business diplomacy.

> **advertising.** The art of making people think they've always wanted something they've never even heard of before.
>
> See mint; poetry[3]; road[2]; Samson.

advertisement. Sweet are the uses of advertisement.

advice. 1. The one thing which is more blessed to give than to receive. 2. What you take for a cold. 3. What we ask for when we want approval. 4. What the wise don't need and fools won't take. 5. Something we give by the bushel but take by the grain. 6. A commodity which is given until it hurts—the other person. 7. A commodity sold by your lawyer, given away by your mother-in-law, but impossible to dispose of yourself. 8. A word of advice: don't give it. 9. You can never tell whether advice is good or bad until you no longer need it.

See don't; old[5]; President[1]; vanity; vice; worst: worst people.

> **fatherly advice.** Economy, son, is anything your mother wants to buy.

> **free advice.** It costs nothing unless you act upon it.

> **good advice.** Something old men give young men when they can no longer give them a bad example.

> **parting advice.** Put a little water on the comb.

advise. See advice.

> **advisory capacity.** 1. The only capacity in which some people are willing to serve. 2. All wives learn to drive their husbands' cars, at least in an advisory capacity.

affairs. None but the brave deserve affairs.

See neighbor[2]; operation; priest; responsible[1]; rheumatism.

> **public affairs.** Women's participation in public affairs keeps the affairs public.
>
> See politics[4].

affected. Modern girls may be affected but they don't put on much.

affection. See hug[2].

afford. A man can afford anything he can get; a woman can afford anything she can get a man to get for her.
See children[1]; gamble; self-denial.

afraid. See kindred; modern: modern girl[1].

after. After man came woman, and she has been after him ever since.
See young[2].

after-dinner speaker. See speak: after-dinner speaker, after-dinner speaking; speech: after-dinner speeches.

afterthought. Second thoughts are best: God created man; woman was an afterthought.

against. Everything you say to a woman will be used against you. See husband[2].

age. 1. Women age quicker than men but less often. 2. Some people have no respect for age unless it's bottled. 3. The best way to tell a woman's age—is a mistake. 4. A man's age commands veneration; a woman's demands tact. 5. The seven ages of woman are: her own and six guesses. 6. The three ages of man are underage, overage, and average. 7. The seven ages of woman are: infancy, childhood, adolescence, junior miss, young woman, young woman, and young woman. 8. Never trust a woman who tells you her real age; she's liable to tell you the truth about anything.
See cake: birthday cake[1]; diplomat[3]; exaggerate[1]; overlook; respectable; shy; truth: truthful woman; women[1]; wood; year: light-years.

middle age. 1. The time in life when your idea of getting ahead is staying even. 2. The time in life when a man begins to lose his hair, his teeth, and his illusions. 3. When you begin to exchange your emotions for symptoms. 4. The period in a man's life when he'd rather not have a good time than have to get over it. 5. About ten years older than you are. 6. The period in life when you'll do anything to feel better, except give up what's hurting you. 7. Women in the Middle Ages used cosmetics; women in the middle ages still use them.
See everything.

old age. 1. The period in life when we go backwards as we advance. 2. Old age brings experience, and some kinds of experience bring old age. **3. The years** pass silently, but old age creaks up on a person.

See year: formative years.

agnostic. 1. One who says he knows nothing about God and, when you agree with him, becomes angry. 2. A learned man who doesn't pretend to know what ignorant men are sure of.

agree. 1. Any man who agrees with his wife can have his way. 2. We like a man that comes right out and says what he thinks, when he agrees with us. 3. There's one point a husband and wife always agree upon: he thinks nothing is too good for her, and so does she.

See argumentative; flatter[3]; harmony: domestic harmony[2]; history[4, 7]; sight: strange sight; unnecessary; view.

agreeable person. One who agrees with you.

agreement. See compact.

> **gentleman's agreement.** One which no gentleman would put in writing.

agriculture. What half the world is engaged in; that's how the other half lives.

agriculturist. Farmers make money on the farm and spend it in town; agriculturists make money in town and spend it on the farm.

ahead. The best way to get ahead is to have one.

See calendar[3]; dandruff; date[3]; general; get: get even; political: political leader; strip-tease: strip-tease dancer; **year:** lean years.

ahem. The seamstress' exclamation.

ailment. Don't speak of your private ailment in public; she might hear you.

aim. See fanatic[2]; name: maiden name.

air. 1. Many a person on the air should get the air. 2. When a woman goes up in the air, she usually lands on her husband. 3. The reason the air is better in summer is because more radio programs are off it.

See bold; breathe; ego: inflated ego; radio[3]; Senate; trifle; wind[1].

> **air-condition.** Science is resourceful: it couldn't open the Pullman windows, so it air-conditioned the trains.
>
> See pregnant: pregnant woman; shop: closed shop.

air program. Too much of it consists of the hot variety.

air raid. Helter-skelter to a shelter.

See raid; siren.

air service. Many a man goes into it because he is no earthly good.

air travel. Its steady increase will soon force the advertisers to lay their billboards flat on the ground.

castles in the air. 1. The only buildings that require no upkeep. 2. They're all right if you don't try to move into them. 3. People who build castles in the air need no architect.

hot air. 1. The most common method of heating used in Washington. 2. Many an apartment is heated by hot air—the landlord's.

See air: air program; Nazi; borrowing[1]; janitor[2]; straw vote.

airplane. If the airplane is ever made foolproof, it will be the only thing that is.

See jump[1].

airport. See aviation[3].

aisle. See elevator: elevator man.

alarm clock. 1. A convenient device if you like that sort of ting. 2. The trouble with alarm clocks is that they go off while you're asleep.

See yeast.

album. See book.

family album. 1. It takes a family album to convince some people that the truth is a terrible thing. 2. The pictures in the family album are all right, but they forgot to print the jokes under them. 3. The man who criticizes modern women's wear should look through the old family album.

photograph album. The strange views people take of things.

alcohol. 1. The stuff that makes the world go round. 2. A liquid for preserving almost everything but secrets.

See dignity; prohibition: Prohibition Era[1]; veneer.

denatured alcohol. Ill-natured alcohol.

alibi. The legal proof that a person wasn't where he was, and therefore couldn't do what he did.

See autobiography[1]; self-made: self-made man[6]; student.

alike. All women are alike except some are more alike than others.

See disrespect; glad; stagger; think[4].

alimentary canal. A receiving set.

alimony. 1. Taxation without representation. 2. A man's cash surrender value. 3. The fine levied on a man guilty of matrimony. 4. A system by which one pays for the mistake of two. 5. The compensation of love. 6. The high cost of loving. 7. The high cost of leaving. 8. A contraction of "all his money." 9. Alimony is like buying oats for a dead horse. 10. Alimony proves that two can live more cheaply as one. 11. Wives get most of the divorces and all of the alimony.
See divorce[5]; proof.

alive. There's no use worrying about life because you'll never get out of it alive.
See convalescent; leave[4]; money[10].

all. Some give all to love and some give love to all.

alligator. The skin that's fashionable for ladies' wear, especially among lady alligators.

allowance. See bail; bankrupt; father: average father; marriage: happy marriage[3].

alluring. When an alluring girl walks, her whole figure makes eyes at you.

alms. A word that has no singular because a solitary act of charity doesn't deserve the name.
See beggar[1].

alone. 1. The reason why men leave home is that they don't like to stay there alone. 2. Never miss an opportunity to make others happy, even if you have to leave them alone to do it.
See Americanize; fire: forest fire; loan; smoke[1]; snore[2].

aloud. In polite society whispering is not aloud.

alphabet. It's as easy as A B C.
See B.A.[2]; soup: alphabet soup.

alphabet of love. The alphabet of love consists of avowals and consents.

altar. See lead; path: bridle path.

alteration. When a self-made man marries, his wife usually makes a lot of alterations.

altruism. 1. The art of doing unselfish things for selfish reasons. 2. The burning desire to help suffering humanity, except those unfortunates we happen to know.

amateur. One who used to get the hook; now he gets the hook-up.
See actor: amateur actor; athlete: professional athlete; club: glee club; gardener; kiss[15].

ambassador. 1. An honest man sent abroad to lie
try. 2. A politician who is given a job abroad in
him out of the country.
See newspaperman.

ambiguity. Telling the truth when you don't mean to.

ambition. 1. The last refuge of a failure. 2. An ir
sation caused by inflammation of the wishbone.
See fire[2]; proud.

ambulance. One reason why so many pedestrians do
where they're going is that they're in an ambulance.
See way: right of way.

amend. If the law of supply and demand is responsible for
ing prices, it ought to be amended.

amendment. A patch on the seat of government.
See constitution: woman's constitution; husband: average
band.

America. 1. The land that's burdened with excess prophe
2. The country where they lock up juries and let the defendai
out. 3. The land of opportunity, which may account for s
much knocking. 4. I.O.U.S.A. 5. The trouble with America
is that it wants to raise nothing but cotton and wear nothing
but silk.
See billboard[1]; carnation; chewing gum[2]; Columbus[1, 2]; communism; Europe; marriage: before & after[3]; Pilgrims; polygamy[3]; prohibition: Prohibition Era[2]; see[1]; Senate; slogan.

history of America. The replacement of the red Indian by
red tape.

American. 1. A man with both feet on the ground and both
hands in the air. 2. One who doesn't know the words to the
Star-Spangled Banner. 3. A person who yells for the government to balance the budget and borrows five dollars till payday.
4. Americans are of two kinds: those who think they are as good
as anybody else, and those who think they are better.
See Bostonian; bullfight; chewing gum[1]; pedestrian[3]; slogan;
statistics: traffic statistics.

all-American. All good Americans should know the names of
good all-Americans.
See football: football fan.

American melting pot. It usually makes it hot for the immigrant.

average American. A person who works himself to death so he can live.

loyal American. One who gets mad when an alien criticizes the United States which he criticizes.

One-hundred-percent American. 1. A person who puts that valuation on himself. 2. Ninety-nine-percent hypocrite.

typical American. See harp².

Americanize. When you become used to never being alone, you may consider yourself Americanized.

amiss. You can't marry amiss if you marry a widow.

ammonia. See pneumonia.

amount. Generally a small amount of anything does not amount to anything.

See man: stingy man; rationing³.

anarchy. Where everyone is so free that no one can do as he would like to do.

ancestor. 1. The man who boasts only of his ancestors belongs to a family better dead than alive. 2. A person shouldn't be blamed for his ancestors; they should be blamed for him.

See back: back up; blood¹; choose¹; road: roadhouse; snob²; thrift.

ancestry. See mule².

anesthetic. See liquor: liquor tax.

angel. 1. A man who backs stars. 2. In heaven an angel is nobody in particular. 3. Nowadays you must go to heaven to meet an angel. 4. An angel with wings is not so desirable as an angel with arms. 5. A woman who is always up in the air and harping on something is not necessarily an angel.

See disguise; geometry²; low; sermon²; widower.

anger. It's never without a reason, but seldom with a good one. See lawyer².

angry. 1. It takes two people to make one person angry. 2. When angry, count ten; when very angry, swear. 3. Two things a person should never be angry at: what he can help, and what he can't.

See mad.

animal. Animals are lower than man in the scale of evolution because they don't keep on grabbing more when they have enough.

See blush; brute; caucus; censor⁵; descend¹,³; Elks²; furs²,⁴;

hash[1]; inferior; mammal; man[2, 4, 5, 8]; mugwump; ruminant; spring[7]; taxidermist[2]; vitamin; widow[1]; woman[1]; zoo, zoological garden.

See also aardvark; cat; chicken; cow; dog; duck; elephant; etc.

anniversary. See birthday.

silver wedding anniversary. The day on which the couple celebrates that twenty-five years of married life are over.

annoy. A thing of duty will annoy forever.

See house[4]; noise[1]; question[3].

anonymous. The most famous of all writers.

answer. 1. No answer is also an answer. 2. Man was made before woman to give him time to think of an answer to her first question.

See coed[4]; indiscreet; maid: old maid[5]; salesman[4]; stop[1]; yes[1].

ant. 1. A small insect that, though always at work, still finds time to go to picnics.

antique. 1. Something superfluous that nobody would want if everybody had it. 2. Something so old that it is worth more than it really is. 3. Something whose price increases as its value decreases.

See furniture: instalment furniture; junk; virtue: old virtues; wood.

romantic antiques. Women like romantic antiques, except those who annoy them with marriage proposals.

anybody. See everybody.

apart. You can tell some twins apart even when they're not apart. See different; stagger.

apartment. 1. A place too small to throw anything in except a party. 2. A place where you start to turn off the radio and find you've been listening to the neighbor's.

See air: hot air[2]; grow.

modern apartment. 1. People who live in one have little room to complain. 2. If the modern apartment gets any smaller, a man will have to marry a wifette to live in it.

apologize. The only time a man has the last word with a woman is when he apologizes.

apology. A man expects an apology if you're in the wrong; a woman expects one if you're in the right.

apparel. The apparel of the woman oft proclaims the man.

appeal. A woman deserted by one man has no remedy but to appeal to twelve.

See sex[1]; worst.

appearance. A great factor in earning money, and vice versa.

See disappearance; keeper; life[6]; ocean[2].

appendix. 1. The only one safe from a doctor is the one in a book. 2. Something which gives you information or inflammation. 3. Many a girl who doesn't get taken out has an appendix that does. 4. The appendix may be useless to man, but think what it has done for the medical profession.

See corn[2]; tonsils.

appetite. 1. The rich suffer from want of appetite, the poor from excess of appetite. 2. When a man loses his appetite temporarily, he's in love; when he loses it permanently, he's married. 3. A wife who likes to cook can forgive her husband almost anything but a poor appetite. 4. Many a man kisses his wife because he didn't have an appetite anyhow.

See boy[1]; pride[2].

appetizer. An appeteaser.

applaud. The people who applaud at the movies probably talk back to their radios.

See encore[2].

applause. 1. The echo of a platitude. 2. At the beginning of a speech, applause expresses faith; in the middle, hope; at the end, charity.

See turn[1].

apple. Adam's experience shows that it's not wise to eat an apple; it should be drunk as cider.

See collector: bill collector[2]; onion[3]; pie: political pie; source[1]; worm[2].

appointment. It's never too late for a woman to keep an appointment.

See receiver.

appreciate. See critic[3]; slim: slim girl; play: modern play; wealth: wealthy people.

approach. See mosquito[5]; pedestrian[16].

approval. See advice[3]; coat: sealskin coat.

archeology. The science that proves you can't keep a good man down.

architect. One who drafts a plan of your house and plans a draft of your money.

See air : castles in the air[3] ; breakfast : breakfast nook ; plan[2].

architect's error. A breakfast nook.

argue. 1. It's not necessary to understand things in order to argue about them. 2. When you argue with a fool, be sure he isn't similarly engaged.

See hungry ; kiss[14] ; neighbor : quarreling neighbors.

argument. 1. It takes one to make an argument, if she's your wife. 2. Many an argument is sound—and only sound. 3. A wife may not be a magician, but she can turn anything into an argument.

See abuse ; bigot ; club[2] ; concur ; plaintiff ; sound.

argumentative. Some people are so argumentative, they won't even eat food that agrees with them.

arithmetic. See cake : birthday cake[2].

ark. See Noah.

arm. See angel[4] ; disarmament ; hold[1] ; marriage : before & after[6] ; tourist[2] ; woman[12].

army. See soldier[1] ; wrestler.

arrest. See Sabbath.

arrive. In fashionable society, nobody arrives until everybody else has.

See thought : second thoughts.

arson. A sure-fire proposition.

art. 1. Art, like morality, consists in drawing the line somewhere. 2. There are only two great blessings in life : the love of art and the art of love. 3. There are moments when art attains almost to the dignity of manual labor.

See artist ; auctioneer[1] ; perfume[2].

work of art. What the public takes no interest in until it is attacked as obscene.

artery. See Broadway[1] ; love[16].

artist. Art is long, but most artists are short.

See drawers[1].

bad artist. One who can't even draw flies.

tonsorial artist. 1. The only man to whom other men always take their hats off. 2. One who usually earns more with his brush than any other artist.

asbestos. See hell[1].

ashamed. The more things a man is ashamed of, the more respectable he is.

See writer: woman writer.

ashes. See athlete; flame: old flame.

ash tray. Something to put tobacco ashes in when the room hasn't got a fine table top or rug.

ask. Many men would do less lying if their wives didn't ask so many questions.

See question[3]; yes[1].

asleep. See alarm clock[2]; bunk; business[2]; famous; sleep.

asparagus. Sparrow grass.

aspirin. Love is like getting drunk, marriage is the hangover, and divorce is the aspirin tablet.

See hangover[4].

ass. In Biblical days it was considered a miracle for an ass to speak; now it would be a miracle if one kept quiet.

See masses; stock: stock market[2].

assault. Every woman likes to be taken with a grain of assault.

assess. A female donkey.

asset. Woman's chief asset is man's imagination.

See bill: twenty-dollar bill; caution; lawyer[6].

asterisks. 1. The little dots the author sprinkles through the novel where the reader is expected to use his own imagination. 2. In the modern novel, asterisks signify to proceed at your own risk.

astray. The advantage of the emotions is that they lead us astray.

asunder. Whom God hath joined together, let no man put asunder; God will take care of that.

atheism. The chief fault with atheism is that it has no future.

atheist. 1. A man who has no invisible means of support. 2. One who thanks God that there is no God.

athlete. A dignified bunch of muscles, unable to split wood or sift the ashes.

See coach.

> **female athletes.** They really came in with the twentieth century; before that time they were all bustle-bound.

> **professional athlete.** The difference between an amateur and a professional athlete is that the latter is paid by check.

attempt. See dial; familiarity[2]; sandwich.

attendance. In burlesque, if the girls' clothes don't drop off, the attendance does.

See club: night club[3].

attention. If a girl who likes a man's attentions doesn't marry him, it's because she likes a man's attentions.

See clutch; disgrace; flirtation; inattention.

attract. What attracts the senses attracts the censors.

See evil.

attractive. See women[4].

auction. You can't pick up anything at an auction unless it has first been knocked down.

auctioneer. 1. The only person who should admire all schools of art. 2. One who always looks forbidding when conducting sales.

See bid.

audience. Leave your audience before they leave you.

See neurotic; hypocrite; indulge; performance.

author. What he doesn't know fills a book.

authority. The chief trouble with this country seems to be too many authorities and not enough authority.

See citizen: law-abiding citizen; umpire[2].

auto. See automobile; car.

autobiography. 1. It's usually an alibiography. 2. The written story of motor cars.

automobile. When automobiles came in, pedestrians went under.

See birth: birth rate; car; death: natural death; recreation; sense: horse sense[5, 7].

   automobile industry. The industry that has the greatest turn-over.

autopsy. It's better to change your attitude and pay some heart balm than be exhumed later for an autopsy.

avenue. The landlord expects more rent where the street is called an avenue.

average. The trouble with the average man is that he seldom increases his average.

   average man. 1. One who thinks he isn't. 2. One who thinks he's above the average. 3. The man who gets mad when you refer to him as the average man. 4. The average man must be a ghost; everybody talks about him but nobody has ever seen him.   5. The average man must be the lowest form of humanity because everybody thinks he's above him.

See braggart.

aviation.   1. People who take up aviation usually start at the bottom.   2. With constant progress in aviation, sooner or later we ought to get to the man higher up.   3. Aviation is not yet safe; you still have the taxi ride from the city to the airport.

See explorer: modern explorer; plane.

aviation industry.   1. It's always on the up and up.   2. Where there will always be plenty of room at the top.

aviator.   1. The most serious aviators are flighty.   2. Aviators can do anything birds can, except sit comfortably on a barbed-wire fence.

avoid.   A man is known by the company he avoids.

awake.   See content; insomnia; lie[7]; maid; story: bedtime story; troublesome.

award.   A client always wonders which one of them was hit by the car when his lawyer deducts his fee from the court's award.

awning.   No matter how high it may be suspended, it's only a shade above the street.

B

B.A.   1. The best way to get it in college is through the support of a P.A.   2. A degree which means that the holder has mastered the first two letters of the alphabet.

baby.   1. An alimentary canal with a loud voice at one end and no responsibility at the other.   2. A native of all countries who speaks the language of none.   3. An inhabitant of Lapland. 4. The most extensive employer of female labor.   5. The morning caller, the noonday crawler, the midnight brawler.   6. A baby that's a healthy pink may also be a loud yeller.

See big; cautious: cautious man; debt: government debt; floor: dance floor[2]; floorwalker; grandmother[1]; male[2]; old: old man; sleep[4, 5]; speech[1]; stork[4]; success: howling success; triangle[2]; wake: wake up[2].

bachelor. 1. A man who's been lucky at love. 2. A man who lost the opportunity of making some woman miserable. 3. The man who knew when to stop. 4. A man who believes that one can live as cheaply as two. 5. A man who looks but does not leap. 6. A man who never makes the same mistake once. 7. A man with enough confidence in his judgment of women to act upon it. 8. A permanent public temptation. 9. A souvenir of some woman who found a better one at the last minute. 10. One who enjoys the chase but does not eat the game. 11. A man who has no children to speak of. 12. A man who thinks before he acts, and then doesn't act. 13. The only man who has never lied to his wife. 14. A selfish, callous, undeserving man who has cheated some worthy woman out of a divorce. 15. Not all men are fools; some are bachelors. 16. A bachelor rarely marries because, when it comes to taking a wife, he doesn't know whose wife to take. 17. Bachelors know more about women than married men do; that's why they're bachelors.

See chance; disappoint[1]; dreams[3]; floor: dance floor[2]; free-thinker; lady: lady in waiting; marry: married man[2]; mind: half a mind; necking[2]; perfect: perfect people; ring[3]; shirt[2]; sign.

confirmed bachelor. One who has been confirmed by a woman.

eligible bachelor. A man of obstinacy entirely surrounded by suspicion.

back. 1. Everybody hates people who talk behind your back, especially at the movies. 2. The old-fashioned wife used to ask her husband to button up her back; the modern wife asks him to powder it.

See bone[1]; bury; flatterer; gardening[2]; horse[3]; mosquito[3]; movement; noise[2]; pessimist[3]; politician[10]; rag.

back up. The person who boasts about his ancestors believes in going forward by backing up.

halfback. A halfback in football is often away back in his college studies.

See requirement.

pat on the back. It develops character if administered often enough, young enough, and low enough.

See acrobat; body; chin[1]; committee: committee-of-five.

backbone. 1. Backbone won't get you anywhere if the knob at the top is made of the same material. 2. Nowadays a woman shows a lot of backbone in her choice of evening gowns.

See bone[2]; chiropractor: successful chiropractor; **column:** spinal column; courage[5]; display; petition.

backside. Southern exposure.

backslapping. It usually terminates in backsliding.

backwards. See life[3]; mule[8].

bacon. See father[1].

bad. 1. Believe everything you hear about the world; nothing is too impossibly bad. 2. To say the good die young is a standing invitation for the small boy to be bad.

See commandment; coquette; dare; egg[1]; good[4]; husband[6]; lawyer: good lawyer[2]; model: artist's model[2]; optimist[9]; pessimist[10]; prose; tie: Christmas ties[2]; trouble[6].

bag. See hotel: hotel guest; kangaroo[3]; reformer[7].

bail. Never give your son all the allowance you can afford; keep back some to bail him out.

bait. 1. Maybe the fish goes home and lies about the size of the bait he stole. 2. At the beach, a girl usually wears a baiting suit.

See celibate; fisherman: fisherman's motto.

bake. Baking a smaller loaf enables the baker to make a larger roll.

half-baked. Those who think they are hard-boiled may only be half-baked.

baker. A man who kneads much and sells everything he kneads himself.

balance. See shop: shopping[2].

balance the budget. See budget: balance the budget.

bald. The advantage of being bald is that, when you expect callers, all you have to do is to straighten your necktie.

See expose; heir; neatness.

bald head. It's like heaven; there is no dying or parting there. See hat[1]; respectability.

bald-headed man. 1. One who has less hair to comb but more face to wash. 2. If parting is such sweet sorrow, a bald man should be very happy.

baldness. The penalty of aspiring to be a highbrow.

ball. See caddie[2]; spring[2].

ban. See rationing[1].

banana. 1. Its skin is a reminder that fall is near. 2. Remember the banana: when it leaves the bunch, it gets skinned.

band. If it's loud and lively, it's probably in full swing.
See cigar[2].

banjo. See musical instrument.

banjo player. A musician who has easy pickings.

bank. 1. An institution where you can borrow money if you can present sufficient evidence to show that you don't need it. 2. A place where they lend you an umbrella in fair weather and ask for it back again when it begins to rain. 3. An institution with so many vice-presidents that, when there's a director's meeting, it looks like a run on the bank. 4. Only the people who work in a bank realize there's no money in it. 5. If you owe a bank enough money, you own it.
See politics[14]; vice-president[2].

bank account. 1. The man without a bank account is of no account. 2. Not every bank account is of much account.

bank balance. The true balance of power.

bankbook. The volume of business.
See checkbook.

bankroll. The bigger the bankroll, the tighter the rubber band.
See money: stage money.

bankrupt. If you make too many allowances for people, you'll soon find yourself bankrupt.
See competition[1]; extravagant: extravagant girl.

banquet. See roast.

bar. 1. Drinking makes strange bar fellows. 2. The man who enters a bar very optimistically often comes out very misty optically.
See tavern; zoo.

behind the bars. Teetotalers believe that drinkers should be behind the bars.
See zebra.

barber. 1. A brilliant conversationalist who occasionally shaves and cuts hair. 2. The town cut-up. 3. Fortunately, barbers, unlike authors, are not paid by the word. 4. When one barber cuts another barber's hair, which one does the talking?
See artist: tonsorial artist; hair: hair cutter; trim.

barber shop. 1. A clip joint. 2. Two heads are better than one—in a barber shop.

See scar.

barber's instruments. They can cut almost everything but conversation.

barber trade. Its business is to see that hair which needs cutting badly gets cutting badly.

bare. See girl[4]; grin; model; tire: old tire.

bareback. Nudists on horses always ride bareback.

bargain. 1. A transaction in which each party thinks he has cheated the other. 2. It takes two to make a bargain, but only one to get stuck. 3. It takes two to make a bargain, but only one gets it. 4. Every woman likes a bargain but dislikes being told she is wearing one.

bargain sale. 1. A chance for a woman to ruin one dress while buying another. 2. Something that often ends up in a counterrevolution. 3. Men fight for what they want, and women attend bargain sales.

See price[2].

bark. Barking dogs never bite—while barking.

See matrimony: matrimonial bark; tree: dogwood tree.

barrel. See cider; elephant[2].

bartender. A fizzical culturist.

baseball. A game in which the young man who bravely strikes out for himself receives no praise for it.

See bawl; homer[1]; strike[3]; ticket; umpire[1].

baseball season. In the summer the baseball season is half gone, and grandmothers are all gone.

bath. From listening to some prudes you'd think they blindfold themselves before taking a bath.

See music: true musician; opportunist[2]; scald; telephone[1].

bathing. A thing of beauty is a joy—until it goes in bathing.

bathing beauty. 1. A girl worth wading for. 2. One who believes in keeping her powder dry. 3. Most men like bathing beauties even though they've never bathed any.

bathing beauty contest. The only jury all men are glad to serve on.

bathing suit. See suit: bathing suit.

battle. See bet[2]; engagement[2]; general.

bawl. There's always too much bawl in baseball.

See nursery[2].

B.C. Adam and Eve lived thousands of years B.C.—before clothing.

beach. A place where people lie upon the sand—about how rich they are in town.

See bait[2]; pebble.

bean. The one that provides the largest number of calories is usually dad's.

bear. If you go hunting bear, you'll catch cold.

See forebears; steer; stock: stock market[2].

bearable. Life is not bearable with a woman until it is unbearable without her.

beard. It doesn't grow on a woman's chin because her tongue would never let her chin be motionless long enough to shave it.

beast. Any girl can handle the beast in a man if she's cagey enough.

See brute; jackass.

beat. If you want noise or silence, the drum is an instrument you can't beat.

See egg[1]; game: childish game; heart[1]; hospital[1]; investor.

beau. The less clothes, the more beaus.

beautiful. See drink[1]; heiress; three; unreasonable; Venus[1].

beautiful girl. See bigamist[4].

beautiful woman. Her face is her fortune, and it runs into a handsome figure.

See whisper[2].

beauty. 1. It's only a skin game. 2. The one thing a woman may lose and never know it's gone. 3. The best substitute for brains. 4. A thing of beauty keeps you broke forever.

See bathing; Christian: Christian endeavor; knee[1]; potent; ride: joy ride; virtue[3].

beauty parlor. 1. It makes a woman look pretty over the weak-end. 2. Women who can pass a beauty test find it hard to pass a beauty parlor.

beaver. See catskin.

bed. No civilized person ever goes to bed the same day he gets up.

See early[1]; floor[1]; generation: rising generation[2]; marriage: common law marriage; nurse[2]; party: dull party; physic; politician[11]; wear[1].

four-poster bed. It seems like a lot of bunk.

bee. Farmers who raise bees have probably been stung by everything else they raised.

See busy[3]; humbug.

beef. See deer.

beer. The difference between a glass of beer and a glass of water is ten cents.

See never; prohibitionist[2]; water[2].

before. See headache[1]; mirror[3]; tell[3]; young[2].

beg. See community chest; panhandler.

beggar. 1. When beggars cease to trouble you for alms, it is high time to improve your clothes. 2. If a wife wants to see a man eat a meal without finding fault with her cooking, she should feed a beggar.

See panhandler.

begin. See love[2, 3]; sight; start.

beginning. In drinking, a good beginning is half the bottle.

See illness; speech: good speech[2].

begrudge. Many a wife wakes up her husband when he talks in his sleep; she even begrudges him those few words.

behavior. See duty[1]; marriage[17].

behind. See general; watch; year: lean years.

believe. 1. Your friends don't believe you make as much as you say you do, and the government doesn't believe you make as little. 2. Believe half of what you see, and nothing of what you hear. 3. The man who believes all he says doesn't always say all he believes. 4. We know that most of us still believe in God, but we don't know if God still believes in most of us.

See conviction[1]; cynic[6]; faith[1, 4]; flattery[2]; hear[1]; heredity[2]; heresy; movies[3]; punishment: capital punishment[4]; repeat[1]; see[2].

bell. Many a husband in a family fight is saved by the bell.

See birth: births, marriages, deaths[2].

bellboy. 1. When people go to summer hotels for a change and rest, the bellboys get the change and the hotels get the rest. 2. In a hotel, you ring for the bellboy; in the water a bell buoy rings for you.

belt. See pessimist[2]; prude[2].

benefit. See doubt[2]; marriage[4]; press: press agent[1]; young[1].

bent. More people get crooked from trying to avoid hard work than become bent from too much of it.

See stigma; straight[2].

berry. You can get along at Christmas time without the holly but you must have the berries.

berth. Marriages are made in heaven, and berths are made in Pullman cars.

best. 1. Get the best of liquor or it will get the best of you. 2. To love and win is the best thing; to love and lose, the next best.

See girl: best girl; manufacturer; mind: best mind; optimist[4]; religion[4]; smell[1]; song: old songs; thought: second thoughts; worst: worst people.

best man. See bridegroom[4].

best people. The ones your wife knew before she married you.

See help; installment: installment collector[1].

best seller. See Bible[2]; experience[5].

bet. 1. It can be lost in more ways than won. 2. The race is not always to the swift nor the battle to the strong, but that's the way to bet. 3. No horse can go as fast as the money you bet on him. 4. It's not wrong to bet on the horses—that is, on the right horses.

See abet; sense: horse sense[1, 6].

betray. Some women never betray a confidence without first imposing the strictest secrecy.

betrothal. Throwing one's hat in the wedding ring.

better. What every young girl should know.

See American[4]; bitter; coquette; divorce; family: family tree[1]; friend[7]; genealogy; good[2]; individualism; love[26]; marry[2]; more: more or less; oleomargarine; pessimist[10]; respect; water: water wagon; worse[2].

better half. See half: better half.

betting. See bet.

beware. When a woman repulses, beware; when a woman beckons, bewarer.

Bible. 1. The Bible begins with a man and a woman in a garden and it ends with Revelations. 2. The Bible continues to be a best-seller even though no effort is made to suppress it. 3. The Bible contains the Book of Numbers but it's not the telephone directory. 4. The Bible is no laughing matter; indeed, there isn't a single laugh in it.

See enemy[6]; monkey[2].

bicycle. See tantrum.

bid. Auctioneers want you to come when you're bid, and bid when you've come.

See auctioneer[2].

bier. John Barleycorn's last order will be a bier.

big. No big men have ever been born in small towns—only little babies.

See bus[1]; fish[3]; forgive[1]; heart: big heart; hunter: big game hunter[2]; man: small man; skirts: mother's skirts; success[2]; wish.

big shot. As a rule, merely a big bore.

bigamist. 1. A man who doesn't know when he's got enough. 2. One who makes the same mistake twice. 3. A man may have one wife too many and still not be a bigamist. 4. The man who is married to a beautiful girl and a good cook is probably a bigamist.

See serve[1].

bigamy. 1. A form of insanity in which a man insists on paying three board bills instead of two. 2. Bigamy may be wonderful, but think of two mothers-in-law.

See monogamy[2]; monotony.

bigot. The person who doesn't agree with you in a religious argument.

See prohibitionist[1].

bilious. Bills make husbands bilious.

bill. 1. Some people have trouble meeting their bills but most people have trouble dodging them. 2. When there's a bill, we're away. 3. There's only one thing harder than paying bills, and that's collecting them. 4. In the Houses of Congress bills must be introduced, but many of the bills that come to the houses of congressmen are old acquaintances.

See bilious; Christmas[7], Christmas gift[2]; Congress[8]; customer; dear; exercise: feminine exercise; honeymoon[3]; insane; lawyer[9]; mosquito[6]; obstetrician; paperweight; repair; settler; stork[1]; summer[3].

twenty-dollar bill. A valuable asset—if it's not due.

billboard. 1. Beyond the Alps lies Italy, and behind the billboards lies America. 2. The roughest roads have the fewest billboards. 3. If all the billboards in the United States were placed end to end, they would not reach as far as they do now. See air: air travel.

billiards. To play billiards well is the sign of a misspent youth.

binding. Don't look a gift book in the binding.

biography. 1. The portrait of a person, usually colored. 2. Biographies are usually written when people are dead because they are so unlike them when they were alive.

bird. 1. Protect the birds: the dove brings peace and the stork brings tax exemptions. 2. A bird in the hand is worth two in the bush, but the bird thinks otherwise.
See aviator[2]; divers; fat: fat woman[2]; feather; flying; manners: table manners[1]; stork[1]; wing[1]; worm[1].

early bird. 1. The early bird has to get his own breakfast. 2. The early bird catches the worm, but what can you do with a worm nowadays? 3. No one should adopt the early bird policy without first finding out whether he classes as a bird or a worm.
See catch[2]; welcome[2].

birth. 1. A vital statistic. 2. Escape from solitary confinement. 3. The only commencement day that takes place in a hospital.

birth control. 1. The aim of birth control is to make our population less dense. 2. What a pity it is that birth control can't be made retroactive. 3. It isn't enough for birth control to safeguard posterity; it must also provide a posterity to safeguard.

birth rate. Thanks to our high birth rate, people are being born faster than the automobile can kill them.

births, marriages, deaths. 1. Hatched, Matched, Snatched. 2. Yells, Bells, Knells.

birthday. 1. When a man has a birthday he takes a day off; but when a woman has a birthday she takes a year off. 2. Among women, every birthday after the twentieth is the plentieth.
See diplomat[3]; husband: tactful husband; remind[2].

father's birthday. The only really quiet affair in most homes.

bit. See horse[2].

bite. If a man bites a dog, he's probably eating a frankfurter.
See bark; chow; dog[3]; editor: newspaper editor; fingernails[2]; mosquito[4]; neck[3]; news[2, 3]; publicity[3]; resort: ideal summer resort; revenge[1].

bitter. Life makes some people bitter and others better.
See defeat; wife[1].

blabbermouth. The woman who listens only when she herself talks.

black. It's dangerous to marry a woman who looks good in black.
See blackberry; bookkeeper[1]; experience: school of experience[2]; optimist[1]; servant[2]; white[1].

blackberry. A fruit which is purple when black and red when green.

blackmail. It's the white male that resorts to blackmail.

blackout. Where you can't see your face in front of your hand.

bladder. A dog's idea of heaven is a mile of trees and a full bladder.

blame. It takes two to make a quarrel, but one gets the blame.
See ancestor[2]; fault; misfortune[2]; self-made: self-made man[2, 6]; swear[3].

blanket. Cover charge or overhead.
baby blanket. It covers up many a woman's mistake.
wet blanket. One that dampens your ardor.
See critic[4].

bleach. Elderly women should not bleach their hair because only the young dye good.

bleed. When war bleeds a nation white, it leaves its people red.
See surgeon.

blend. Some gentlemen prefer blondes; others prefer blends.

bless. See poverty[2].

blind. 1. Love may be blind but the neighbors aren't. 2. When the blind leads the blind, they both fall into—matrimony.
See defendant[2]; diamond[3]; eye: eye opener; justice[2]; mother-in-law[4]; see[4]; touch: sense of touch.
blindman's buff. A fellow feeling for a fellow creature.

blinds. See house: glass houses[3].
Venetian blinds. They have a shady reputation.

blink. A girl with beautiful eyes soon puts a man on the blink.

bliss. If ignorance is bliss, there must be a lot of happy people in the world.
See blister; folly; infatuation; intelligence: intelligence test[2]; kiss[3].

blister. All is not bliss that blisters.

bloc. A minority group often led by a bloc head.
See Congress[7].
farm bloc. The farm bloc in Congress does more blocking than farming.

block. See resist.

blonde. 1. The outstanding contribution of chemistry to the world. 2. Not every blonde is light-headed. 3. Just because a fellow prefers blondes, that doesn't make him a gentleman. 4. Gentlemen prefer blondes because where there's light, there's heat. 5. Gentlemen prefer blondes because blondes are always fair to them.
See blend; brunette[2]; dye; mutual; pressure; story: off-color story.
decided blonde. A girl that decided to dye her hair.

blood. 1. Good from ancestors, better from parents, best from transfusion. 2. People with the best blood in their veins usually get it by transfusion.

blot. The fountain pen writes, and having writ, blots.

blotter. Something you look for while the ink dries.

blow. See Florida; inflation; saxophone[1, 3, 5]; scandal[1]; trumpet; straw vote; wind[2].

blowout. See forecast.

blue. See colorful; experience: school of experience[2]; reformer[8].

bluffer. See cliff: cliff dweller.

blunt. Blunt women are usually dull.

blush. Man is the only animal that blushes—or needs to.
See corporation[3].

board. See bigamy[1]; free[3]; matrimony[3].
boarding house. 1. A house that usually provides poor quarters for good dollars. 2. If all the people who eat at boarding houses were put at one long table, they would reach.
See skeleton.

boarder. See fly[1].

boast. 1. With people who boast, it's no sooner done than said. 2. The man who has the right to boast doesn't have to.
See brag; past[4]; side: shady side.

boaster. A person who, every time he opens his mouth, puts his feats in.

boat. Many people who get sick on a boat are well off.
See ferryboat.

body. The human body is a wonderful thing: pat a man on the back and he gets a swelled head.

See accident[1]; caucus; doctor[3]; rib; skeleton[2]; stomach[1].

boil. One in the pot is worth two on the neck.

bold. The brave deserve the fair, but if too bold, they deserve the air.

See careful; pebble.

bonanza. A hole in the ground owned by a champion liar.

bond. When a man gives his word to another man, it's his bond; when he gives his word to a woman, it's his bondage.

See finance; matrimony: bonds of matrimony; vagabond.

bone. 1. Most of our troubles are caused by too much bone in the head and not enough in the back. 2. The man who makes no bones about anything probably has no backbone.

See dice; heal; knit; osteopath; osteopathy[2]; skeleton[1], skeleton in the closet[3]; spinach; woman[9].

book. 1. Never judge a book by its movie. 2. Most new books are forgotten within a year, especially by those who borrow them. 3. Don't give a person a book for a gift; he may have one. 4. Books are friends; that's why some people never cut them.

See author; binding; checkbook; chewing gum[5]; critic: literary critic; egotist[3]; friend: good friend; index; libel; library; pocketbook; read: reading[2]; shut: shut up; suppress.

book ends. The parts of books that many people read first.

bookcase. 1. A piece of furniture that should be carefully protected against dry rot. 2. Circumstances alter bookcases.

bookkeeper. 1. A person who feels good when things start looking black again. 2. A person who borrows books is not his brother's keeper, but his brother's bookkeeper.

See Adam: Adam & Eve[1]; football: football team.

bookworm. A person who would rather read than eat, or a worm that would rather eat than read.

boost. When a man gets to the top everybody is willing to give him a boost.

boot. See accelerator.

bootblack. The man who always takes a shine to us.

booty. In considering marriage, a girl is often torn between love and booty.

bore. 1. A person who talks when you want him to listen.

2. One who, when you ask him how he feels, tells you. **3.** One who insists upon talking about himself when you want to talk about yourself. **4.** A person who never tries to make a long story short. **5.** A person who lacks the power of conversation but not the power of speech. **6.** The secret of being a bore is to tell everything.

See depend; ear; endurance: endurance test; filibuster; hero[2]; progress[3]; public speaker[3]; rain[2]; resort: summer resort[4]; speech: after-dinner speeches[2]; success: social success; thick[1].

big bore. A person of small caliber.

See big: big shot.

boredom. See ennui.

born. The only excuse some men have for not being married is that they were born that way.

See Adam: Adam & Eve; chicken[1]; nudist[7]; poet[3]; song: song writer[1]; spoon[1]; stupid; sucker[2].

borrow. See acquaintance; bank[1]; book[2]; bookkeeper[2]; happiness[3]; library; means[1]; money[8]; neighbor[1]; pessimist[13]; promise: promising people; tax: income tax; trouble[1, 3]; umbrella[3]; untouchable; value.

borrowing. **1.** The exchange of hot air for cold cash. **2.** Some men spend half their lives borrowing money and the other half in not paying it back.

bosom. See brassiere[1]; buttocks; shirt[1].

boss. **1.** A man always shows himself in his work, especially if the boss is around. **2.** By working faithfully eight hours a day, you may eventually get to be a boss, and work twelve hours a day. **3.** The real boss of the family is the one who can spend a few dollars without having to say anything about it.

See dictation; freedom[2]; hesitate[1]; household; imagination[2]; love[19]; marriage: successful marriage[1]; stone: rolling stone[1]; yes[1].

Bostonian. An American, broadly speaking.

bottle. **1.** Men who don't use glasses generally prefer to drink out of bottles. **2.** There's many a slip 'twixt the cup and the lip; the safest way is to drink out of a bottle.

See age[2]; boy[1]; cream; liquor[1]; live; pneumonia; skeleton: skeleton in the closet[1].

bottom. **1.** There are two sides to every question, and no bottom.

2. The habit of going to the bottom of things usually lands a man on top.

See aviation[1]; college: college graduate[1]; gravedigger; heart[2]; skier; subway: subway contractor; successful: successful man[1]; trousers; well.

bow. What Cupid fortunately places on a girl's lips rather than on her legs.

bowels. A good set of bowels is worth more to a man than any amount of brains.

See cold[3].

bowling alley. The only place where people bother to pick up all the pins.

box. See fighter: prize fighter.

boxing. The less a fighter knows of boxing, the more he knows the ropes.

boxer. The only person who wakes up and finds himself rich.

boy. 1. An appetite with a skin pulled over it. 2. Merely a noise with dirt on it. 3. One-tenth joys and nine-tenths noise. 4. Boys will be noise. 5. A boy loves his dog because it's the only thing around the house that doesn't find fault with him. 6. Boys will be boys, but the girls are giving them close competition. 7. When a boy marries, his mother thinks he is throwing himself away, and his sisters think the girl is.

See bad[2]; college[4]; spring[5].

bracelet. There is no end to the rings and bracelets some women wear.

brag. The man who never boasts is always bragging about it.

See duty[2]; press: press agent[2]; self-made: self-made man[7]; traveler.

braggart. The average man away from home.

brain. The brain is wonderful: it starts working the moment you get up, and doesn't stop until you get to the office.

See also beauty[3]; bowels; diplomacy[7]; dry[1]; fish[5]; fugitive; muscle; professor: absent-minded professor; silence[1].

brains. Many a man has more brains in his little finger than he has in his own head.

See brawn; coed[6]; eloquence; mob[2]; tax: income tax[1].

brakes. 1. When the brakes of your car give way, the best thing to do is to hit something cheap. 2. The better your brakes, the greater the danger to your rear fenders.

See break[2]; clutch; pedestrian[22].

brass. The main component in a knocker.

brassie. Women who play golf must use a brassie even if they don't wear one.

brassiere. 1. A girl's bosom friend. 2. A hammock for two. 3. Next to herself a woman likes her brassiere best. 4. The old-fashioned bustle has worked its way to the front, been streamlined, and is now called a brassiere. 5. No matter how much the styles change, they wear the same things in brassieres every season.

See brassie; hangover[4]; molehill; upkeep.

brat. The triumph of mind over mater.

brave. None but the brave deserve the fair, and none but the brave can live with some of them.

See affairs; bold; frankfurter.

brawn. Brains may be mightier than brawn but they don't show up so well in a bathing suit.

bread. Half a loaf is better than no bread, and so is a whole one. See roll; sandwich: garlic sandwich, western sandwich; zwieback.

breadline. See economics.

break. 1. Clothes don't make a man, but they can break a husband. 2. There will be no break in prices until the government applies the brake.

See dish; gold: gold digger[7]; heal; nose[5]; retailer; roll; useless; will[4].

break even. To owe money to as many people as you don't owe. See marry: married life[3].

even break. Whether the pedestrian gets an even break depends largely on where the car hit him.

breakfast. A man is as old as he feels before breakfast, and a woman is as old as she looks before breakfast.

See bird: early bird[1]; coffee[2]; lunch.

breakfast nook. The little corner that modern architects have to measure their patrons for.

See architect: architect's error.

Sunday breakfast. A meal where the cream is sour.

breath. See colorful; dimension; expense: running expenses; garlic; halitosis; temperance.

breathe. Air is still free, but it costs more to be able to breathe it.

breeding. The only evidence of breeding that some children show is when they scratch their heads.

See familiarity; fat.

good breeding. Concealing how much we think of ourselves and how little we think of others.

well-bred man. One who steps on his cigarette so it won't burn the rug.

brevity. The soul of style.

See lingerie; suit: bathing suit[3, 5]; wear: women's wear[2].

bribe. See politician[4].

bride. 1. One who should make sacrifices for her husband, but not in the form of burnt offerings. 2. First the bride selects the bridesmaids; then the church; then the trousseau; then her lawyer; then her detective.

See ceremony; groom[1]; honeymoon[1, 4]; June; path: bridle path; triumphant; trousseau; wedding[4].

beautiful bride. One who is well-groomed at a wedding.

bridal day. The day on which a woman leads a man to the halter.

bride's father. Men hate to display emotion, but the bride's father may be pardoned if he sheds a few cheers.

modern bride. What she doesn't know would fill a cookbook.

bridegroom. 1. A thing they have at weddings. 2. A man who exchanges good quarters for a better half. 3. The proof that a woman can take a joke. 4. One who is never the best man at a wedding.

See honeymoon[1].

bridesmaid. There are two kinds of girls: those who neck, and bridesmaids.

See bride[2].

bridge. 1. Next to love, the greatest indoor sport in America. 2. A structure built over a river to get one across, or a card game to get one cross. 3. Two's company, three's a crowd—unless someone comes along to make a fourth at bridge. 4. The only time a husband and wife get fun out of holding hands is when they are playing bridge.

See cards: good card trick; map: road map[2]; million[2]; musician[2]; servant: servant problem.

bad bridge partner. The person who has a one-trick mind.

bad bridge player.   Early to bid and early to raise makes a bad bridge player.

bridge expert.   One who can keep a kibitzer quiet all evening.

bridge partner.   See partner: life partner.

bridge player.   A person who learns to take it on the shin. See slam. .

good bridge game.   The triumph of mind over chatter.

bridle.   See groom[1].

bright.   See future[2]; glasses: sunglasses; inside; light: dim lights; optimist[7]; shoplifter; speech: after-dinner speeches[2].

broad.   The way of a man with a broad eventually leads to Broadway.

See joke: broad jokes; narrow.

broadcasting.   What it needs is a cough medicine for radios.

broaden.   Marriage broadens a man; it also flattens him. See travel.

Broadway.   1. American's hardened artery.   2. The double crossroad of the world.   3. Fraudway.   4. If the straight and narrow path leads to virtue, Broadway is well named.   5. A place where people spend money they haven't earned, to buy things they don't need, to impress people they don't like. See broad.

broker.   A person who's seldom original but great in quotations.

brood.   1. When a girl broods about a lover, it's because she hasn't got one.   2. If you brood over your troubles, you'll have a perfect hatch.

See dog[4].

Brooklyn.   The bedroom of New York.

broom.   See courtship[3].

brother.   See sister.

brown.   See colorful.

browse.   The superficial reading done by lowbrows.

brunette.   1. All's fair in love, unless it's a brunette.   2. Gentlemen prefer blondes, at least those who have married brunettes.

brush.   See artist: tonsorial artist; hair[3].

brutal.   In order not to show anything brutal on the screen, most movies end just as the couples are about to get married.

See theory: beautiful theory.

brute.   An imperfect animal, whereas man is a perfect beast.

buck.   A drink in the hand is worth two bucks in a night club.

pass the buck. The reason our dollar bills wear out quickly is because Americans are continually passing the buck.

See politics[7].

budget. 1. A family quarrel. 2. A system of worrying before you spend instead of afterwards. 3. People who live on a budget tell their money where to go instead of wondering where it went.

See desire; income: fixed income.

balance the budget. 1. A budget system saves money because by the time you've balanced it, it's too late to go anywhere. 2. After the government takes enough to balance the budget, the citizen has to budget the balance.

See American[3].

bug. See ant; fly.

bugbear. An insect that crawls on bears.

buggy. A carriage swarming with bugs.

build. 1. Home was not built in a day. 2. The best way to be contented with your lot is to build a house on it.

See straddle.

building. When building materials come down, buildings will go up.

See air: castles in the air.

bulb. In some gardens the bulbs seem to think they're buried instead of planted.

bulk. If people would leave the bulk of their fortunes to lawyers, a lot of time would be saved.

bull. 1. A buttermilk cow. 2. It's remarkable how a little bull will cow a man.

See bullfight; golf[2]; news[3]; shoot; steer; stock: stock market[2].

bull ring. Americans haven't anything like a bull ring unless you count the one candidates throw their hats into.

bullfight. It's easy to recognize an American at a bullfight; he's the one who cheers for the bull.

bumper. A bumper crop bumps the farmer.

bunion. The girl who turns you down on the dance floor probably knows her bunions.

bunk. No wonder the world's asleep, with so much bunk.

See bed: four-poster bed; politician[11]; politics[9].

bureau. See old: old-timer; Washington, D. C.[1].

bureaucrat. A red tapeworm.

burglar.   1. A man who is always ready to take advantage of an opening.   2. A man who isn't as rich as he thinks he ought to be. See police.

burlesque.   It isn't a show; it's a take-off.
See attendance; outstrip.

burlesque dancers.   They do little more than stand around and twiddle their tums.

burlesque girl.   One whose clothes are so designed that she is always seen in the best places.

burlesque show.   A riot of off-color.

young burlesque girl.   A mere stripling.

burn.   The burning question in this country is whether to burn coal or oil.
See breeding: well-bred man; bride[1]; cake: birthday cake[3]; fire[2]; flame: old flame[2]; fuel; grease; match: good match; schoolboy.

bury.   When you bury the hatchet, don't bury it in your enemy's back.
See bulb; mistake[1]; telephone: telephone booth[2]; undertaker[2].

burial ground.   A place where a person is aged in wood.

bus.   1. If buses get any bigger, locomotives will have to stop, look, and listen, at crossings.   2. The bus may be putting some railroad trains out of business, but not when they meet at a grade crossing.
See modern: modern man; newspaper; politeness[1, 3]; run: run after; seat.

bus driver.   The man who isn't afraid to tell a woman where to get off.

bus motto.   The public be jammed!

bush.   See bird[2].

bushel.   See advice[5].

business.   1. What is everybody's business is nobody's business. 2. Many a business reputed to be sound is sound—asleep. 3. There are two reasons why some people don't mind their own business: either they haven't any mind or they haven't any business.
See bankbook; complaint; eccentric[1]; expert: efficiency expert; finance: finance company; gentleman[7]; half; hell[2]; honest: honest man; imagination[2]; level; oculist; patriotism; pawnbroker[4]; pleasure[2]; politics[16]; prosperity[3]; racketeer[2]; reformer[2]; run[1]; statistician[5]; tie: Christmas ties[2]; unnecessary.

shaky business.   Playing with dice.

businessman.   1. One who talks golf all morning at the office, and business all afternoon on the links.   2. One who, when given enough rope, will be tied up at the office.   3. A businessman is judged by the company he keeps solvent.

See dig; dodge; stenographer: fast stenographer.

big businessman.   He may be down but he's never out—of a conference.

ethical businessman.   One who never goes back on his word without consulting his lawyer.

tired businessman.   One who can hardly lift his feet to the top of the desk.

bust.   Nations must trust one another or bust one another.

See front[2]; sculptor.

bustle.   1. Another word that doesn't mean what it used to. 2. A bustle is like a historical novel: it's a fictitious tale based on stern reality.

See brassiere[4].

busy.   1. No one is so busy as the person who has nothing to do. 2. Women are like money: keep them busy or they lose interest. 3. The husband who is as busy as a bee may wake up to find that some one else has his honey.

See politician[5]; undertaker[2]; women[3]; word: few words[1].

busybody.   A person who burns the scandal at both ends.

butcher.   The person least likely to put on extra weight.

butler.   One who often lives to serve his third degeneration.

butter.   See fly[1].

butterfly.   1. A flutterby.   2. If all the butterflies in the world were placed end to end, there would be more caterpillars.

buttocks.   The bosom of the pants.

button.   Something whose hole is greater than itself.

See collection: collection plate; shirt[2].

buy.   1. The reason women buy so much clothes is because they can't get them for nothing.   2. Buying what you don't need often ends in needing what you can't buy.

See advice: fatherly advice; bargain: bargain sale[1]; Congress[5]; court: American courts; dress[1]; experience[5]; hat[2]; home[14]; love[18, 24]; novel; politician: honest politician; price: present prices; prosperity[1, 2]; time: on time[3]; Wall Street[2]; young: young girl.

buyer. See cellar; water[4].

by-product. A substance usually made into breakfast foods or wallboard.

See prosperity[2].

C

cabbage. The best way to raise it is with a knife and fork.
See cauliflower.

caddie. 1. Just one of those little things that count. 2. A small boy employed to lose balls for others and find them for himself.
See golfer: woman golfer[1].

Caesar, Julius. The Roman conqueror who was hailed while he reigned.

cage. See beast; prison[1].

cake. 1. You can't eat your cake unless you have it. 2. You can eat your cake and have it too by making two cakes. 3. Beware the kind of girl who likes to eat her cake and have yours too. 4. You can't eat your cake and have *it* too.
See heart: hard-hearted man; waffle.

  birthday cake. 1. If you want to make light of your age, put candles on your birthday cake. 2. The design on a woman's birthday cake is often beautiful, but the arithmetic is terrible. 3. When a woman puts candles on her birthday cake, she should be burning most of them at both ends.

calendar. 1. It's always up-to-date. 2. A system which plans its work a whole year ahead and never fails to finish on time. 3. What a speaker goes by if he forgets his watch.

calf. Many a girl has a calf that only a cow can love.
See sheep.

caliber. See bore: big bore.

California. 1. It's much like Florida, except that part of it isn't for sale. 2. There's nothing more tragic than a citizen of California dying in Florida.

  California climate. The tourists have done more for it than nature.

call. Many are called but few get up.

See collector: bill collector[3]; drop; telephone: telephone operator[2]; tickle; visionary; youth[1].

calm. See collect; song: song writer[2].

calories. See bean.

camel. See jail[3].

camera. All the world's a camera—smile, please.

camp. See grasshopper.

camp life. 1. Camp life is just one canned thing after another. 2. Youngsters appreciate camp life, and so do the mosquitoes.

old campground. The trouble with the old campground is that it is more often the old damp ground.

camper. Only in Utopia do the mosquito and the camper lie down together.

can. What people can't eat, they can.

See camp: camp life[1]; cat[2]; housekeeping; kitchen; liberty[6]; milk[1]; old[3]; teaching[2]; uncanny.

garbage can. A good example of a collective noun.

candidate. 1. A man who stands for what he thinks the people will fall for. 2. A modest man who shrinks from the publicity of private life to seek the obscurity of public office. 3. One who gives the people platitudes without fear or favor and straight-from-the-shoulder generalities. 4. When a candidate votes for himself, it's an aye for an I. 5. A candidate needs three hats: one to cover his head with, one to toss into the ring, and one to talk through.

See bull: bull ring; majority[4]; test: mental test; voter[2].

hopeless candidate. In politics, even the hopeless candidate is a promising one.

candle. If you burn the candle at both ends, you'll make both ends meet.

See cake: birthday cake[1, 3]; grease.

candy. See heart: hard-hearted man; opinion: candid opinion.

cane. The stick a man carries because it can't walk.

cannibal. 1. One who loves his fellowmen—with gravy. 2. One who lives in the uninhibited parts of the earth. 3. A person who shows his hospitality by constantly having people for dinner. 4. Religion can't explain what happens when a missionary on his way to heaven is eaten by a cannibal on his way to hell.

See missionary[1]; serve[2]; taste[3].

canoe. See paddle.

capacity. Man's eternal struggle is to keep his earning capacity up to his wife's yearning capacity.

See develop.

capital. See capitalism; clever: clever man; collective bargaining; credit[1]; labor, labor union.

  capital & labor. 1. The money the other fellow has is capital; getting it away from him is labor. 2. Capital and labor should be one—but which one?

  See lockout.

  capital punishment. See punishment: capital punishment.

capitalism. Capitalism capitalizes on capital.

capitalist. One who continues to spend less than his income.

car. 1. A machine that can go twice as fast on weekdays as it goes on Sundays and holidays. 2. A device intended to take both drivers and pedestrians off their feet. 3. Something a man keeps clean and vice versa. 4. After the horse came the car, and after the car came the collector. 5. In the early days, more drivers than pedestrians were seen under cars.

NOTE: This word has not been cross-referenced because it occurs very often throughout this dictionary.

  second-hand car. 1. It passeth nothing but understanding. 2. The world of second-hand cars is divided into two parts: those who ride and those who deride.

  See pedestrian[9].

  streamlined car. It was invented to prevent the pedestrian from telling whether he had been run over or backed into.

  used car. 1. It's not what it used to be. 2. It will give you no trouble if you're the first one to use it. 3. It's rarely what it's jacked up to be. 4. Many a used car is in first crash condition.

cards. See bridge; deal; pinochle; sleeve; spade.

  good card trick. Knowing how to get out of making a fourth hand at bridge.

care. Care will kill a cat, but a cat doesn't care.

See gentleman[3].

career. See chiseler; grafter; politics[1].

  checkered career. It usually ends in a striped suit.

careful. Be bold in what you stand for but careful in what you fall for.

See enemy[1].

careless. See accident: auto accident[3]; payment: easy payment plan.

caress. Catch as catch can.

See accident: auto accident[3].

carnation. America's national flower.

carriage. It ended with the car age.

carry. See cane; song: song writer[5]; telegram[2]; tune[1].

  carry out. 1. Youth must be served, and then carried out. 2. Singers who can carry a tune should carry it out.

cartel. A business that's known by the companies it keeps.

carve. See chiseler; grafter.

case. See censorship; doctor: grasping doctor; driver: backseat driver[1]; lawsuit[5].

  case history. The case history of the modern woman consists of a vanity case, a cigarette case, and a divorce case.

  legal cases. Circumstances alter legal cases.

cash. See vote.

  cold cash. 1. It often warms a girl's heart. 2. So-called because we can't keep it long enough to warm it up.

  See borrow: borrowing[1].

cashier. The man who counts in this world.

  See criminal[3].

cat. 1. Every dog has his day but the nights are reserved for the cats. 2. A cat's idea of heaven is a can full of garbage.

  See care; indigestion[2]; king[1]; reformer[7]; skunk[1]; spitz; violin; weather: beastly weather.

  black cat. If a black cat crosses the path of a car, it's a lucky cat.

  catty woman. One whose husband leads a dog's life.

catalogue. When one woman talks, it's a monologue; when two women talk, it's a cat-alogue.

catch. 1. Only a dog knows what it would do if it did catch the car. 2. The early bird catches the worm, but the early fish catches the worm, hook and all. 3. When a henpecked husband misses his usual homeward train, he catches it.

  See caress; chase[1]; fisherman[1]; flypaper; germs[1]; heart: faint heart; heat; installment: installment buying[1]; marriage: before & after[6]; religion[7]; spoils; thief; train[2].

caterpillar. An upholstered worm.

See butterfly[2].

catskin. A fur sold as rabbit skin to be used in making imitation beaver.

caucus. The dead body of an animal.

cauliflower. Cabbage with a college education.

caution. A great asset in fishing, especially if you are the fish.

cautious man. One who hasn't let a woman pin anything on him since he was a baby.

cave. See centaur.

celebrate. See anniversary: silver wedding anniversary; Thanksgiving[3].

celebrity. A swellebrity.

celibate. Love has no bait for a celibate.

cell. Life started from a cell and, if justice is done, a lot of it is going to end there.

See parole.

cellar. The purchase of coal goes not only to the buyer but also to the cellar.

See prohibitionist[3].

cellist. A person who should have bowlegs.

cellophane. Men are as transparent as cellophane and as hard to remove once you get wrapped up in them.

cemetery. 1. A place of last resort. 2. A place filled with people who thought the world couldn't get along without them.

See equality[1]; fence[2]; skinflint.

censer. Censers smell sweet, censors foul.

censor. 1. A person who thinks all people are as nasty as himself, and hates them for it. 2. A man who knows more than he thinks he ought to. 3. One who loves morality so well that he will commit any crime to maintain it. 4. The only thing some towns have in the way of a good show. 5. If censors had their way they'd put pants on animals. 6. Censors are always trying to tie the nation into hard nots. 7. A censor always tries to root out evil with his noes. 8. It's hard for women to satisfy the censor; he attacks them when they're loose, and also when they're tight. 9. What makes no sense makes censors.

See attract; censer; goods; Hollywood[3]; innocence; practice[1]; suit: bathing suit.

censorship. In the movies, just a case of stop, look, and less sin.

census. See triplets.

census taker. A man who goes from door to door increasing the population.

cent. See collector[2].

centaur. A monster that was half horse because it lived in damp caves.

centenarian. There's nothing so wonderful about a centenarian; look how long it took him to get there.
See light[2].

center. The center of the stage is where all good actors go when they die.

ceremony. Even in the old days a lot of fellows kissed the bride, but not so many before the ceremony.
See wedding[3].

certain. 1. Nothing is certain but uncertainty. 2. Nothing is certain but death and higher taxes.
See gamble: gambling[1]; guess: woman's guess; sure.

chair. It's odd how chairs never move in the daytime but at night tiptoe up and kick you in the shins.
See housewife: typical housewife; tack.

electric chair. 1. A good example of period furniture because it ends the sentence. 2. Beware of the girl with the baby stare; a man is safer in the electric chair.

high chair. The little boy who hides behind his mother's skirt nowadays has to get into his high chair to do it.

champagne. A beverage which makes you see double but feel single.

champion. Some champions make great price fighters.
See rumor[2].

world's heavyweight champion. The fat man in the circus.

chance. Most bachelors have lots of chances to get married but they are not taking any chances.
See chancery; ghost[2]; marriage[26]; optimist[10]; political: political platform[3].

game of chance. One in which you haven't got much of a chance.

chancery. A court of equity in which all the parties take chances.

change. 1. A man's opinions all change, except the one he has of himself. 2. A man will never change his mind if he has no mind to change. 3. The greater the change in men's clothing, the less the change in their pockets.

See bellboy[1]; changeable; clothing; fanatic[3]; fashion[4]; leopard; mind: woman's mind; name: maiden name; opinion[4]; ordeal; pickpocket; pocket[1]; prescribe[1]; religion[6]; rudness; stenographer; view.

changeable. To swear to love always is to promise that two changeable persons will never change.

character. 1. What you have left when you've lost everything you can lose. 2. What a man is in the dark. 3. Your character depends largely upon what the public doesn't know about you. 4. Many a man's reputation would not know his character if they met on the street.

See back: pat on the back; conceit[1]; snore[3].

charge. In business, you charge a thing and pay for it later; in politics, the payments come first and the charges are filed later. See power: power companies; resort: summer resort[1]; shaving[1]; storage.

charity. 1. Charity begins at home and usually ends there. 2. Charity suffereth long, and so does the man who tries to live on it. 3. Charity covers a multitude of church lotteries.

See alms; philanthropist[4].

charm. A charm in the personality is worth two on the neck.

See enlarge; suit: bathing suit[5].

chase. 1. A man always chases a woman until she catches him. 2. A man never gets into trouble chasing a woman; it's only after she is caught that the trouble begins.

See chastity: chaste woman; opportunity[4].

chastity. 1. Chastity in the female is merely lack of temptation; in the male, merely lack of opportunity. 2. Chastity thinks that Cupid is stupid.

See couch.

chaste woman. One who is seldom chased.

chatter. See bridge: good bridge game; talk: talkative woman.

chatterbox. A person who suffers from chronic palpitation of the tongue.

cheap. 1. Two can live as cheaply as one if one doesn't eat. 2. Two can live as cheaply as one can drink. 3. Two can live as cheaply as one; they usually have to. 4. The only two who can live as cheaply as one are a flea and a dog.

See alimony[10]; bachelor[4]: brakes[1]; diner; expensive[1]; golf[5];

money[8]; politician: cheap politician; production: mass production; single; talk[1, 3].

cheat. See bargain[1]; peace[3].

check. 1. Every woman has a secret desire to write—checks.
2. Many people never know where the next check is coming from or when the last one is coming back.

See athlete: professional athlete; club: night club[5]; college: college boy[1], college cheer; date[3]; hat[4]; spendthrift; subscription; town: small town[1].

bad check. The only crime greater than writing a bad poem is writing a bad check.

returned check. A matter of no account.

rubber check. 1. So-called because it bounces back. 2. Something that will give you a long stretch.

checkbook. One of the books with unhappy endings.

See bankbook; marriage: successful marriage[2].

checkmate. The girl you marry for her money.

cheek. The man with plenty of cheek probably has a fat head too.

cheer. See bride: bride's father; mirror: woman's mirror.

cheer leader. See kangaroo[2].

cheese. The holes in Swiss cheese should have been put in Limburger because that's the cheese that needs the ventilation.

cheese business. It's still going strong.

Limburger cheese. 1. A variety of cheese whose odor puts it easily in the first rank. 2. A cheese composed of what's decomposed. 3. A type of cheese that should be made out of—doors.

chemistry. See blonde[1].

cherry. The only fishing through the ice that some people ever do is for cherries.

chess. A game always played on the square.

chess player. See suit: two-pants suit[1].

chest. See pneumonia.

chew. See ruminant.

chewing gum. 1. The most common impediment in the speech of Americans. 2. It's changing America from the wide-open spaces to the wide-open faces. 3. The fulfillment of the idea that, since jaws must wag, they should have something to wag against. 4. Chewing gum is hard to get rid of, but not so hard as some of the people who chew it. 5. More money is spent on chewing gum than on books, but one can borrow books if necessary.

See cover; foothold; mouth: gum chewer's mouth; typewriter: noiseless typewriter.

chic. When a man spends his evenings away from home, he has probably been sitting up with a chic friend.

chic woman. One who is always ready to take what's becoming to her.

chicken. 1. The only animal you can eat before it's born. 2. Many a man has gone to the dogs chasing chickens.

See coupé; duck[1]; highway[1]; neck[1]; weeds[2].

child. 1. A stomach entirely surrounded by curiosity. 2. A pain in the neck when he's around; a pain in the heart when he isn't. 3. First he is taught to talk, then he is spanked for not being silent. 4. The child is father to the man, but not when the child's a girl.

See children; curious[2]; egg[1]; exemption; fill: filling station; often[1]; placenta; self-defense; tabloid[6]; vanity: extreme vanity.

illegitimate child. A sinfant.

only child. A shining example of what not to be.

child labor. What we need is a child labor law to keep children from working their parents to death.

childhood. See cleanliness.

children. 1. Children have become so expensive that only the poor can afford them. 2. Small children give you a headache; large children, a heartache. 3. Children first love their parents, then judge them, then forgive them.

See breeding; Christmas[1]; diet: soft diet; divorce: ideal divorce; drum[1]; elevate; familiarity[1]; fatherland; fruit; glasses: sunglasses; grandmother[2]; grow; heredity; illegitimate; indigestion[2]; life[8]; maintain; manners: table manners[2]; mimic; obscene; old[5]; orphanage; paddle; parents; question[3]; Reno; sin; smart[2]; spanking[2]; support[3]; switch; will: will power[4].

ill-bred children. They always display their pest manners.

smart children. The behavior of smart children often indicates that they don't smart in the right places.

Chile. About the hottest country on the globe.

chimney. See Santa Claus.

chimney sweep. A person who does things to soot himself.

chin. 1. When a woman reaches forty, she stops patting herself on the back and begins under the chin.   2. Many a fat person has two chins going on three.

See beard; fat: fat woman[1]; scandal[2]; violinist.

receding chin.   It's marvellous for eating corn on the cob.

Chinese.   The only way an American can read Chinese is when it's printed in English.

chip.   See face: poker face.

chiropodist.   1. A man who, when given an inch, will take a foot. 2. A man who is down at the heel even when he is prosperous.

chiropractor.   A man who gets paid for what another man would get slapped for.

   successful chiropractor.   It takes backbone to become one.

chisel.   See grafter.

chiseler.   The man who carves out a career for himself.

See chivalry: age of chivalry.

chivalry.   The courtesy and respect of a man for a strange woman.

See driver: woman driver[7].

   age of chivalry.   It has now been succeeded by the age of chiselry.

choose.   1. You can't choose your ancestors, but that's fair enough for they probably wouldn't have chosen you.   2. Generally the woman chooses the man who will choose her.

See friend[8]; pick[1, 2]; vice[1].

chorine.   A girl who usually kicks best after her salary is cut.

chorus.   In union there is strength; that's why weak-voiced singers form choruses.

See safety.

   chorus girl.   Chorus girls are always indecorous.

See education[2]; kick[1].

chow.   When a man bites a dog, it's his wife's pet chow.

chowder.   With clams, two is company and three is chowder.

Christian.   A person who is supposed to love those he heartily dislikes.

   Christian endeavor.   It is notoriously hard on female pulchritude.

Christianity.   1. Primitive peoples can learn almost everything from the Christian nations except Christianity.   2. The greatest service that could be rendered to Christian peoples would be to convert them to Christianity.

See church[7].

Christmas. 1. The season when we must get the children something for their father to play with. 2. When people keep their radios on all hours of the morning playing *Silent Night*. 3. The season when fowl murder promotes peace and good will. 4. A widely observed holiday on which neither the past nor the future is of so much interest as the present. 5. An annual celebration when every girl wants her past forgotten and her present remembered. 6. Christmas comes but once a year—is enough. 7. If Christmas comes, can bills be far behind?
See berry; cigar[3]; give[1]; hint; lionize.

Christmas gifts. 1. They prove that it's better to give than to receive. 2. The husband who receives a Christmas gift usually receives the bill a month later.

Christmas shopping. Do your Christmas shopping early or you'll do it surly.

chromium. It covers a multitude of tins.

church. 1. An organization supported by the husbands of its members. 2. If absence makes the heart grow fonder, then a lot of people certainly love the church. 3. The old go to church to close their eyes, the young to eye their clothes. 4. When the churches discover that they can't successfully compete with the movies, they might try religion. 5. To stop crime is the work of the church, but which church? 6. It's hard for a rich man to enter the kingdom of heaven, but it's easy for him to get on the church board of trustees. 7. Don't attack the church; it's the last bulwark against Christianity. 8. Most people have some sort of religion; at least they know what church they're staying away from.
See bride[2]; charity[2]; collection; driving[3]; fair: fair exchange; liberalism; nickel[2]; sermon: drowsy sermon.

skyscraper churches. The building of skyscraper churches is a move in the right direction.

cider. The last barrel of cider is the hardest.
See apple.

cigar. 1. The man who says his cigars are the best thing out, may be telling the truth. 2. The man who always smokes cigars without bands enjoys a quiet smoke. 3. If women ever take to cigars as they have to cigarettes, the men can get even at Christmas.

See pen: fountain pen; smoke: smoking.

cigar box. If you take a cigar out of a cigar box, the cigar box will become a cigar lighter.

cigar-lighter. If matches were made in heaven, where did the cigar-lighter come from?

five-cent cigar. 1. What the five-cent cigar needs is a good country. 2. There are several good five-cent cigars on the market but they are sold at higher prices. 3. The five-cent cigar has come back but it takes five cents' worth of matches to keep it going.

cigarette. Some people smoke one pack of cigarettes a day; others smoke any given amount.

See breeding: well-bred man; cigar[3]; fire: forest fire; light[3]; mother: modern mother; smoke: smoking; tobacco[1].

circle. 1. A line of no depth running around a dot forever. 2. A round line with no kinks in it. 3. A line which meets its other end without ending. 4. A round straight line with a hole in the middle.

See geometry[1]; progress[2]; straight[3]; triangle[3].

family circle. You can't keep the family circle square with a triangle.

sewing circle. In a ladies' sewing circle, more husbands are darned than socks.

circulation. Tight clothes stop circulation, but the tighter a woman's clothes, the more she is in circulation.

See secret[6].

circumstance. Witnesses must lie because circumstances can't.

See bookcase[2]; case: legal case; face[5].

circus. An amusing performance that carries on in competition with Congress.

See champion: world's heavyweight champion.

citizen. See budget: balance the budget; immigrant; schoolhouse.

law-abiding citizen. One who obeys all duly constipated authorities.

city. A large town made up of millions of people being lonesome together.

See expensive[2]; farmer; life: wild life; simmer.

civilization. 1. What the human race will eventually die from. 2. The question is not where civilization began, but when will it.

3. In another century civilization will have reached all peoples except those that have no resources worth stealing.

civilize. See evolution[5]; padlock.

claim. Most women claim to be dresstitute.

clam. See chowder; noise[1].

clamdigger. One who is generally mussel bound.

claptrap. The world will beat a path to your door if you build a better claptrap than your neighbor.

clarinet. It's no fun; it's a funnel.

class. Society consists of two classes: the lower class cultivates the dignity of labor, the upper class the labor of dignity.
See coed[4]; college: college boy[3]; earn[2]; experience: school of experience[1]; mankind; masses; poor[2]; seat: aisle seats; work[2].

classic. A millstone on the road to learning.

clean. See car[3]; dirty; fingers; gold: gold digger[4]; grit; groom[2]; Hollywood[3]; mind: woman's mind; pan; room; sponger; towel; wash.

cleanliness. Cleanliness is next to godliness, but in childhood it's next to impossible.
See godliness.

clear. Making light of troubles will help you see the way clear.

clergyman. One who still preaches against modern dress even though there's not enough left to talk about.
See cop[1].

clever. See ideal: ideal man[2]; liar: clever liar; manage[2]; three.
  clever girl. One who knows how to refuse a kiss without being deprived of it.
  clever man. He who lives by his wits must be a clever man to live upon so small a capital.
  See understand[1].
  clever person. One who puts his problems aside for a brainy day.
  clever woman. One who knows how to give a man her own way.

client. See millionaire: scared millionaire.

cliff. A pushover.
See dummy.
  cliff dweller. Not the only bluffer.

climate. See heaven[3].

temperate climate. One which is freezing cold in winter and sizzling hot in summer.

clock. 1. The man who watches the clock generally remains one of the hands. 2. Some people's faces would stop a clock; others would make one run.

See alarm clock; shirker.

close. You can generally tell how close your closest friend is if you ask him for a loan.

See detour[4]; eyes[3]; mind: open mind[3]; miser[3]; shaving: clean-shaven man; speech: good speech[2].

closet. See mink; wear[2].

clothes. 1. Fine clothes make the man—if the girl wears them. 2. The clothes that make the women are the clothes that make the men. 3. Clothes make the man, and they also help him to make the woman. 4. Clothes make the man, but when it comes to a woman, clothes merely show how she is made. 5. Modern girls are fond of nice clothes but they are not entirely wrapped up in them.

See beau; beggar[1]; break[1]; burlesque: burlesque girl; buy[1]; church[3]; circulation; drown; extreme; fake; formal; frat; habit: loose habits; laundry; matrimony: matrimonial bureau; party: informal party; pocket[2]; problem: girl's problem; show; stare; stylist; tease[2]; uncomfortable.

loud clothes. When louder clothes are made, college men will wear them.

smart clothes. Much of the smart in smart clothes is when a woman sees them on another.

clothesline. Fashion has lifted a considerable burden off the clothesline.

clothing. Many a man has only two changes of clothing—with and without.

See B.C.; change[3]; fashion[3].

club. 1. Some men believe in clubs for women—when kindness fails. 2. During a domestic argument, the husband either goes to his club or reaches for it.

See golf[4], golf ball[2].

glee club. It's easy to start an amateur glee club; the difficulty lies in stopping it.

night club. 1. A place where the tables are reserved and the guests aren't. 2. A place that knows the relation between

gauze and effect.   3. A place that always has a full attendance.
4. A place where they have taken the rest out of restaurant
and put the din in dinner.   5. They can check people's hats
and coats in night clubs, but they can't check their drinking.
See buck; night, nightcap[2]; pin: rolling pin.

clue. What detectives boast about when they can't find the
criminal.
See detective: ideal detective; hobby: detective's hobby; murder.

clutch. You can't pay attention to your brakes when your mind
is on your clutch.
See accident: auto accidents[2]; straw.

coach. An athlete who will gladly lay down your life for the
school.

coal. 1. No matter what kind of coal you use, it always goes up in
smoke.   2. There is enough coal in the United States to last
thousands of years, but one would never think so from present
prices.   3. The consumer shakes down the coal in the furnace,
but the coal dealer shakes down the consumer.
See burn; cellar; diamond[1]; storage.

> **coal dealers.** Coal dealers are in a position to forecast where
> prices may go, but the consumers can only predict where coal
> dealers should go.
> See coal[3]; winter[4].

coat. See club: night club[5]; house[3]; naked; pants[3]; rabbit[2];
restaurant[2].

> **fur coat.** Something given to a woman to keep her warm or
> quiet.
> See opportunist[1].

> **mink coat.** It takes dozens of rabbits to make one.

> **sealskin coat.** The best way to get one from a man is to
> have his seal of approval.

cockroach. See grasshopper.

cocktail. People drink cocktails because they don't like to eat
on an empty stomach.

coed. 1. A girl who also goes to college.   2. Some coeds pursue
learning while others learn pursuing.   3. Where there's smoke,
there's a coed.   4. A coed answers more questions over the
phone than she does in class.   5. A coed believes in every man
for herself.   6. A coed with brains goes to the head of the pro-

fessor's class, but a coed with class goes to the head of the professor.

See garden: Garden of Eden; language: romance languages; matrimony[5].

coeducation. It was once a race for supremacy between the sexes, but now it's neck to neck.

coffee. 1. People who give up drinking coffee have good grounds for doing so. 2. Half the world's supply of coffee is consumed in the United States in spite of what some of us have to drink at breakfast.

See degree[1]; ground: grounds.

coffin. It's not the cough that carries you off, but the coffin they carry you off in.

See telephone: telephone booth[2].

cold. 1. The only thing that can stay in some people's heads more than a day. 2. Don't feel bad if you have a cold in the head; even that's something. 3. The best way to get rid of a cold is to keep your mouth shut and your bowels open. 4. The more the years that have passed over a person's head, the more the colds that have passed through it.

See advice[2]; bear; climate: temperate climate; exercise[2]; feather[1]; frozen; hat[4]; heat; horse: race horse; hotel[2]; laryngitis; weather: zero weather.

bad cold. It's not to be sneezed at.

collaboration. What every sin is the result of.

collect. The wife who knew how to ask her husband for money remained calm—and collected.

See collective bargaining; hobby: detective's hobby.

collection. A church function in which many people take only a passing interest.

See installment: installment buying[3].

collection plate. When better times come, there'll be better buttons in the collection plate.

collective bargaining. In collective bargaining, capital bargains and labor tries to collect.

collector. 1. Not an occupation but a pursuit. 2. The only fellow who will stick to a man when he hasn't got a cent. 3. Never put off till tomorrow, unless it's the collector.

See car[4].

bill collector. 1. No man is a hero to a bill collector. 2. An apple a day keeps the doctor away, but only money keeps the bill collector away. 3. The way to have some of the best families ask you to call again is to be a bill collector.

college. 1. A fountain of knowledge where all go to drink. 2. A place where too many students learn too little. 3. The more we go to college, the more we go to college. 4. You can lead a boy to college but you can't make him think. 5. It's hard to select a college because you can't be sure which one would make father wiser. 6. Sometimes the only thing a man gets out of college is himself. 7. Fathers send their sons to college either because they went to college or because they didn't. See ability; B.A.[1]; clothes: loud clothes; coed[1]; dad; father: average father, self-made father; fever; fugitive; graduation; habit[1]; professor[3]; requirement; sap[3]; shirk; son; waste[2]; wealth: wealthy man.

college boy. 1. One who likes ties with dots, suits with stripes, and letters with checks. 2. One who likes to be treated with kindness by his parents, but not with unremitting kindness. 3. If all the college boys who sleep in class were placed end to end, they would be much more comfortable.

See flunk; irk.

college-bred. A four-year loaf made with father's dough.

college career. Dad may not be able to estimate the value of a college career, but he can tell you the cost.

college cheer. The check from home.

college courses. These days they include not only Greek but a little Scotch.

college girl. See coed; education[2].

college graduate. 1. One who starts at the bottom and wakes up. 2. One who is presented with a sheepskin to cover his intellectual nakedness. 3. If nobody dropped out before the eighth grade, what persons would be found to hire the college graduates?

See ladder.

college students. 1. When better money is made, college students will write home for it. 2. It wouldn't hurt any if the colleges would work their way through some of the students. See ability[1]; skin[3].

college yell. Thanks to civilization, mankind was enabled to develop the college yell from what was once only a feeble war whoop.

collision. What occurs when two motorists go after the same pedestrian.

color. Something which is fast when it doesn't run, but not fast when it does.

See baby[6]; biography[1]; experience: school of experience[2]; teetotaler.

off-color. See burlesque: burlesque show; story: off-color story.

colorful. Alcohol makes a man colorful: it gives him a red nose, a white liver, a yellow streak, a dark brown breath, and a blue outlook.

Columbus. 1. All Columbus did was to discover America; now look what other people have done to it. 2. It cost Columbus only a few thousand dollars to discover America, but then he didn't have to live in it afterwards.

column. Some people marry in an inside paragraph and repent in a front page column.

See Samson.

spinal column. A backbone where your head sits on one end and you sit on the other.

columnist. 1. Sometimes spelled calumnist. 2. A two-eyed creature who uses one eye for peeking and the other *I* for writing the column.

See keyhole[2].

coma. A coma interrupts the thought of a person; a comma interrupts the thought of a sentence.

comb. See bald: bald-headed man[1]; irony.

combination. The best combination for a woman is an old head, a young heart, and a baby face.

come. See opportunity[2, 4]; optimist[6]; profiteer[1].

comedian. 1. One who has a good memory for old jokes and hopes others haven't. 2. Usually a man with hair on his jest. 3. One whose life is no laughing matter. 4. One who, even when he feels good, is often out of humor.

See indulge.

radio comedians. They wouldn't laugh so hard at their own jokes if they had made them up.

comedy. A serious business.

See world[1].

comfort. Money may not buy happiness but with it you can be unhappy in comfort.

See newspaper: newspaper's duty.

comfortable. See college: college boy[3]; fashionable.

comics. See mind: serious-minded people.

comma. A mark of punctuality.

See coma; period.

command. When a man commands a good salary, the chances are his wife commandeers it.

commandment. Some people aren't wholly bad; they've only broken nine commandments.

See Ten Commandments.

commission. See radio[4].

commit. There would be fewer murders committed in the country if the murderers were.

committee. 1. A body that keeps minutes and wastes hours. 2. A group of important persons who, singly, think they can do nothing, but who, together, agree that nothing can be done. See idea[2].

    committee-of-five. It consists of one man who does the work, three others who pat him on the back, and one who brings in a minority report.

    standing committee. One that just sits.

common. Some people have nothing in common except that they both are.

See Main Street.

common sense. See sense: common sense.

commonwealth. A joint checking account.

communication. See conversation[1].

communism. Communism in America isn't new; the first American Reds were the Indians.

communist. A person always on his Marx.

community chest. An organization that puts all its begs in one ask it.

commuter. 1. One who spends his life in riding to and from his wife. 2. A traveling man who pays short visits to his home and office.

compact. Women may not always keep their agreements, but they certainly keep their compacts.

company. 1. In marriage, three's company and two's none. 2. A man is known not so much by the company he keeps but by the company he keeps out of. 3. People may like your company and still not like you. 4. A man is judged by the company he keeps; a woman, by how late she keeps company. 5. If you drop knives and forks, it means company is coming; if you miss them, it means they have gone.

See avoid; bridge[3]; businessman[3]; cartel; heaven[3]; hero[1]; misery; pajamas; pleasant[1]; producer: theatrical producer; rheumatism[2]; sandwich: garlic sandwich; stay[2]; tact: social tact; wait[2].

competition. 1. The life of trade and the bankruptcy of many engaged in it. 2. The life of trade but the death of profit.

See boy[6]; church[4]; circus; honesty[2].

complain. People who complain about not being themselves are always the gainer.

See crow; law[3]; parachute; sick: sick people.

complaint. Even when business is sound, the sound is mostly complaint.

See ground: grounds; life[2]; organ: organ recital; straphanger.

complex. See meddler.

complexion. Women get wrinkles in their complexions by worrying about their complexions.

See cosmetics[1]; drug store[3]; smoke[2].

exotic complexion. A bleaches and cream complexion.

schoolgirl complexion. Keep your schoolgirl complexion and your schoolgirl complexion will keep you.

compliment. 1. Something which you say to another and which both of you know is not true. 2. The naked truth arrayed in full dress. 3. The only thing we can pay in hard times. 4. The man who gives a compliment, gives nothing; and the person who accepts it, gets less.

See receipt; self-made.

compose. See cheese: Limburger cheese[2]; song: song writer[2, 4].

compositor. A person who has set ways.

compulsory. See liquor[2].

conceit. 1. The character of others. 2. A form of I-strain. 3. The feeling that you are the constant subject of admiration by people who are not even thinking of you. 4. Everyone has a right to be conceited until he's successful.

conceited man. One who suffers from too much vitamin I in his system.

conceited person. One whose I's are too close together.
See crossword puzzle[1].

conclusion. The logical way of reaching a conclusion is by following a train of thought.
See exercise: mental exercise; hurdle; jump[3]; statistician[1, 4].

concur. Argument with a woman is a case of: *He came, he saw, he concurred.*
See yes: yes man[1].

conduct. See etiquette[1]; vulgarity.

conference. 1. An organized method of not doing business. 2. A meeting of representatives who sit until they settle. 3. Some people tell the truth, and some say he's in conference now.
See businessman: big businessman.

confession. Confession is nine points of the law.
See sin: wages of sin[3]; past[4]; wedding[5].

open confession. 1. An open confession is not good for the sale. 2. An open confession is good for the soul, but bad for the reputation.

confidence. All that's necessary to enjoy love or frankfurters.
See betray.

confuse. You must always explain things frankly and simply to your lawyer; it is for him to confuse them afterwards.

confusion. See statistician[3].

Congress. 1. A national body that allows for a great deal of breakage when it makes laws. 2. Congress has some of the best members that money can buy. 3. When Congress takes a vacation it doesn't do anything then either. 4. Talk is cheap, except in Congress. 5. Many a man is elected to Congress—anything to get him out of town. 6. You can lead a man to Congress but you can't make him think. 7. Operations in Congress are usually directed by bloc heads. 8. Every man thinks his wife should be in Congress; she brings so many bills into the house.
See bill[4]; bloc: farm bloc; circus; death; inflation; man[2]; tax[3]; test: mental test.

chaplain of Congress. Members of Congress make the laws, and the chaplain of Congress prays for the country.

congressman. 1. One who as soon as he is elected, either grows or swells. 2. One who, every time he opens his mouth, steps on the gas. 3. One who votes for all appropriations and against all taxes.

See bill[4]; Congress: chaplain of Congress; dodge; news[3]; promise: breach of promise[1].

crooked congressmen. Representathieves.

conjecture. Something that keeps a lot of people guessing.

connection. Many a live wire would be a dead one if it weren't for his connections.

See telephone[2].

conscience. 1. The fear of being found out. 2. A guilt-edged knife. 3. The anticipation of the opinion of others. 4. The wholesome fear of the police. 5. The voice that tells you not to do something after you have done it. 6. The still, small voice that warns us someone is watching. 7. Something that feels terrible when everything else feels wonderful. 8. Conscience doesn't keep you from doing anything; it merely keeps you from enjoying it. 9. The man whose conscience never troubles him must have it pretty well trained.

See reformer[1]; self-made: self-made man[11].

clear conscience. The man with a clear conscience probably has a poor memory.

conscience-stricken people. They should strengthen their will power or weaken their conscience.

international conscience. The still, small voice that tells a country when another country is stronger.

liberty of conscience. Doing wrong and not worrying about it afterwards.

See prudence.

voice of conscience. It isn't a speaking voice but it has a telling effect.

conservative. 1. A person who has something to conserve. 2. One who has got his. 3. A man who is too cowardly to fight and too fat to run. 4. One who believes in the present what liberals forced on the world in the past.

See liberal; radical[2, 4]; right[3].

consistent. See inconsistency.

consolation. There's one consolation about both life and taxes: when you finish one, you're through with the other.

constant. There is nothing constant in this world except inconstancy.

constipate. See citizen: law-abiding citizen.

constitution. Something that determines the state of one's health or the health of one's State.

United States Constitution. Under it every man has the right to make a fool of himself as he sees fit.

See happiness: pursuit of happiness; test: mental test.

woman's constitution. The only one that doesn't take amendments.

consumer. One who has been hit by everything except falling prices.

See coal[3]; coal: coal dealer; soar; squeal.

contempt. See familiarity.

content. Drinking may not cure insomnia but it makes one more content to stay awake.

See corner.

contest. See girl: unpopular girl; weather: weather bureau.

bathing beauty contest. See bathing: bathing beauty contest.

contract. The more debts a man contracts, the more he enlarges them.

See debt[2, 3]; self-made: self-made man[8]; street.

contralto. 1. A low woman who sings. 2. A low form of music that only women sing.

contribute. Some people always contribute heat, but not light, to a discussion.

control. See public utility; weight: weight control.

convalescent. A patient who is still alive.

convenience. What the telephone used to be.

convention. 1. The road to hell is paved with good conventions. 2. At a convention, the delegate-at-large is the man who has come without his wife.

See mother[1].

political convention. Its basic nature is sound.

conversation. 1. The slowest form of human communication. 2. In conversation, when a man can't break in, it's because a woman can't break off.

See barber: barber's instruments; bore[5]; corkscrew; filibuster; library: public library; monologue[1, 3, 4]; monopolize; music: bad

music; operation: surgical operation; silence[5]; travel[2]; war[2];
weather: bad weather.

thin conversation. Usually made by a person with a thick
head.

conversationalist. One who, rather than listen, uses the interval
to plan his next remark.
See barber[1].

good conversationalist. One who can disagree without being
disagreeable.

convert. See Christianity[2].

convict. A felon who needs a friend.
See skip.

conviction. 1. A belief that you hold or that holds you. 2. Many
a man has the courage of his friends' convictions. 3. Judges
without conviction are the most generous in handing it out.
See graft; idea[3]; jury[4]; mind: open mind[1]; prejudice[3]; racketeer[1].

cook. 1. Heaven sends us good meat but the devil sends us cooks.
2. Some women can dish it out but they can't cook it. 3. There's
nothing more exasperating than a wife who can cook and won't,
except a wife who can't cook and will.
See appetite[3]; beggar[2]; delicatessen; dish; graveyard; hash[5];
missionary[1]; seat: back seat[2]; spaghetti.

cookbook. See bride: modern bride; marriage: successful
marriage[2].

good cook. The trouble with divorce is that you can't keep a
good cook now even by marrying her.
See bigamist[4].

coolness. It's usually created by hot words.

cooling system. See dancer: fan dancer[1].

co-operation. All the pedestrian asks is a little more co-operation
between horsepower and horse sense.

cop. 1. When a man flirts with a woman, and she calls a cop, he
is lucky; she might have called a clergyman. 2. Hear no evil,
speak no evil, see no evil, would be a good motto if so many
cops didn't follow it.
See policeman; racketeer[3].

traffic cop. Even though he whistles at his work, that doesn't
mean he's good-natured.

copy. People seldom improve when they have no model but themselves to copy.

See copyright; resolution: New Year's resolution[2].

copyright. It does not give a person the right to copy.

coquette. When she's good, she's very, very good, but when she's bad, she's better.

See flirt.

co-respondent. The difference between a co-respondent and a correspondent is just one letter.

cork. The average man has a corking good time uncorking.

See propose[2].

corkscrew. The best thing with which to open a conversation.

See drunkard[2].

corn. 1. Any surgeon can remove an appendix but it takes a genius to remove a corn. 2. Great aches from little toe corns grow.

    corn borer. A person who bores you with old jokes.

    corn on the cob. See chin: receding chin.

corncrib. Where all the old gags come from.

corner. Be content with your lot, especially if it's a corner one.

See gas: gas station[1].

coroner. Many a person approaches the coroner at sixty miles an hour.

corporation. 1. Something which is neither flesh nor fish but often foul. 2. A group of persons formed for individual profit without individual responsibility. 3. A corporation cannot blush.

corpse. A morgue-aged property.

corpulence. The survival of the fattest.

corset. 1. Something like love: it binds us together and makes us better than we are by nature. 2. There's a skeleton in every corset. 3. Women who wear corsets don't have loose habits.

See course.

cosmetician. Woman's face is his fortune.

cosmetics. 1. Beauty products which help women face the world with bright complexions. 2. It's only skin dope.

See age: middle age[7]; wrinkle[2].

    cosmetic dealer. See cosmetician; face[1].

cost. See breathe; college: college career; dimension; fun[2]; give; love[25]; ship; sympathizer; tax: income tax[1]; upkeep.

coterie. In one's old coterie may one sport the old pantry and vestry.

cotton. 1. Alabama wool. 2. City people make many things out of cotton, but all the farmer wants to make out of it is a profit. See America[5]; sheepish.

couch. A chaste longue.
See sofa.

cough. Something you can't drop with a cough drop.
See coffin.

cough medicine. See broadcasting.

count. 1. An old maid counts on her fingers, but a young one counts on her legs. 2. We do not count a man's years until he has nothing else to count.
See angry[2]; caddie[1]; cashier; highway[1]; man: suspicious man; teacher: kindergarten teacher; telegram[1]; word[2].

counterfeiter. One who proves that it's not always right to imitate a good example.
See time[1].

counter-irritant. A woman who looks at everything and buys nothing.

country. 1. What this country needs is fewer people telling us what this country needs. 2. People who live in the country always know how the land lies.
See cigar: five-cent cigar; conscience: international conscience; diplomacy[4]; expensive[2]; life: rural life; marriage: happy marriage[2]; patriot; President[2]; reformer[4]; simmer; tariff.
See also Chile; Czechoslovakia; Greece; Ireland; etc.

adopted country. Stepfatherland.

uncivilized country. One in which a payroll can be delivered safely without an armored car.

countryman. Most people love their country; it's their countrymen they can't bear.

coupé. Don't count your chickens until they're in the coupé.

couple. See marry: married couple.

courage. 1. Fear holding on one minute longer. 2. Fear that has said its prayers. 3. There are few persons with courage enough to admit that they haven't got any. 4. It is better to have courage than a wife; a man can't have both. 5. Man may have more courage than woman, but he doesn't get half the chance to show his backbone.

See conviction[2]; coward[1]; misfortune[3]; racketeer[1]; try: try on[1].

course. The size of the course eaten determines the size of the corset.

See golf: golf course; dessert; roast; smooth; tabloid[4].

court. 1. He who courts and does not wed, has to come to court instead. 2. In these days of frequent divorce, most of the courting is done after marriage.

See chancery; lawyer[3]; peer[2]; receiver; separate; strain; tabloid[7].

American courts. The best that money can buy.

Supreme Court. 1. It corrects the errors of the lower courts and perpetuates its own. 2. Where people go if they have anything left after getting out of the lower courts.

courtroom. A place where justice is usually dispensed—with.

courtship. 1. The period during which the girl decides whether or not she can do any better. 2. It begins when a man whispers sweet nothings, and ends when he says nothing sweet. 3. That part of a girl's life which comes between the lipstick and the broomstick.

See trial.

cousin. See husband: second husband[2]; rich[2].

cover. Many a general who is covered with medals has never been covered with guns.

See diapers; politician[8]; society[1]; spats[2]; stockings; tabloid[3]; trousseau.

cover charge. 1. Something a restaurant tries to keep under cover. 2. Even a restaurant without tablecloths may have a cover charge.

covered wagon. It was covered with many things but never with mortgages.

cow. An animal that doesn't give milk; you've got to take it from her.

See bull; calf; cream; farmer: good farmer; giraffe[2]; golf[2]; milk[1, 2], evaporated milk; never[2]; pull; sour[1].

contented cows. There are many contented cows, but who has ever heard of a contented farmer?

coward. 1. What many a man would be if he had enough courage. 2. No coward is small enough to hide behind a woman's skirts these days.

See magician.

cowbell. You can hear cowbells, but you can't hear cow horns.

crab. See pearl; shellfish.

crack. It's a wise crack that knows its own father.

See ice; installment: installment collector[2]; wit: half wit[1].

crank. A person or thing that makes revolutions.

See organ: hand organ.

crash. If you stop, look, and listen when approaching a railroad crossing, all you'll hear is the car behind crashing into you.

See car: used car[4].

crazy. It's not necessary for a writer to be crazy, but it does help.

See fame: test of fame; hobby; insane: insane asylum[1, 3]; newspaper: newspaper function; plane; steam.

cream. It costs more than milk because it's harder for the cows to sit on the smaller bottles.

See breakfast: Sunday breakfast; complexion; exotic complexion; fly[1].

create. Did nature create man to show that she is big enough to make mistakes, or was it pure ignorance?

See poetry[2]; rest; science.

Creation. Woman was only a side issue at the Creation, but now she's the whole works.

See man[1].

credit. 1. The capital of a rich man's son. 2. The easiest way to get it is not to need it. 3. One can get everything on credit nowadays except money. 4. Some men are so generous, they give their wives everything credit can buy. 5. Give a man credit for anything today and he will take it.

See language: sign language; prosperity[3, 5]; rabbit[2].

creditor. 1. One who has a better memory than a debtor. 2. A great observer of set days and times. 3. The man who cannot meet his creditors probably doesn't want to. 4. Running into debt isn't so bad; it's running into creditors that's so upsetting.

See keep: keep up; summer[3]; want[5].

crime. 1. The true story of crime cannot be told in sentences. 2. Crime too has its permanent wave.

See censor[3]; church[5]; dishonest; number; optional; tabloid[8]; wave: crime wave.

criminal. 1. One who gets caught. 2. No one is a criminal before he is caught. 3. Give a criminal enough rope and he'll tie up a cashier.

See clue; executor; judge[2]; pen.

critic. 1. A man who expects miracles. 2. One who writes about things he doesn't like. 3. A person who can appreciate something he doesn't like and depreciate something everybody else likes. 4. A wet blanket that soaks everything it touches. 5. One who would have you write it, sing it, play it, or paint it, as he would do it—if he could. 6. The fate of critics is to be remembered by what they failed to understand. 7. Critics are people who go places and boo things.
See gold[1]; relatives[1].

drama critic. 1. One who gives the best jeers of his life to the theatre. 2. One who believes in the policy that the flay's the thing.
See actor: ham actor.

literary critic. One who usually finds meanings in a book that the author didn't know were there.

criticism. 1. It can be avoided by saying nothing, doing nothing, and being nothing. 2. The disapproval of people not for having faults, but for having faults different from ours.

criticize. See American: loyal American; pleasure[1].

crockery. See ping-pong; resolution: New Year's resolution[1].

crooked. What many a man is, straight through.
See bent; congressman: crooked congressmen; manufacturer: pretzel manufacturer; repeat[6].

croon. See sing: radio singing.

crop. As soon as a crop starts coming up in the fields, it starts going down in the market.
See bumper; family: family tree[1]; wild: wild oats.

marriage crops. The trouble with them is that they're too divorcified.

croquette. See meat[2].

cross. You can't put things across by getting cross.
See bridge[2]; ferryboat; pedestrian[22]; tracks: railroad tracks.

crossing. Where it is better to be dead sure than sure dead.
See bus[1]; front[1]; heat: dead heat; race; railroad: railroad crossing; sober.

grade crossing. People who haven't time to stop at a grade crossing always find time to attend the funeral.
See bus[2].

crossroad. 1. Often the meeting place of headlights and light

heads.   2. The safest thing to do at a crossroad is to humor it.
See Broadway[2].

crossword puzzle.   1. Something a conceited person does with a
fountain pen.   2. A problem made up of a few crosswords and
many crossed out words.
See gnu[1].

crow.   A bird that never complains without caws.

crowd.   See bridge[3]; pickpocket; resort: summer resort[4]; statesman[3]; subway[1]; swim: swimming pool.

crown.   About the only crowns worn by kings nowadays are on
their hats.
See king[2]; tooth.

cry.   1. If at first you don't succeed, cry, cry again.   2. Some
women try and get it; others cry and get it.   3. You never know
what you can get till you cry.
See milk: spilt milk; transplanting; vegetable.

cub.   See ruminant.

cue.   See pool.

cultivate.   Cultivate vices when you are young, and when you are
old they will not forsake you.

culture.   Some people have culture, but most have varnish.

cultured man.   One who has a lot of information that isn't
worth anything to him.

cup.   There's many a cup 'twixt the lip and the slip.
See bottle[2]; sailor[2]; sip.

Cupid.   1. He always tries to make a hit with every Miss.
2. When he hits the mark, he usually Mrs. it.
See bow; chastity[2]; cupidity.

cupidity.   Cupidity causes more marriages than Cupid.

cure.   What a doctor often does to a disease while killing the
patient.
See doctor[4]; fee; guillotine[1]; medicine; procure; psychoanalysis;
psychologist; quit; snore: snoring[5]; swear[2]; tobacco: tobacco
habit.

curiosity.   Bright eyes indicate curiosity, and black eyes indicate
too much curiosity.
See child[1]; love: first love[1]; run[2].

woman's curiosity.   It's almost as great as a man's.

curious.   1. The most curious thing in the world is a woman who is not curious.   2. Many a child is so curious, he tries to take his nose apart to see what makes it run.

See disappoint[2].

currency.   Money which isn't current enough.

  confederate currency.   Time is money, but a lot of it is about as valuable as confederate currency.

current.   See electricity[2].

curve.   1. Time often changes a woman's dangerous curves to extended contours.   2. Many an auto accident is caused by the driver's hugging the wrong curve.

See liquor[6]; suit: bathing suit[4]; triangle: domestic triangle.

cushions.   The only underthings nudists go for.

custom.   The difference between law and custom is that it takes a lot of nerve to violate a custom.

customer.   The customer is always right, until his bill is overdue. See drink: soft drink; power: power companies; taxi: taxi driver[1].

cut.   See barber[1, 2, 4], barber's instruments, barber trade; book[4]; chorine; tailor[1]; tax: tax cut; tongue: fool's tongue.

  cut off.   See talk: talking machine; telephone: telephone booth[5].

  short cut.   After shaving, a fellow's map generally shows a lot of short cuts.

cyclone.   Wind exceeding the speed limit.

See trifle.

cynic.   1. One who thinks it is better to have loved and lost. 2. One who is married to his first love.   3. A man bored with sinning.   4. One who suffers from skeptic poisoning.   5. A person who knows the price of everything and the value of nothing.   6. A man who doesn't believe in anything and wants other people to share his beliefs.

Czechoslovakia.   The land of Czech and double Czech.

D

dachshund.   1. A low-down dog.   2. Half a dog high by a dog and a half long.   3. A dog who wags his tail by remote control.

4. A good family dog because all the members of the family can pat him at the same time.

dad. In every university there are many young men diligently working their dads through college.

See bean; college: college career; education: liberal education[2]; father; owe[1]; son.

daddy. Every male parent is a daddy, but not every daddy is a male parent.

dairyman. All that he is he owes to udders.

dalliance. Neck-romancy.

damages. People who go to law for damages are sure to get them.

See fire: fire department.

damp. A home doesn't have to be damp even if there is much due on it.

See blanket: wet blanket; camp: old campground; centaur.

dance. 1. Hugging set to music. 2. If a man can't dance, the least he can do is hold you while you dance.

See feet[1]; generation: younger generation[1]; restaurant[5].

dance floor. See floor: dance floor.

modern dance. 1. It has developed in leaps and bounds. 2. Wonderful exercise; the reformers are certainly exercised about it.

new dances. Some people grow old gracefully; others attempt the new dances.

dancer. Good dancers are light on their feet; poor dancers alight on their partners'.

fan dancer. 1. A dancer with a cooling system. 2. One who never lacks fans.

tap dancer. A person with a shaky future.

toe dancer. A person who dances all over her partner's toes.

dandruff. Small, whitish scales trying to get ahead.

See guillotine[1].

dangerous. A little loving is a dangerous thing.

See little: little woman; lying[2]; run: running; widow[1], little widow.

Daniel. The only man who was not spoiled by being lionized.

dare. A man is as good as he has to be, and a woman as bad as she dares.

dark. If you can't make light of your troubles, keep them in the dark.

See character[2]; hand[3]; house: glass houses; merger; pawn; poker.

darkroom. Where many a girl with a negative personality is developed.

darn. 1. Women who have no holes in their stockings don't give a darn. 2. The old-fashioned wife darned her hubby's socks, but the modern wife socks her darned hubby.

See circle: sewing circle.

Darwin. A scientist who got his idea of evolution from observing peoples' relatives.

See evolution[3].

date. 1. The only dates some old maids ever get are the ones on their tombstones. 2. Girls with good figures make the best dates. 3. This would be a great world if you could date your checks as far ahead as the publishers date their magazines.

See line: good line; popular: popular girl; room: waiting room.

heavy date. The girl with a heavy date usually wears something light.

out of date. See fashion[2].

daughter. 1. A father is afraid all young men want to marry his daughter; a mother is afraid they don't. 2. As long as a woman can look ten years younger than her own daughter, she is perfectly satisfied. 3. Still daughters run deep. 4. If the folks don't keep up the old home, their daughters won't have anywhere to stay between marriages.

See fact: facts of life; rise: early rising[1]; turn: turn out[2]; wedding: wedding dress.

dawn. See nudist: nudist camp[1].

day. 1. In some homes it starts with the sunrise; in others, with the son-rise. 2. After a few months of work, Eskimos call it a day.

See Adam: Adam & Eve[2, 3]; build[1]; cat[1]; clever: clever person; cold[1]; dissipation; nudist: nudist camp[1]; resolution: New Year's resolution[1]; Sabbath; sheep; strong[2]; tomorrow; weak[1]; world[3].

daily dozen. 1. What a fat person should take every day, but not with his knife and fork. 2. It's usually the daily doesn't.

day off. It's generally followed by an off day.

Father's Day. The day to remember the forgotten man.

good old days. See Adam: Adam & Eve[4]; driving[1]; time: times.

Mother's Day. The holiday that proves that everybody loves mother—on Mother's Day.

rainy day. See rain: rainy day.

daydream. Women daydream but men dame-dream.

daylight. 1. About all that anybody can save these days. 2. The best way to save it is to use it.

daylight-saving time. During daylight-saving time, the only chance you get to see the night is in the morning.

daytime. See chair: miss[3].

deacon. A guiding light to warn the people.

dead. See crossing; mankind; medium; money[10]; often[1]; opinion[4]; praise[1]; relatives[6]; secret[4]; widow[3]; work[3].

deaf. See speaker: loud speaker[1].

deal. 1. In cards, a good deal depends upon a good deal. 2. In cards, a good deal depends on luck, and luck depends on a good deal.
See reform[3].

dean. A person who doesn't know enough to be a professor but who is too smart to be a president.

dear. Time makes most women dearer to their husbands—time and clothing bills.
See deer; girl[4].

death. Two things are certain: death and taxes; but death doesn't get worse every time Congress meets.
See Adam; certain; executor; inevitable; painless; punishment: capital punishment[2]; taxpayer; time[4]; together.

natural death. Being killed by an automobile.
See profession: medical profession.

debt. 1. What most people run into. 2. The only thing that doesn't become smaller when it is contracted. 3. People who run into it usually try to crawl out of it. 4. The wages of sin is debt. 5. A new way to contract debts—pay them off. 6. In the midst of life we are in debt.
See contract; creditor[4]; finance; generation: passing generation; liquidate; marriage: marriage vows; owe[1]; prompt; prosperity[4]; raise[1]; round[2]; shoemaker; sting.

college debts. Obligations that, with economy, thrift and self-denial, father will be able to pay.

government debt. When you think of the government debt the next generation must pay off, no wonder a baby yells when it's born.

public debt. The trouble with it is that the private individual has to pay it.

debtor. See creditor[1].

deceit. To deceive a deceiver is no deceit.

See deception; disappearance; oneself; romance[2].

decency. 1. Indecency's conspiracy of silence. 2. A man never becomes so lost to decency and righteousness that he can't see the other fellow's duty.

See suit: bathing suit[2].

decent. Truth is stranger than fiction, and more decent.

deception. The one charm of marriage is that it makes a life of deception absolutely necessary for both parties.

See deceit.

decide. See jury[1]; polls[1].

decline. Declining to pay high prices will make them decline.

Decoration Day. What many women think Easter Sunday is.

deed. See misdeed; mortgage[2]; realtor; telegram[1].

deep. See daughter[3]; education: college education[4].

deer. Deer is not beef but beef is dear.

See hunter: wise hunter.

defeat. It isn't bitter if you don't swallow it.

defend. It is easier for a woman to defend her virtue against men than her reputation against women.

defendant. 1. A person who should always have a lawyer unless he has friends on the jury. 2. Justice may be blind, but seldom too blind to distinguish between the defendant who has money and the one who hasn't. 3. Many a defendant is not half as guilty as the judge and jury—take him to be.

See America[2].

definition. A word that's not a definition.

See dictionary: comic dictionary; optimist[5]; wage: living wage[1].

defraud. See gold: gold digger[2].

deft. The musician who plays by ear is quite deft.

degree. 1. A man with a degree and ten cents can get a cup of coffee anywhere. 2. No matter how many degrees a man has, he can never equal a thermometer.

See B.A.[1,2]; M.A.; education[2]; matrimony[6].

delicatessen. The only way to teach some women how to cook is to burn down all the delicatessen stores.

delirium. Something that's different from love, but it's hard to tell the difference.

deliver. Remarks that are uncalled for are usually delivered.
See hearse[1]; introducer; speech[1].

demand. See supply: supply & demand.

democracy. 1. The bludgeoning of the people, by the people, for the people. 2. A form of government in which the rich get every consideration granted the poor. 3. Where you can say what you please but don't have to listen unless you want to. 4. A form of government that is run by all the people and run down by some of them.
See faith[2].

Democrat. See party[3].

dense. The population of the United States is most dense from the neck up.
See birth: birth control[1].

dentist. 1. The greatest Yank of them all. 2. One who pulls the tooth, the whole tooth, and nothing but the tooth. 3. One who pulls out the teeth of others to obtain employment for his own. 4. One who, at work, always looks down in the mouth. 5. One who lives from hand to mouth. 6. The only man who can tell a woman to shut her mouth and get away with it. 7. A man who runs a filling station. 8. If you plan to be a dentist, start saving up old magazines.
See extraction; painstaking; room: waiting room.

depart. See dress: silk dress; hair[2]; hiccough.

departure. Nothing makes a woman in love happier than the departure of a rival.

depend. You can always depend upon a bore never to have a previous engagement.
See feeling[2]; salad; subject[1].

deposit. 1. Woman is the one who pays and pays; the man merely deposits. 2. Time is money, but just try to deposit it.

depression. 1. A period when people do without the things their parents never had. 2. The times that try men's soles. 3. Good times gone bad. 4. A period when you can't spend money you don't have. 5. A period when all wages go down except the wages of sin.

See prosperity[6].

depth. Height turned upside down.

See grave; loan: loan shark; public speaker[1].

dermatology. The best specialty; the patient never dies, and never gets well.

descend. 1. Man descended from the animals, but some men descended much further than others. 2. The trouble is not what man descended from but what he descends to. 3. Man must be descended from some kind of animal because one-half of the world goose-steps and the other half pussyfoots.

See inferior; descent.

descendant. See pioneer; road: roadhouse.

descent. 1. The further back you can trace your descent, the longer you have been descending. 2. Some people doubt whether man's descent from the monkey has started yet.

desertion. The poor man's method of divorce.

See appeal.

deserve. The man who marries a second time doesn't deserve to lose his first wife.

See bold; brave; mate; successful: successful man[3].

design. Women's styles may change but their designs remain the same.

See cake: birthday cake[2]; flagrant.

designers. They had better be careful or they'll work themselves out of a job someday.

style designer. One who has mode in his eye.

desire. It's often nipped in the budget.

See tragedy.

desk. See businessman: tired businessman; pile; salesman[2].

despise. If the world despises a hypocrite, what must they think cf him in heaven?

See suicide[2].

dessert. The course that people with upset stomachs should eat first.

destroy. See memory.

destruction. See pride[4].

detail. See liar: clever liar; sympathy.

detective. A person who never runs down anything but his heels.

See bride[2]; clue; swindler.

detective stories. See story: detective stories.

ideal detective. One who follows the culprit and not the clue.

detest. A woman detests flattery, especially when it is directed toward another woman.

detour. 1. The roughest distance between two points. 2. Something open for summer driving. 3. The longest distance between two points. 4. It's fortunate that whenever a road is closed, a detour is open.
See scenery.

develop. No woman really makes a fool out of a man; she merely gives him an opportunity to develop his natural capacities.
See college: college yell; darkroom; sweets; tax: income tax[1].

development. See evolution[1]; fiction[2]; progress[3]; wishbone.

devil. Women give themselves to God when the devil wants nothing more to do with them.
See cook[1].

devour. The man who devours his wife with kisses often finds that she disagrees with him.

diagnose. See doctor: grasping doctor.

dial. A man in love will phone his girl every day or dial in the attempt.
See story: radio story.

diamond. 1. A chunk of coal that stuck to its job. 2. A woman's idea of a stepping stone to success. 3. A gem whose bright sparkle renders a woman stone-blind to the defects of the man offering it. 4. The diamond proves that all that glitters is not gold. 5. There's nothing harder than a diamond, except making the payments on it. 6. Diamonds don't grow on trees but they are found on the right kind of limbs.
See hand[2]; hard[1]; money: pin money; pearl; umpire[2].

> **diamond jubilee.** When the last installment is paid on the engagement ring.

diapers. Changeable seat covers.

diary. Some people can't even tell the truth in a diary.

dice. In dice, rolling bones gather no moss.
See business: shaky business.

dictaphone. Its advantage is that it never takes a man's mind off his work by crossing its knees.

dictation. When a stenographer marries her boss, she stops taking dictation from him.

dictator. 1. One who thinks he can take it, no matter to whom it belongs. 2. A person who has an easy time reaching a misunderstanding with other countries.

See fascism[1].

dictionary. It always has the first and last word.

See drug store[2]; investigate; office[2]; pride[4].

comic dictionary. A book containing daffynitions.

die. The good die young, and the old dye for various reasons.

See accelerator; California[2]; center; civilization[1]; exposure; fame[1]; flowers[4]; grouch[2]; insurance: life insurance[2]; leave[4]; liar[2]; longevity; lot[2]; millionaire; property; relatives[3, 5]; resolution; statistics: traffic statistics; wicked.

diet. 1. Eat, drink and be merry, for tomorrow you diet. 2. Diets vary: vegetarians live on vegetables, and sailors live on the sea.

See board: board of health; onion[2].

balanced diet. See walk: tightrope walker.

dieting. 1. A form of fad reducing. 2. The art of letting the hips fall where they sway.

reducing diet. 1. A diet that does so much for the will power and so little for the waistline. 2. The best one is to live on hope. 3. Women on reducing diets like to have their weigh.

soft diet. Parents who are too hard on their children should be put on a soft diet.

dietetics. The triumph of mind over platter.

differ. See love[6]; radical[1]; savage.

difference. See delirium; horse: horse race[1]; preacher[3]; single; size.

different. All husbands are alike, but they have different faces so you can tell them apart.

See criticism[2]; divorce[11]; ignorant[1]; neighbor: quarreling neighbors; news[1].

difficult. See nothing: do nothing[4].

difficulty. 1. The best way out of one is through it. 2. The chief difference between the movies and real life is that in the movies the difficulties come before marriage.

dig. If you want a tired businessman to do any spring digging, give him a golf club.

See grave: marital grave.

dignity. The one thing that can't be preserved in alcohol. See class.

dimple. Many a man who falls in love with a dimple makes the mistake of marrying the whole girl.

dimension. There are four dimensions: length, breadth, thickness, and cost.

diner. A restaurant where you can eat dirt cheap, but who wants to eat dirt?

dinner. See cannibal[3]; club: night club[4]; forgive[2]; girl: shrewd girl; guest[3]; hungry; lunch; serve[2, 3]; speaker: after-dinner speaker[2]; swamp; thirteen[1].

diplomacy. 1. Lying in state. 2. The art of letting someone else have your way. 3. The non-publicity of duplicity. 4. The patriotic art of lying for one's country. 5. The art of convincing a man he's a liar without actually telling him so. 6. The art of getting something as though you were giving it. 7. It's easy on the brain but hell on the feet.

business diplomacy. The art of never saying no but always taking the matter under advisement.

secret diplomacy. The best way to end it is to admit women to the diplomatic corps.

diplomat. 1. One who pours banana oil on troubled waters. 2. An international liar, with an elastic conscience and a rubber neck. 3. A man who always remembers a woman's birthday, but never her age. 4. One who never heard that old joke before. 5. When a diplomat says *yes,* he means *perhaps;* when he says *perhaps,* he means *no;* and when he says *no,* he's no diplomat. See sleeve.

dipsomaniac. One who drinks like a fish, but not the same thing.

direction. See pin[3]; political: political leader; rumor[1]; street: one-way street[2]; wages[1].

right direction. See church: skyscraper churches; mind: one-track mind.

wrong direction. It will do no good to get on the right track if you then go in the wrong direction.

dirt. Simply matter out of place.

See boy[2]; diner; press: press agent[1]; soap; suit: bathing suit[6].

dirty. The girl with the cleanest mind gives you the dirtiest looks.

See soap: soft soap; towel.

disagree. See conversationalist: good conversationalist; devour; harmony: domestic harmony[2]; history[7].

disappearance. Appearances are deceitful, but disappearances are often more so.

See pin[3].

disappoint. 1. When a man is disappointed in love, he remains a bachelor; a woman marries. 2. Men marry because they are hopeful; women because they are curious; both are disappointed.

See dreams[3]; expect; party: two-party system; sign.

disappointment. See fishing[1]; opportunity[1]; year[1].

disarmament. If the female statue with the scales represents Justice, then the one minus the arms must represent Disarmament.

discharge. The best way to get rid of your duties is to discharge them.

See report.

disclose. Man proposes but woman discloses.

discourage. No wonder a hen gets discouraged; she can never find things where she lays them.

discover. Better sit in the back row and be discovered than sit in the front row and be found out.

See Columbus[1, 2]; explorer: modern explorer; reputation[1].

discretion. The age of discretion is reached when one has learned to be indiscreet discreetly.

discussion. The better part of valor.

See contribute.

disease. See cure; medicine; osteopathy[2]; psychoanalysis; wife[6]; writer: writer's cramp.

disgrace. It's no disgrace to be poor; it doesn't attract that much attention.

See inconvenient; poverty[3].

disgraceful. Some people grow old gracefully; others keep disgracefully young.

disguise. 1. The woman who thinks she's an angel in disguise is probably a perfect disguise. 2. An angel in disguise is not always in the skies.

See hunter: wise hunter; poverty[2].

dish. Something often hard to cook but always easy to break.

See cook[2]; modern: modern girl[1]; pan.

chafing dish. A frying pan that has gotten into society.

washing dishes. The only way to avoid it is to have your husband eating out of your hand.

See swim.

dishonest. It's queer that men should take up crime when there are so many legal ways to be dishonest.

disillusion. The attainment of an ideal.

disillusioned people. They should have their faith lifted.

dislike. Usually a husband and wife both like and dislike the same things; they both like to fight, and they both dislike each other.

See Christian; reason[2].

display. Today women display more backbone than men.

See wife: modern wife.

displease. Women dress not to please men but to displease other women.

disposition. The position of your nature.

See happiness[1]; telephone: telephone booth[2].

disrespect. Members of the younger generation are alike in many disrespects.

dissatisfy. Where there's a will, there are dissatisfied relatives.

dissipation. They who lengthen their nights by dissipation usually shorten their days.

distance. 1. Very often the girl who looks good at a distance should stay at a distance. 2. Most girls who look good from a distance owe it to the distance.

See detour[1, 3]; hear[2]; manners; relative: distant relative; sight: far-sighted; telephone[4]; witness: witness stand[2].

diva. A woman swimmer.

divers. Birds of a feather flock together, but ducks are found in divers places.

divide. The world is divided into people who think they are right.

See spoils.

dividends. See hen[2].

division. See political: political troubles.

divorce. 1. Hash made from domestic scraps. 2. The future tense of marriage. 3. The proof that one man's mate is another man's poison. 4. A legal formula ending a marriage and preceding a wedding. 5. Its two chief causes: matrimony and alimony. 6. Nowadays a couple marries and the first thing you know they have a little divorce. 7. After a divorce, a woman feels like a new man. 8. The girl who marries for money often divorces for love.   9. Statistics show that divorces almost equal marriages; love is evidently finding a way—out.   10. The best way to decrease the number of divorces is for folks to stay divorced.   11. Divorces have become so common that the really smart folks are staying married in order to be different.

See alimony[11]; bachelor[14]; cook: good cook; court[2]; desertion; earth[1]; fast[1]; fight[4]; June; marry[4], unhappy married man; mirage; morning; originate; promise: breach of promise[2]; publicity[4]; quest; reason: trivial reasons; state; strain; tabloid[7]; wedding[1].

divorce evil.   One reason for the divorce evil is that people don't divorce evil.

divorce suit.   It's always pressed with the seamy side out.

ideal divorce.   Where the wife gets the children and the husband gets the maid.

divorcee.   A person who married for better or worse, but not for good.

do.   1. Do others or they will do you.   2. No man lives long enough to do all the things his wife wants him to do.

See boast[1]; explain; first[1]; happiness: secret of happiness[1]; health[1]; keep: keep on; marriage: marriage ritual; marry[6]; nothing: do nothing; nowadays; payment: easy payments; reason[1]; Rome; seasickness[2]; suicide[1]; taste[2]; teaching[2]; think[5]; well: well-to-do.

doctor.   1. One who kills you today to prevent you from dying tomorrow.   2. A man who suffers from good health—in his community.   3. A man who prescribes drugs of which he knows little, for a body of which he knows less.   4. If the doctor cures, the sun sees it; if he kills, the earth hides it.

See appendix[1]; collector: bill collector[1]; cure; double: double jeopardy; fee; heal; illness; insane; mistake[1]; onion[3]; organ: organ recital; osteopath[2, 3]; owe[1]; practice[2]; prescribe; quit; recover; seasickness[2]; specialist; tonsils.

best doctor.   The one you run for and can't find.

grasping doctor.   One who diagnoses your case by feeling your purse.

doctrine.   The skin of truth set up and stuffed.

dodge.   If he dodges cars, he's a pedestrian; if he dodges taxes, he's a businessman; if he dodges responsibility, he's a congressman.

dog. 1. The only animal that has seen his god. 2. An animal that perspires through his pants. 3. The more you see of men, the more you admire dogs. 4. The difference between a dog and a man is that if you pick up a starving dog and make him prosperous, he won't bite you. 5. A reasonable number of fleas is good for a dog; it keeps him from brooding over being a dog. See bark; bite; bladder; boy[5]; cat[1], catty woman; catch[1]; cheap[4]; chicken; chow; dachshund[1, 2, 3]; editor: newspaper editor; fleas; love: puppy love[1]; news[2, 3]; offer; publicity[3]; revenge[1]; smell[2]; spitz; tease[1]; Utopia; water[1]; weather: beastly weather.

dog fancier. A person who takes a fancy to fancy dogs.

doggerel. A little dog.

dogmatism. Puppyism come to its full growth.

See stigma.

doings. Newspapers play up the doings of rich people, it being only natural that money should draw interest.

doldrums. They always succeed the war drums.

dollar. 1. The jack of all trades. 2. It goes very fast nowadays, but not very far. 3. Something that can never fall so low as the means some people adopt to get it. 4. A dollar doesn't buy much of anything nowadays without a partner.

See board: boarding house[1]; hotel[1]; installment: installment buying[2]; lawsuit[3]; menace; nickel[2]; odds; owe[2]; perfume: expensive perfume; same[2]; sense[3, 4]; squander[2]; writer[2].

dollar bills. Famous men get their heads on them but women would rather get their hands on them.

See buck: pass the buck.

dollar sign. An S that's been double-crossed.

silver dollar. Another proof that money talks is that a man's head never appears on a silver dollar.

domestic. See divorce[1]; triangle: domestic triangle.

donkey. See assess.

don't. The best advice to give a man about to marry.

door. One never knows whether it's opportunity at the door or just another salesman.

See census: census taker; cheese: Limburger cheese[2]; claptrap; keyhole[3]; knocker; mink; opportunist[1]; Oriental; push; stork[3].

revolving door. 1. It goes around with a lot of people. 2. It's constantly making revolutions.

dormitory. Some people sleep in pajamas; others sleep in dormitories.

dot. See circle; college: college boy[1].

dotage. A condition characterized by anecdotage.

double. The only way to double your money is to fold it and put it in your hip pocket.

See champagne; life: double life; trouble[7].

double cross. See Broadway[2]; dollar: dollar sign.

double jeopardy. When your doctor calls in a consulting physician.

doubt. 1. When in doubt, tell the truth. 2. If you're in doubt whether to kiss a pretty girl, give her the benefit of the doubt.

dough. 1. Man wants but little here but dough. 2. Strange that men call money dough; dough sticks to your fingers.

See college: college-bred; manufacturer: pretzel manufacturer; miser[1]; politics[7].

doughnut. It proves that the hole is greater than any of its parts.

See miser[1]; odds; pessimist[1].

doughnut hole. 1. Nothing in the way of food. 2. It was invented by a fresh air fiend.

dove. See bird[1].

down. 1. A man is never down till he's down in the mouth. 2. So much down usually means so much to keep up.

See farm[3, 4]; hit[1]; hold[2]; living: cost of living[5]; lying[1]; mustache: young man's mustache; pedestrian[6]; prejudice[1]; tombstone[2]; up: up & down; whale.

down & out. See businessman: big businessman; flyer: flyer's wife.

downfall. The upkeep of woman is the downfall of man.

downtown. You can't keep a good golfer downtown.

draft. See architect[1].

drama. See actor: amateur actor.

dramatist. Usually a man of all work and no play.

draw. See art[1]; artist: bad artist; interest[1]; lipstick[3]; poker.

drawers. 1. A single artist may be nothing in particular, but two artists are a pair of drawers. 2. Summer is ending, winter drawers on.

See matrimony: matrimonial bureau; resolution: New Year's resolution[2].

dream. See dreams.

dreamer. A person who leads a dreamatic existence.

practical dreamer. One who has an ear for music and a nose for pork chops.

dreams. 1. Where you meet a better class of people. 2. What some men believe in until they marry one. 3. When a married man dreams he's a bachelor, it's a sign he's going to be disappointed when he wakes up.

See daydream; insomnia[3]; money[7]; nightmare; professor: absent-minded professor; sign; troublesome; vague; wake: wake up[1].

dress. 1. A woman never knows what kind of dress she doesn't want until she buys it. 2. The dress that makes one girl look slim often makes others look round. 3. There are a million or more reasons why modern women dress as they do, and every one is a man. 4. You can always see a woman's dress without seeing her dress.

See bargain: bargain sale[1]; clergyman; displease; Europe; gown: evening gown[2]; inch; installment: installment plan[2]; modest; naked; night; nothing[2]; please[2]; pour; salad; slacks[3]; strip-tease: stripper; try: try on[2].

coming-out dress. It isn't always a low-cut gown.

evening dress. A dress that's more gone than gown.

house dress. The cheapest garment in the long run because it's seldom worn out.

short dress. See miss: junior miss.

silk dress. It has departed; it's probably better off.

dressmaker. 1. One who knows the seamy side of life. 2. One who is never what she seams.

drink. 1. After a few drinks every woman looks beautiful. 2. It was a woman who first prompted man to eat, but he took to drink on his own account thereafter. 3. First the man takes a drink; then the drink takes a drink; then the drink takes the man.

See bottle[1, 2]; buck; cheap[2]; college[1]; diet[1]; dipsomaniac; drunkard[1]; end[3]; eyesight; graveyard; health[1, 3]; impunity; irrigate; kidney; liquor[7]; man: abstemious man, stingy man; milk: spilt milk[2]; night: nightcap[2]; old-fashioned: old-fashioned girl[3]; schooner; souse; thirteen[2]; throat; water[2]; whiskey; wine; work[2].

mixed drink. 1. A mixed drink is not harmful unless you drink it. 2. Blessed are the pure in spirits for there is nothing worse than a mixed drink.

soft drink. A soft drink turneth away customers.

See heart: soft-hearted woman.

drinking. 1. What a man does to forget, but the only thing he forgets is when to stop. 2. They who can stand drinking usually drink standing. 3. There are two reasons for drinking: one is, when you are thirsty, to cure it; the other, when you are not thirsty, to prevent it.

See bar[1]; beginning; club: night club[5]; cocktail; content; hangover[2]; water[5].

hard drinking. The easiest thing some men do.

occasional drink. Nothing can be more frequent.

regular drinking. Drinking between drinks.

drive. See driving.

driver. One who horns in.

See accident: auto accidents[1]; car[2, 5]; curve[2]; fender[2]; flat; golf; golf links[2]; knock; next; safety; safety zone; speed: speed up; street; thick[2]; traffic: traffic jam; wreck.

backseat driver. 1. When better cars are built, the backseat driver will be enclosed in a soundproof case. 2. Not all women are backseat drivers; some sit up front where they can grab the wheel if their husbands don't obey them.

See rear admiral; seat: back seat.

bad driver. 1. An accident going somewhere to happen. 2. One who never takes the street and narrow path.

careless drivers. In the old days there were just as many careless drivers but the horses had better sense.

See run: run down[2].

reckless driver. 1. He's seldom wreckless long. 2. The reckless driver must go, but why must he go so fast? 3. A reckless driver is rarely a wreckless driver.

See lifetime.

woman driver. 1. One who refuses to take the straight and narrow path. 2. When she holds out her hand, you can be certain she is either going to turn left, turn right, back up, or stop. 3. She doesn't let her right hand know what her left hand has signaled. 4. A man is always glad to give her half the road if he could find out which half she wants. 5. Time, tide, and women drivers wait for no man. 6. Among women drivers, one bad turn deserves another. 7. Allowing the woman driver the right of way is chivalry, to say nothing of prudence.

See road[4]; signal.

driving. 1. It proves that much of the horse sense of the good old days was possessed by the horse. 2. Drive like hell, and you'll get there. 3. It's dangerous to drive a car with one hand; many a man has run into a church that way. 4. The majority of Americans know how to drive a car, but the police records prove otherwise. 5. Everyone should learn how to drive a car, especially those behind the steering wheel.

See advise: advisory capacity[2]; detour[2]; fill[2]; fog; hit[2]; minute; rehearse; seat: back seat; sober; speeder; truck; turn[2]; youth[3].

backseat driving. See hearse: hearse driver.

driving dangers. Hic, hike, hug.

reckless driving. The solution of this problem can't be given in a short sentence.

drop. Some guests drop in for a call; others call in for a drop. See company[5]; cough; high; million[2]; pick: pick up; prohibitionist[5]; prohibitive; waterfall.

drown. When you go to drown yourself, always pull off your clothes; they may fit your wife's second husband.

See straw.

drug. See doctor[3]; druggist; restaurant[4].

druggist. A man who used to sell drugs.

drug store. 1. An establishment where a person can get indigestion and a remedy for it at the same time. 2. If you can't find a thing in the dictionary or the encyclopedia, ask for it in the drug store. 3. The only way to get women to take long walks for their complexions is to put the drug stores further apart.

See medicine: medicine cabinet.

drum. 1. If thine enemy wrong thee, buy each of his children a drum. 2. Two heads are better than one—in a drum.

See beat; doldrums; fiddle.

drunk. It's as easy to get drunk on water as it is on land.

See aspirin; fight[3]; flesh; sober; sophisticated; zwieback.

drunkard. 1. One who is always out of spirits between drinks.

2. One who attempts to pull himself out of trouble with a corkscrew.

See liquor[4]; stagger.

sad drunkard. One who is in a state of melancoholism.

dry. 1. One who has water on the brain. 2. In modern society, the drys get most of the boos.

See talk: dry talker; towel: paper towel.

dry dock. The place that launched a thousand ships.

duck. 1. A chicken on snowshoes. 2. An animal that walks as if it had just gotten out of a rumble seat.

dude. When a dude marries, he becomes subdued.

See nudist: nudist colony.

due. See bill: twenty-dollar bill; customer; damp; winter[5].

dull. All work and no pay makes Jack a dull boy.

See blunt; jack[3]; temper[5]; yawn[2].

dull people. People with too much polish.

dumb. The stupid half of wisdom.

See laugh: laugh last[3]; oyster[2]; Venus[1].

dumb people. The trouble with them is that they don't stay dumb.

dummy. All the dummies in the movies don't get thrown over cliffs.

dust. 1. Mud with the juice squeezed out. 2. The only thing you can be sure of getting on your radio. 3. Man is but dust, and woman settles him.

See gold: gold-dust; janitor[1].

duty. 1. The behavior that one expects from others. 2. A task we look forward to with distaste, perform with reluctance, and brag about ever after.

See annoy; decency[2]; discharge; importer; marriage[21]; Mrs.; snob[4]; tariff: tariff supporter; whisper[2].

painful duties. The taxes on imports and exports.

dye. Many a blonde dyes by her own hand.

See bleach; die.

dyspepsia. 1. The remorse of a guilty stomach. 2. Many people think they have religion when they are merely troubled with dyspepsia.

See restaurant[1].

E

ear. The wife who has her ears pierced has a husband who has his bored.

See deft; dreamer: practical dreamer; love: puppy love[2]; music: true musician; shut[2]; spectacles[2]; telephone: telephone operator[1]; tell[4]; wife[4].

early. 1. Early to bed and early to rise makes a man a farmer. 2. The man who is early of late used to be behind before, and now is first at last.

See advertise[1]; bridge: bad bridge player; Christmas: Christmas shopping; head[2]; hint; marry[5]; miss[3]; pawnbroker[5]; worm[1].

early bird. See bird: early bird.

earn. 1. The woman who marries a man for his money usually earns it. 2. Society is made up of two classes: those who get more than they earn, and those who earn more than they get.

See appearance; capacity; money[9]; Mrs.; musician[1]; save[3]; successful: successful man[2]; work[1].

earth. 1. Marriages may be made in heaven but divorce occurs when the parties get down to earth. 2. In the beginning the earth was made round, and it's never been square since.

See air: air service; doctor[4]; equator; exterior; flat; goat[2]; inherit; meek; polls[2]; pure; revolve; war[3]; woman: woman's sphere.

earthquake. An earthshake.

Easter. See Decoration Day.

easy. Men who take things easy are often taken for easy things. See alphabet; drinking: hard drinking; payment: easy payment plan; photography; tax[3].

eat. 1. What to eat in hot weather is a problem to some people, but how to eat in any kind of weather is a problem to others. 2. The girl who looks sweet enough to eat probably does.

See board: boarding house[2]; bookworm; cake; can; cheap[1]; chicken[1]; cocktail; dessert; diet[1]; diner; dish: washing dishes; drink[2]; fast[2]; fat: fat woman[2]; fingers; frankfurter; garlic; girl: petite girl; health[1]; horse[2]; indigestion[3]; moth[1]; onion[4]; pan; restaurant[3]; tiger; vitamin.

eccentric. 1. The kind of person who minds his own business. 2. Be virtuous and you will be eccentric.

eccentricity. Originality without sense.

See rudness.

echo. 1. No sooner said than said. 2. The only thing that can cheat a woman out of the last word.

eclipse. It gives the sun time for reflection.

economics. Studying economics won't keep you out of the breadline, but at least you'll know why you're there.

See idea: theoretical ideas.

department of economics. Many a college practices economy by curtailing its department of economics.

home economics. Going home to mother.

economist. 1. Somebody who has a plan to do something with somebody else's money. 2. A man who tells you what to do with your money after you have done something else with it. 3. Usually a man who can save money by cutting down some other person's expenses. 4. One who has never been able to convince his wife that economy should begin at home. 5. One who would be more convincing if he were less extravagant with his words.

economy. 1. The reduction in some other fellow's salary. 2. Denying ourselves a necessity today in order to buy a luxury tomorrow. 3. A way of spending money without getting any fun out of it.

See advice: fatherly advice; truth[3].

economical man. The type most girls want to marry but few want to be engaged to.

edgewise. The only time some husbands can get a word in edgewise is when they talk in their sleep.

See sharp; talk[2].

Edison. See talk: talking machine.

editor. To read some magazines makes one wonder what the editors could have rejected.

See poetry[1].

newspaper editor. If a dog bites a man, it's not news, unless he's a newspaper editor.

education. 1. The training that enables people to get along without intelligence. 2. The knowledge that a chorus girl gets by stages and a college girl by degrees.

See educator; examination; graduation; highbrow[3]; waste[2].

board of education. In the old days, a shingle.

college education. 1. Something that never hurt anyone who was willing to learn something afterwards. 2. What enables a person to get a job as secretary to a man who never went to college at all. 3. A polish that shows mostly on shoes and hair. 4. It's only sheepskin deep.

See cauliflower; quarterback; ticket.

educated person. One who knows something about everything and everything about something.

liberal education. 1. You can't get a liberal education nowadays unless you have a liberal father. 2. While a college man is getting a liberal education, his dad is getting an education in liberality.

educator. Education pays, unless you become an educator.

effect. Take not God's name in vain; select a time when it will have effect.

See club: night club[2]; conscience: voice of conscience; living: cost of living[6]; salesman[4]; thought[1].

efficiency expert. See expert: efficiency expert.

efficient. No man has ever been able to convince his wife that a pretty stenographer is as efficient as an ugly one.

effort. See fanatic[2]; rheumatism[1].

egg. 1. Unlike a child, it never gets beaten when it's bad. 2. Something that isn't always as good as it's cracked up to be. 3. An egg a day keeps the axe away.

See heart: soft-hearted woman; hen[3]; lay; shell.

ego. The only thing that can keep growing without nourishment.

inflated ego. Nothing gets you up in the air quicker than an inflated ego.

egotism. The attitude of a young man in love, who thinks that nothing is good enough for her except himself.

egotist. 1. A person who tells you those things about himself which you intended to tell him about yourself. 2. When two egotists meet, it's a case of an I for an I. 3. One who, when he doesn't understand something in a book, decides it's a misprint. 4. One who brazenly tells the world that he thinks as much of himself as you silently think of yourself.

elect. See government: representative government.

election. 1. You don't have to fool all the people all the time;

during elections is sufficient. 2. Every four years we have a national election, and every forty years a rational one.

See majority[4]; political: political platform[2]; politician: active politician; statesman[6]; tariff: protective tariff; Thanksgiving[1].

electric chair. See chair: electric chair.

electrician. A man who wires for money.

electricity. 1. The chief difference between it and lightning is that you don't have to pay anything for lightning. 2. Its future depends on current matters.

elephant. 1. An animal with a vacuum cleaner in front and a rug beater in back. 2. If an elephant charges, the best thing to do is to let him have both barrels at once—and the gun too. See size.

elevate. The best way to elevate the masses is to raise children properly.

elevator. If a man takes off his hat in an elevator, it means he has good manners and hair.

elevator man. One who has his ups and downs, like the chap who chooses the aisle seat at the movies.

elf. See gremlin.

Elks. 1. The only teeth some men have are those they got when they joined the Elks. 2. Elks have what no other animals have —parades.

elocution. See punishment: capital punishment.

elope. The best thing some eloping couples can do is not to come home and all will be forgiven.

See run: run away.

eloquence. God gave eloquence to some, brains to others.

embarrassment. The only thing the modern girl takes the trouble to hide.

See stitch; tell[5].

embrace. See necking[1].

emotion. Many a woman has discovered the secret of perpetual emotion.

See astray; bride: bride's father.

empty. See glass; pessimist[15]; shirt: stuffed shirt; thought: train of thought.

encore. 1. A greedy theater-goer's desire to get more than his money's worth. 2. In the movies you can applaud safely without fear of an encore.

encyclopedia. See drug store[2].

end. 1. All's well that ends. 2. Many a movie that doesn't end happily ends—happily. 3. The reason some men can't make both ends meet is because they are too busy making one end drink.

See adult[2]; bracelet; cake: birthday cake[3]; candle; checkbook; circle[3]; column: spinal column; diplomacy: secret diplomacy; fight[4]; flyer: stunt flyer; football: football player; frankfurter; friendship[2]; grease; hysterics; illness; love[23]; match[1]; necking[2]; neighbor[3]; requirement; romance[1]; sandwich; serve[3]; sight; spanking[1]; speech: good speech[2]; spread: middle-age spread; story: radio story; success[1]; twins: Siamese twins; weekend.

end to end. See butterfly[2]; college: college boy[3]; road: road hog[2]; statistician[4]; Sunday: Sunday afternoon.

endow. Men are endowed by their Creator with certain inalienable rights, all of which they must fight for.

endurance. A virtue if your judgment is bad.

See golfer[3].

endurance test. Entertaining a pest who says nothing, or listening to a bore who does all the talking.

enduring. To be enduring, a peace must be endurable.

enema. A patient in the hospital may have few friends, but he has plenty of enemas.

enemy. 1. A man cannot be too careful in the choice of his enemies. 2. If you've simply got to make some enemies, pick on the lazy ones. 3. Only a friend can become an enemy; your relatives are that way from the start. 4. Love your enemies, for they tell you your faults. 5. Always forgive your enemies, especially the ones you can't lick. 6. The Bible tells us to love our neighbors and also to love our enemies, probably because they are generally the same people.

See drum; forgive[1]; friend[1, 7]; hate; legislation: class legislation; outline; whiskey[3]; wife[10].

engage. When a man's engaged, the lucky woman is—the girl's mother.

See economy: economical man.

engagement. 1. A lull before the storm. 2. In war, a battle; in courtship, a surrender.

See depend.

English. See Chinese.

enjoy. See conscience[8]; hypochondriac[1]; Thanksgiving[1]; ticket.

enjoyment. Never put off enjoyment, for there's no time like the pleasant.

enlarge. When a woman gains weight, her charms are enlarged without being enhanced.

ennui. Plain boredom on a hundred thousand a year.

enough. Money buys everything, if you have enough of it. See bigamist[1]; Christmas[6]; kiss[8]; monogamy[1]; tongue[3].

enthusiasm. 1. A nervous disorder afflicting the young and the inexperienced. 2. Faith with a tin can tied to its tail. See gardening[2]; wave: permanent wave[2].

entrance. See stenographer.

entrust. The only woman who never betrays a friend's secret is she who has never been entrusted with it.

envelope. See letter[1]; pay: pay envelope.

environment. Some people believe in environment; others believe in heredity—especially those who got all their money that way.

envy. See jealous: jealous people.

epicene. An obscene epigram.

epidemic. See public opinion[2].

epigram. See epicene.

epigrammatist. One who flips quips.

epistle. The wife of an apostle.

epitaph. A statement that lies above about the one who lies below. See liar: monumental liar; wicked.

equal. All men are born free and equal but some of them grow up and get married. See leg: bowlegs[2]; occasion.

equality. 1. He who seeks it should go to a cemetery. 2. Once women merely asked equality with men, but now they have outstripped them.

equator. A menagerie lion running around the middle of the earth.

equity. 1. It follows the law, but seldom overtakes it. 2. Equity and law are two things which God hath joined together, but which man hath put asunder. See chancery.

Eros. See love[8].

err. To err is human. when *we* make the mistake.

See human.

error. See court: Supreme Court[1]; expert[1]; prohibition: Prohibition Era[3].

Eskimos. God's frozen people.

See day[2].

estate. See lawyer[1].

etc. A sign used to make others believe you know more than you do.

ether. Persons should be given ether twice for every operation; once before, and again afterwards to stop them from talking about it.

See radio: radio announcer[1].

etiquette. 1. A code of conduct which makes lying a virtue. 2. The difference between table manners and stable manners.

See fingers.

>**book of etiquette.** The book of etiquette doesn't mention it but it is considered good form to return the book of etiquette you borrow.

Europe. In Europe girls dress like their mothers, but in America it's the other way around.

Eve. The only woman who couldn't throw up to her husband the better men she might have married.

See Adam: Adam & Eve.

even. See break: break even; temper: even-tempered person.

evening. With some people you spend an evening; with others you invest it.

See girl[2]; hay; moral: morals[1]; sucker[1]; toper.

evening gown. See gown: evening gown.

event. See history[2]; prophet.

eventually. Many a man doesn't speak to his wife for a long time, but his turn will eventually come.

everybody. When everybody is somebody, then nobody is anybody.

See game; onion[3]; statesman[4]; weather[1]; worse[1].

everything. The old believe everything; the middle-aged suspect everything; the young know everything.

See education: educated person; money[12]; newlywed; philosopher[2]; store: general store; taxi: taxi driver[4]; tell[1, 2]; temptation[3].

everywhere. The woman who trusts her husband everywhere is the one who goes everywhere with her husband.

See unmentionables.

evil. A myth invented by good people to explain the attraction of others.

See censor[7]; cop[2]; divorce: divorce evil; heredity[1]; history[1]; matrimony[2]; money[1]; party[1]; pessimist[7]; saxophone[4]; source[1]; virtuous; wife: small wives.

evolution. 1. The development of man from monkey, which some people forgot to make. 2. A theory which can be proved by one's relatives. 3. A clever trick performed by Darwin who made a monkey of Adam. 4. There is too much talk of evolution and not enough of it. 5. Perhaps in time evolution will produce men too civilized to quarrel about it. 6. The best thing to do about evolution is to try to live it down.

See animal; Darwin; pedestrian[21]; prove; slow.

exaggerate. 1. The only time a woman will not exaggerate is when she is talking about her own age. 2. There are people so addicted to exaggeration that they can't tell the truth without lying.

See tooth: tooth cavity.

examination. The sad part about education is that some of the final examinations are final.

bar examination. A test to determine how much you can hold.

example. See advice: good advice; set.

good example. See counterfeiter; hypocrite.

shining example. Another shining example of married life is the pair of trousers many a husband has to wear.

See child: only child; nose: unpowdered nose.

exception. 1. It proves the rule—to be an exception. 2. If you save half your salary every week for ten years, at the end of that time you'll be an exception.

See rule.

excess. Nothing succeeds like excess.

exchange. You are bound to get the worst of the bargain when you exchange ideas with a fool.

See liberty[1]; fair: fair exchange; restaurant[2]; sympathy.

excuse. 1. The man who is good at making excuses is seldom good at anything else. 2. Every man has his uses, and every woman her excuses.

See friend[3]; late; law[4]; politician[13].

execution. Learning to play the saxophone should either improve the execution of players or hasten it.

executive. One who hires somebody else to do it.

See ability: executive ability.

executor. A person who puts criminals to death with a will.

exemption. No matter how bad a child is, he's still good for an exemption on the income tax return.

See bird[1].

exercise. 1. When you feel like exercising, just lie down till the feeling goes away. 2. The only exercise some people take is when they have colds and their noses run.

See dance: modern dance[2]; germs[2]; pallbearer; sleep: sleepwalker.

feminine exercise. Running up bills.

mental exercise. Jumping at conclusions.

reducing exercise. See reducing: reducing exercise.

strenuous exercise. After forty it's harmful, especially if you do it with a knife and fork.

existence. See motion: perpetual motion; popular: popular girl; resistance.

exit. See performance.

expanse. Children laugh at a fat man; they have fun at his expanse.

expect. Blessed is he who expects nothing, for he shall never be disappointed.

See fishing[1]; husband: conceited husband; life[5]; remorse; unexpected.

expense. It's not difficult to meet expenses these days; one meets them everywhere.

See economist[3]; keeper; lawsuit[1]; life[6]; love[9]; tour: all-expense tour.

running expenses. It's the running expenses that keep father out of breath.

expensive. 1. It used to be that two could live as cheaply as one; now one can live as expensively as two. 2. It's always too expensive for the country man to live in the city, and too expensive for the city man to live in the country.

See children[1]; impress; wear: women's wear[1].

experience. 1. The name men give to their mistakes. 2. What you get when you are looking for something else.   3. Knowledge acquired when it is too late.   4. What you have left after everything else is gone.   5. The one perpetual best-seller; everybody is continually buying it.   6. Experience is a dear teacher; the rest are underpaid.   7. Experience is a preacher as well as a teacher.

See ability: executive ability; age: old age[2]; fender[1]; kiss[15]; marriage: second marriage.

school of experience.   1. Its class yell is *Ouch.*   2. Its class colors are black and blue.   3. You don't get a sheepskin in the school of experience; you just have your own removed.

expert.   1. A man who avoids the small errors while he sweeps on to the grand fallacy.   2. One who is just beginning to understand how little he knows about the subject.

efficiency expert.   1. One who has no business of his own to wreck.   2. One who is smart enough to tell you how to run your business, and too smart to start one of his own.

See layman.

military expert.   A man who tells you today what's going to happen tomorrow, and who tells you tomorrow why it didn't happen today.

explain.   It's easier to do a good job than to explain why you didn't.

explorer.   A person who gets enough material for a lecture.

See find.

modern explorers.   With the aid of aviation, modern explorers have discovered everything but the way to get back.

explosion.   See powder[2].

export.   See duty: painful duties.

expose.   If a bald man doesn't raise his hat and expose his head, he exposes his bad manners.

exposure.   The only persons liable to die from exposure are tramps and politicians.

See backside; stitch.

expression.   'Tis love that makes the world go round—with that worried expression.

See tee; trial.

exterior.   The interior of the earth is very hot, but the exterior is not so hot.

extraction. Dentists spare no pains to make extractions satisfactory.

See tooth: infected tooth.

extravagant. One reason why so many people are extravagant is that there are a thousand ways to spend money and only one way to save it.

See economist[5].

extravagant girl. She usually makes a poor mother and a bankrupt father.

extreme. Women's clothes go to extremes but seldom to extremities.

See streamline.

extremist. The man who is always having his shoes shined and his hair cut.

eyebrow. See mustache[2].

eyes. 1. Keep them wide open before marriage, and half shut afterwards. 2. A girl may shut her eyes when she is being kissed, but she certainly doesn't when anyone else is. 3. Some girls close their eyes when you kiss them, but others close yours. See blind; church[3]; cold[5]; columnist[2]; designer: style designer; figure[1]; fireman; flu; grapefruit[3]; mind: narrow-minded man; oculist; preacher[5]; spectacles[1]; suit: bathing suit[1]; undo; vague; wink[2]; wool.

black eyes. 1. They usually indicate a strong character, but more often a weak defense. 2. Some are born with black eyes; others have to fight for them. 3. The hand is quicker than the eye, which explains why there are so many black eyes. See curiosity.

eye opener. Love is blind, and marriage is an eye opener.

eyesight. When it begins to blur, you should use stronger glasses and weaker drinks.

See umpire[1].

eyewash. See grapefruit[2].

F

face. 1. Something very important to Oriental peoples, and to cosmetic dealers. 2. Be it ever so homely, there's no face like one's own. 3. God gives a woman one face, and she makes herself another. 4. Circumstances alter faces. 5. You can't save your face if you lose your head. 6. The woman whose face is her fortune doesn't want it lifted.

See bald: bald-headed man[1]; beautiful: beautiful woman; black-out; chewing gum[2]; clock[2]; cosmetician; cosmetics[1]; different; flatterer; homely: homely girl; kiss[4]; make-up[1]; mold; money[10]; nudist: nudist camp[2]; pick[1]; pose; red; sculptor; shaving; towel; value: face value; wash; wrinkle[2].

baby face. See chair: electric chair[2]; combination.

face-lifting. 1. It isn't necessary for a man to have his face lifted; if he is patient it will grow up through his hair. 2. People who pull long faces should have their faces lifted. 3. The earliest known method of face-lifting was done with a rope around the neck.

See lift[2]; repair; snob[1].

poker face. The face that launched a thousand chips.

two-faced. Most women are two-faced: one for home and one for street wear.

fact. Women are facts because facts are stubborn things.

See imagination[5]; model; statistician[2, 3]; statistics[2]; theory: beautiful theory.

bare facts. They make up the naked truth.

See nudism[4].

facts of life. When a mother explains the facts of life to her daughter, the daughter learns a great deal—about her mother's ignorance.

fad. See diet: dieting.

failure. One who fails to keep on trying.

See ambition[1]; inexperience.

world of failure. It's marked by lassitude and longitude.

faint. See heart: faint heart; praise[3].

fair. All is fair in love and golf.

See blonde[5]; bold; brave; brunette[1]; fare; frat: fraternity house; radio: radio program; support[1].

fair exchange. A fair exchange is no robbery, unless it's a church fair.

fair sex. See sex: fair sex.

fairway. In golf, only the brave deserve the fairway.

faith. 1. An illogical belief in the occurrence of the improbable. 2. The basis of three great enterprises: love, democracy, and hash. 3. The boast of the man who is too lazy to investigate. 4. Believing what you know to be untrue. 5. You can't do much with faith and you can't do much without it. 6. If men had no faith in one another, all of us would have to live within our incomes.

See disillusion: disillusioned people; enthusiasm[2]; plodder.

faith, hope & charity. If you put too much faith and hope in some schemes, you'll have to call for charity.

See applause[2]; kiss[7]; play.

faithful. Girls who are good are faithful, except when they're too good to be true.

faithless. Young men want to be faithful and are not; old men want to be faithless and cannot.

fake. Clothes fake the man.

fall. The bigger the summer vacation, the harder the fall.

See banana[1]; candidate[1]; careful; ideal: man's ideal; pedestrian[7]; pride[1, 3]; repair; stop: sudden stop; swallow[1].

early fall. The prediction of an early fall does not refer to prices.

fall out. A man's hair and teeth are his best friends, but even the best of friends will fall out.

See top[2].

false. See generalization; stock: stock market[1]; teeth, false teeth.

fame. 1. Chiefly a matter of dying at the right moment. 2. It often proves you can make something out of nothing.

See folly: height of folly; niche; pinochle.

test of fame. When a crazy person imagines he is you.

familiarity. 1. Familiarity breeds contempt—and children. 2. Familiarity breeds attempt. 3. Familiarity breeds.

family. 1. The thing most needed in the American home today. 2. A husband doesn't mind if his wife comes from a fine old family so long as she doesn't bring them with her.

See ancestor[1]; budget[1]; father[2]; genealogist; kindred; marriage[9]; radio: radio serial; settle; stay[2].

family life. Matrimony, acrimony, alimony.

family tree. 1. The better it is, the worse the crop. 2. The best part of it is always underground. 3. Something that often starts with grafting. 4. Something you pay a little to have looked up, and then pay more to have it hushed up. 5. A man can't make a place for himself in the sun if he keeps taking refuge under the family tree.

See money[2]; sap[1, 2]; side: shady side; tree[2].

large family. The advantage of a large family is that one of them at least may not turn out like the others.

famous. The man who wakes up to find himself famous hasn't been asleep.

See acquaintanceship; notorious; wake: wake up[3].

fan. See dancer: fan dancer[2]; golf: golf ball[2].

fanatic. 1. One who has never found any other way to have fun. 2. A person who redoubles his efforts after having forgotten his aims. 3. One who can't change his opinion and won't change the subject.

fancy. In the spring a young man's fancy lightly turns to what the girls have been seriously thinking of all winter.

See dog: dog fancier; jazz.

fantastic. See fashion[1].

far. Tact consists of knowing how far is too far.

See get: get back; minister; mother-in-law[2]; pay: payday; pin[2]; speedometer; trust[3]; tune[1].

farce. It takes dozens of pages to write a historical play, but only two sheets to make a bedroom farce.

See police: police force.

fare. You can't convince the railroads that less fare would be more fair.

See save[2].

farm. 1. A portion of land entirely covered by a mortgage. 2. A neglected body of land entirely surrounded by prosperity. 3. Young people would stay down on the farm if prices wouldn't. 4. You can't keep young people down on the farm so long as everybody is down on the farmer.

See agriculturist; bloc: farm bloc; movement.

farm hand. One thing the farmers are not raising enough of.

farm relief. The only farm relief that will ever benefit the farmer will be to relieve him of his farm.

farmer. 1. The only way a farmer can keep his sons home is to move to the city. 2. Farmers can solve their farm problems by moving to the city. 3. As a last resort, the farmer can go to town where his sons and his profits went.

See agriculturist; bee; bumper; cotton[2]; cow: contented cow; early[1]; farm[4], farm relief; middleman; milk[1]; reins; soil; spring[4].

gentleman farmer. One who never raises anything but his hat.

good farmer. One who knows how long cows should be milked; the same as short ones.

See Wall Street: Wall Street men.

fascism. 1. A form of government where you can say what you please as long as you please—the dictator. 2. Fascism is dictated but not red. 3. Under fascism a person can say anything he pleases so long as he says it to himself.

See Nazism; obligatory.

fascist. A person whose opinions are sound—and fury.

fashion. 1. When the fantastic becomes universal. 2. Style which becomes out of date as soon as adopted. 3. The tax on vanity imposed by the clothing industry. 4. A form of ugliness so intolerable that we have to change it every few months.

See clothesline; leg[2]; moth[3].

fashionable. There are two kinds of women: the fashionable ones and those who are comfortable.

fast. 1. How fast it takes for a man to get a divorce depends upon how fast his wife is. 2. If you want to get fat, don't eat fast; if you want to get thin, don't eat, fast.

See bet[3]; car[1]; color; dollar[2]; driver: reckless driver[2]; friend: fast friends; light[1]; shoplifter; spendthrift; statistics: traffic statistics; street; think[7]; throw; tongue[1]; Washington, D. C.[3].

fast woman. One who has been on more laps than a napkin.

hunger fast. It usually takes less time than restaurant service.

fat. If you want to grow fat, breed swine.

See chin[2]; corpulence; fast[2]; girdle: girdle manufacturer; inclined; reducing[1], reducing expert.

fat man. One who cuts a wide swath among the women.

See champion: world's heavyweight champion; expanse.

fat people. They are usually good-natured because it takes them so long to get mad clear through.

See day: daily dozen[1]; lean.

fat woman. 1. One who should always put her best chin forward. 2. One who eats like a bird—a peck at a time.

See scales[2].

fate. See critic[6].

father. 1. The fellow who is put on the pan if he doesn't bring home the bacon. 2. The head of the family, so he's the one that gets the headaches. 3. No one knows his own father, but most of us have some idea.

See advance: advances; child[4]; Christmas[1]; college[5, 7], college-bred; crack; debt: college debts; education: liberal education[1]; expense: running expenses; extravagant: extravagant girl; floorwalker; girl[3]; habit[1]; heredity[2]; modern: modern girl[5]; necessity[2]; quarterback; responsible; sin; stepfather; support[3]; waste[2].

average father. One who knows he has to make allowances when he has a son at college.

Father's Day. See day: Father's Day.

self-made father. One who works his son's way through college.

wise father. Nowadays it's a wise father who knows as much as his own son.

father-in-law. Marry in haste, and repent at your father-in-law's.

fatherland. It's a wise fatherland that knows its own children.

See country: adopted country.

fault. Blaming your faults on your nature will not change the nature of your faults.

See beggar[2]; boy[5]; criticism[2]; enemy[4]; generous; philosopher[3].

fault-finding woman. One who goes through life demanding to see the manager.

greatest fault. To be conscious of none.

woman's faults. If you want to know a woman's faults, just praise her among her female acquaintances.

favor. There's a lot to be said in every woman's favor, but it's not nearly so interesting.

See gentleman[6]; gratitude[1].

fear. See courage[1, 2]; microbe; religion[3]; right[1].

feat. See boaster; feet[1].

feather. 1. Birds of one feather catch cold. 2. Fine feathers make fine birds, but it's usually the other way round.

See divers.

February. See never[1].

fee. God cures, but the doctor takes the fee.

See gigolo[2].

feed. See mosquito[4]; tapeworm.

feel. See breakfast; champagne; doctor: grasping doctor; gloves; hat: straw hat; liquor[3]; old[6]; pessimist[10]; water: water wagon; world[1].

feeling. 1. The poor feel want, the rich want feeling. 2. Love is blind; that's why lovers depend so much on their sense of feeling.

See blind: blindman's buff; forty-five; radio[3]; scales[2].

feet. 1. It's no feat to dance on feet, unless they're your own. 2. The easiest way to get back on your feet is to get rid of your car.

See businessman: tired businessman; car[2]; chiropodist[1]; dancer; diplomacy[7]; generation: younger generation[1]; hand[5]; rug; sailor[3]; salesman[2]; Star-Spangled Banner; thief: car thieves; think[7].

    big feet. Some women have such big feet that when they take off their shoes and stockings, they are half undressed.

fellow. See blind: blindman's buff; blonde[3]; worker: fellow worker.

female. The last letter in female is silent; it's the only thing about her that is.

See fault: woman's faults; mail; speech[3]; woman[4].

feminine. See lady: lady in waiting.

fence. 1. The first resort of stolen goods and politicians. 2. Something built to keep people in or out, except around cemeteries. 3. In politics, a fence will never give offense.

See aviator[2]; hedge; insomnia[4]; mugwump; politician[6]; politics[2, 15]; straddle; suit: bathing suit[8]; tell[4].

fender. 1. The one thing that never learns from experience. 2. Give a driver an inch and he'll take a fender.

See brakes[2]; parking: parking lot; taxi: taxi fare.

ferryboat. A boat that makes every passenger cross.

fever. The father who sends his son to college is liable to be struck with a remittent fever.

hay fever season. The hay fever sneezin'.

few. See individualism: rugged individualism; leg: bowlegs[1]; word: few words.

fiancé. See lover: fickle lover.

fiction. 1. Modern fiction runs too much to love, and modern love runs too much to fiction. 2. The chap who said truth is stranger than fiction died before fiction reached its present state of development.

See decent; friction; history[7]; lawsuit[6]; publicity[5]; story: detective stories[1]; tax: income tax return[1]; truth[4, 6].

fiddle. You can't feel fit as a fiddle if you get tight as a drum.

second fiddle. See harmony: domestic harmony[1].

field. See crop; football[4]; plow.

fifty. An American woman at fifty is neither old nor fifty.

See same[2].

fight. 1. The most intelligent way to fight is to find a smaller man. 2. In love, a man fights for his girl; in marriage, he fights with her. 3. The only difference between getting married and getting drunk is that when you get drunk you don't have to fight. 4. One marriage in every five ends in divorce, but the other four couples fight it out to the bitter end.

See bargain: bargain sale[3]; bell; dislike; endow; eyes: black eyes[2]; grab; left[1]; pacifist[2]; peace[1, 3]; side: winning side; wrong[2].

prize fighting. 1. A sport in which the only honor is to be on the top of the scrap heap. 2. A man has to fight to stay on top in every field except in prize fighting. 3. Marriage is like a prize fight: the preliminaries are generally better than the main event.

fighter. Right is might, but a good left never hurt a fighter.

See box: boxing.

prize fighter. The prize fighter boxes his man before he lays him out; the undertaker lays out his man before he boxes him. See champion.

figure. 1. The man who had a good head for figures now has a son who has a good eye for them. 2. Figures don't lie but those of some women do. 3. Figures don't lie, and under examination some of them won't stand up either.

See alluring; beautiful: beautiful woman; date[2]; filibuster; keep[3]; liar[3]; overweight; run: running; salary.

file. Some people file their nails; others cut them off and throw them away.

filibuster. A bore's idea of conversation.

filibusterer. A figure of speech.

fill. 1. The bigger a man's head gets, the easier it is to fill his shoes. 2. What a woman doesn't know about driving a car would fill a street.

See author; bride: modern bride; head: swelled head; tax: tax suggestions; vegetarianism.

> **filling station.** A child's idea of home.
> See dentist[7].

films. The old silent films had their advantages: you could see women open their mouths without talking.

final. See examination.

finance. Governments are financed by a generation which pays the last generation's debts by issuing bonds payable by the next generation.

> **finance company.** A conspiracy to extend the modest business established by Captain Kidd.

financier. One whose wife never finds out when he gets a raise in salary.

find. Finding little-known lands is always less trouble than finding the explorers.

See caddie[2]; friend: real friend; golf: golf links[1]; miss: missing link; wake: wake up[3].

> **find out.** 1. Some husbands have clever wives; others also have wives who find out. 2. The way of the transgressor is hard —to find out. 3. A man can love more than one woman at the same time, if they don't find it out.
> See conscience[1]; discover; guest: unwelcome guest[3]; installment: installment collector[3]; sinner[1]; wash; wisdom[4].

fine. See alimony[3]; feather[2]; speed.

fingers. Etiquette condemns eating with the fingers; but if food isn't clean enough to pick up with the fingers, it's not fit to eat.
See brain: brains; count[1]; dough[2]; hand[2]; man: suspicious man; osteopath[2]; remember; ring[2]; wedding[3]; wife: peevish wife.

fingernails. 1. Hit the nail on the head, but be sure it's not your fingernail. 2. The best thing for biting fingernails is sharp teeth.

See file; nail; polish.

finish. See man[11]; son.

fire. 1. It makes light of everything. 2. The man with a burning ambition is seldom fired.

See arson; poet[1]; religion[1].

fire department. Most fires are put out before much damage is done by the fire department.

fire escape. All that religion means to some people.

forest fire. What happens when a man lets his cigarettes go out alone.

fireman. A man who never takes his eyes off the hose.

firmness. That admirable quality in ourselves which is detestable stubbornness in others.

first. 1. Do unto the other fellow the way he'd like to do unto you—and do it first. 2. When the girl you kiss gives as good as you give, you are not getting firsts.

See car: used car[2]; early[2]; husband: second husband[1]; love: first love; mint; olive; pants[3]; see[1]; sight, second sight; souse; talk: talking machine; think[4]; throw; toes.

fish. 1. The animal that seems to go for a vacation about the same time most fishermen do. 2. An animal that grows fastest between the time it is caught and the time the fisherman describes it to his friends. 3. It's always the biggest fish you catch that gets away. 4. One man's fish is another man's *poisson*. 5. Fish must be brain food because they travel in schools.

See accordion; bait[1]; catch[2]; caution; dipsomaniac; guest[2]; oyster[1]; resort: ideal summer resort; rod; smell[3]; truth[2].

fishermen. 1. There are two kinds: those who fish for sport and those who catch something. 2. African natives fish lying down but in this country fishermen lie standing up with the arms outstretched.

See fish[2]; golfer[5].

fisherman's motto. Bait and see.

fishing. 1. Eternal expectation and perpetual disappointment. 2. The one solitary vice which men may enjoy without shame. 3. Some men don't fish; they just drown worms. 4. A sport played with a long pole, a worm at one end and a fool at the other.

See caution; cherry.

fishnet. A lot of little holes tied together with string.

fist. See manicurist[1]; pacifist[1].

fit. See fiddle; prove; repeat[3]; sour[2]; tailor[3].

fix. See jury[3].

flag. Some people wave the American flag so they can waive what it stands for.

See flagrant.

flagrant. Some people use the flag to hide their flagrant designs.

flail. Every time a husband quarrels with his wife, words flail him.

flame. See kindle.

old flame. 1. He usually turns out to be a silly ash. 2. Many a girl uses her old flame to burn up her new boyfriend.

flat. 1. What the earth is not, as every car driver knows. 2. Nobody loves a flat man.

See flattery[4]; pawnbroker; polls[2].

flatten. Marriage flatters the woman but flattens the man.

See broaden; travel[1].

flatter. 1. When a woman says, "You flatter me"—do so! 2. The best way to flatter a man is to tell him he's the kind of man who can't be flattered. 3. When a woman says she can't be flattered, agree with her; this will flatter her.

See flatten; situation.

flatterer. One who says things to your face that he wouldn't say behind your back.

flattery. 1. Like perfume, it should be smelled but not swallowed. 2. Something which you say even if you don't believe so, and which the other person believes even if you don't say so. 3. A form of soft soap, and soft soap is mostly lye. 4. Flattery seldom falls flat. 5. Flattery is obnoxious to all except the flattered.

See detest; immigration.

flavor. See meat[1].

flea. 1. He who goes to the dogs is sure to get fleas. 2. Even the best of fleas, sooner or later, will go to the dogs.

See cheap[4]; dog[4]; God[3]; hound; size; Utopia.

fleet. See navy.

flesh. It's hard to get drunk when the flesh is willing but the spirits are weak.

flies. See fly.

flirt. 1. A hit-and-run lover. 2. A woman without a heart who makes a fool of a man without a head.

See cop[1]; waitress[2].

flirtation. Attention without intention.

See passion.

floor. 1. Remember you can't fall out of bed if you sleep on the floor. 2. A husband has a right to mop up the floor with a wife who won't mop up the floor.

See intoxicate; spit[3]; top[3].

> **dance floor.** 1. Some dance floors are so crowded, you can't tell who your partner is. 2. The difference between a bachelor and a married man is that when a bachelor walks the floor with a baby, it's a dance floor.
>
> See bunion.

floorwalker. The father of a new-born babe.

Florida. The hurricane season isn't the only time when there's too much blowing in Florida.

See California[1, 2]; weather: fair weather; winter[3].

florist. The man most likely to go to seed.

flowers. 1. They have more scents than people. 2. When a man brings them to his wife for no reason, there's a reason. 3. Only the man who's been married a long time knows that there are some things you can't say with flowers. 4. You have to die before some people will say it with flowers.

See carnation; provision; wedding[2]; weeds[3].

> **flower bed.** The man who makes his own flower bed has to lie about it.

flu. It's both affirmative and negative; sometimes the eyes have it and sometimes the nose.

flunk. He who knows not, and is sure he knows, is a college youth; flunk him.

fly. 1. A familiar summer boarder who mingles with the cream of society, gets stuck on the butter, and leaves his specs behind. 2. Flies annoy some people more than others: some people shoo them while others just let them run around barefoot.

See artist: bad artist; germs[1]; mosquito[1]; progeny; rumor[1]; swat; time[2].

house flies. Summer guests.

flypaper. There's a catch to it.

flyer. In war, it's best to say it with flyers.

See jump[3].

> **flyer's wife.** The only woman who is always glad to see her husband down and out.

> **stunt flyer.** The end of the stunt flyer is near, but then it always has been.

flying. The impression that men will never fly like birds seems to be aeroneous.

fog. It's dangerous to drive in a fog, especially if it's mental.

fold. If you want to learn how to fold up a road map, learn to play the accordion.

See double; map: road map[1].

follow. The horses some people follow usually follow the other horses.

See map: road map[2]; mob[3]; nudist[6]; shadow[1]; street: street cleaner[2].

follower. He who is a leader of men is rarely a follower of women.

See adherent; virtue[2].

folly. Where singleness is bliss, 'tis folly to be married.

> **height of folly.** While some people rise upward to the pinnacle of fame, others reach the height of folly.

fond. Absence makes the heart grow fonder—of the other fellow.

See absinthe; church[2]; present[1, 2].

food. A matter of taste.

See argumentative; by-product; fingers; fish[5]; paunch; prescribe[2]; price[1]; rationing[3]; restaurant[5]; sermon; soup[1]; waitress[1].

fool. 1. One who always finds a bigger fool to admire him. 2. One who knows not, and knows not that he knows not. 3. It's a poor fool that won't work both ways. 4. A fool and his money are soon partied. 5. Life is just one fool thing after another; love is just two fool things after each other. 6. For every woman who makes a fool out of some man, there's another who makes a man out of some fool.

See advice[4]; argue[2]; bachelor[15]; constitution: United States Constitution; develop; election[1]; exchange; fishing[4]; flirt[2]; fun[1]; heredity[2]; honey; imitate; kiss[13]; love[13]; majority[2]; make; man: man about town; manage[2]; manners; marry[7]; mortal; mouth[3];

opinion[4]; part; party[2]; peer[2]; pet; physician; pick[3]; politician: average politician; run[1]; stock: stock market[4]; subject[2]; voter[2]; wisdom[4]; wise: wise man[4].

old fool. There's no fool like an old fool because he's had more practice.

foolish. See ideal: ideal man[2].

foot. See feet; rug; walking[1].

football. 1. Legal mayhem. 2. A clean sport because it's the only one that's known to have scrub teams. 3. A game in which some players take home the goal posts while others take home a good share of the gate. 4. As long as football is played on muddy fields it will never be a clean sport.

See back: halfback; kick[2]; score; ticket.

football fan. One who knows the nationality of every man on the all-American team.

football player. A contortionist because he is always going around his own end.

football team. Eleven players and a bookkeeper.

See plaster: plaster cast.

foothold. The widespread practice of chewing gum is due to its power of getting a foothold everywhere.

forebears. Quadruplets born from a bear.

forecast. Science can predict an eclipse of the sun years in advance but cannot forecast a blowout over the weekend.

See thermometer[2].

forehead. See heel: higher heel.

foreign. See tariff.

foreign policy. It would be a good thing if other countries understood our foreign policy, but a better thing if we understood it ourselves.

See honesty[3].

foreign relations. Our foreign relations seem to be poor relations.

forest. See fire: forest fire; mortgage[1].

forger. One who is ever ready to write a wrong.

forgery. When a man tries to make a name for himself.

forget. 1. Some people give and forgive; others get and forget. 2. Some men divide their lives between trying to forget and trying to recover from the effects of trying to forget. 3. A man must get a thing before he can forget it.

See drinking[1]; get[3]; husband: tactful husband; kiss: first kiss; lady[4]; memory: good memory[1]; prophesy; reader; refer; remember; tombstone[1]; work[6]; zeal.

forgive. 1. Always forgive your enemies, especially if they are bigger than you. 2. After a good dinner one can forgive anybody, even one's own relatives.

See elope; enemy[5]; marriage: happy marriage[1]; refer; willing.

fork. See cabbage; company[5]; day: daily dozen[1]; exercise: strenuous exercise.

form. Modern girls would rather be well-formed than well-informed.

See nudism[3].

formal. Some parties are formal; at others you wear your own clothes.

forsake. A man usually forsakes sin after sin forsakes him.

fortune. The man who wants to marry a fortune should go widow-shopping.

See beautiful: beautiful woman; bulk; cosmetician; face[6]; redistribute; relatives[6]; successful: successful man[3].

fortune hunter. The man who seeks a girl for her pa value.

fortune-teller. One who looks in the bottom of the teacup, and tells that the cook didn't use a strainer.

See psalmist.

forty. Before forty, a man is too young to marry; after forty, he is too old.

See insurance: insurance company; physician; thirty[1]; women[4]; youth[2].

forty-five. After forty-five a man begins to have thoughts about women; before that he has feelings.

forward. The forward type of girl seems to be coming back.

See heaven[2]; life[3]; mule[3].

foul. See corporation[1].

foul play. The stage is reported to be in a critical condition; foul play is suspected.

fountain pen. See pen: fountain pen.

fowl. See Christmas[3].

frame. See picture.

frankfurter. 1. A sausage sold in the open and eaten by the brave. 2. Everything has an end, except a frankfurter which has two.

See bite; indigestion[1]; law[2].

frankness. The modern girl's long suit, the only long suit she has.

frat. It's a wise frat man that knows his own clothes.

fraternity house. All is fair in love and fraternity houses.

frau. Many a man lives by the sweat of his frau.

fraud. A fraud in need is a fraud indeed.

See Broadway[3].

freckle. A sunspot.

free. 1. The best things in life are free—and the worst people. 2. Free with her lips, free with her hips. 3. The man who is always trying to get something for nothing usually ends by getting free board and clothes.

See anarchy; breathe; equal; matrimony: state of matrimony; screech; train: train pass.

free speech. See speech: free speech.

freedom. 1. The power to do as you please if you don't offend reformers and if you pay racketeers for protection. 2. The ability to do as you please without considering anyone except the wife, boss, police, neighbors and the government.

See liberty.

freethinker. A bachelor or widower.

freight. When the will of the people is expressed, it is carried through by slow freight.

frequent. See drink: occasional drink.

fret. The more smokers fume, the less they fret.

friction. Truth is stranger than fiction but not a stranger to friction.

See political: political machine[3].

friend. 1. One who has the same enemies as you have. 2. One who likes you in spite of your virtues. 3. A person who will not help you because he knows your love will excuse him. 4. Never go back on a friend as long as you can use him to advantage. 5. In prosperity our friends know us; in adversity we know our friends. 6. A friend in need is a friend to keep away from. 7. Instead of loving your enemies, treat your friends a little better. 8. God gives us our relatives; thank God we can choose our friends.

See advantage[2]; believe[1]; book[4]; chic; close; convict; enema;

enemy[3]; give: give away; gold: gold digger[4]; hate; home[8]; lend; shun; thick[1]; wife[10].

best friend. Many a man loses his best friend by marrying her. See fall: fall out; mirror[1]; mother[2]; mustache.

close friend. A person who is very convenient in a tight squeeze.

fast friends. It's better to make ₁riends fast than to make fast friends.

good friend. One who will do almost anything for you except read the books you insist upon lending him.

real friend. He's hard to find and harder to lose.

friendly. When two women suddenly become friendly, it is a sign that some third woman has lost two friends.

friendship. 1. Between women, only a suspension of hostilities. 2. When begun for an end, it will not continue to the end. 3. The quickest way to wipe it out is to sponge on it. 4. The best way to be sure of a man's friendship is not to put it to the test. 5. Friendship is impossible between a man and a woman because, unless he becomes more than a friend, she becomes less. See jealousy.

frog. One swallow doesn't make a summer but one frog can make a spring.

front. 1. There are ten persons to every car in America, and they are always in front of it at street crossings. 2. Girls nowadays put up a good front or bust. See driver: backseat driver[2]; noise[2]; speed: speed up; statesman[3]; walking[1]; watch.

frown. Uneasy lies the king that wears a frown.

frozen. Many are cold, but few are frozen. See Eskimos.

fruit. The best way to preserve it is to keep it away from the children. See blackberry; peanut; plum; uncanny.

fuel. The man who is burning with love is liable to make a fuel of himself.

fugitive. Not everyone who quits college is a fugitive from a brain gang.

full. See club: night club[3]; matrimony: matrimonial bureau; pessimist[15].

fullback. Two halves make a hole, and the fullback goes through.

fun. 1. It's fun to be fooled—with. 2. Fun is like life insurance: the older you get, the more it costs.

See clarinet; economy[3]; expanse; fanatic[1]; fundamentalist; king[3]; syntax.

fundamentalist. One who wants funds to suppress fun.

funds. See fundamentalist; punishment: capital punishment[1].

funeral. What men prize most is a privilege, even if it is that of chief mourner at a funeral.

See crossing: grade crossing; pallbearer; wedding[2].

funny. Everything is funny so long as it is happening to somebody else.

See humor: sense of humor[1]; wear: women's wear[2].

fur. Faint heart never won fur, lady.

See catskin; furs; moth[2]; rabbit[2].

fur coat. See coat: fur coat, mink coat, sealskin coat; tact[2].

furnace. See coal[3].

furniture. Nobody knows what becomes of furniture that is too old even for poor folks and not yet old enough for rich folks. See bookcase[1]; old: old-timer.

installment furniture. By the time installment furniture has been paid for, it has become genuine antique.

period furniture. See chair: electric chair.

furs. 1. Some are sheep at any price. 2. The reason furs wear only a short time is because the animals had worn them a long time first. 3. Women are criticized for wearing furs in summer though they are merely following the fashion of the original owners. 4. If it wasn't for the installment plan, a lot of animals would be wearing their own furs this winter.

future. 1. Something you shouldn't worry about because it may not last long. 2. It's often bright for those who work hard, but that can scarcely be called bright. 3. The girl with a future avoids the man with a past.

See atheism; Christmas[4]; divorce[2]; interesting: interesting people; politics[13]; profit[2]; sinner[2]; turkey: turkey gobbler.

G

gadabout. Usually a gab-about.

tired gadabout. Hither, thither, and **yawn.**

gag. Something shoved down a person's throat whether he likes it or not.

See corncrib.

gamble. There are two times in a man's life when he shouldn't gamble: when he can't afford it, and when he can.

See abet; stock.

gambling. 1. Converting certainty into uncertainty. 2. Getting nothing for something.

See grumble[1].

game. Be game, but not everybody's.

See beauty[1]; love[10, 20].

See also baseball; bridge; cards; chess; football; golf; etc.

childish game. A husband's idea of a childish game is the one at which his wife can beat him.

gang. See fugitive; theory: beautiful theory.

gangster. A man with gunning little ways.

See shot.

garage. The modern idea of home is the place one goes to from the garage.

See puncture; walking[2].

garbage. See can: garbage can; cat[2].

garden. Something you can't live off without almost living in it.

See bulb; zoo: zoological garden.

Garden of Eden. The first coeducational institution.

See Adam: Adam & Eve[4]; Bible[1]; party: third party; radio[2].

gardener. Man reaps what he sows, unless he's an amateur gardener.

See middleman.

gardening. 1. People who write on gardening aren't the only ones who call a spade a spade. 2. The objection to gardening is that by the time your back gets used to it your enthusiasm is gone.

garlic. Don't eat it if you practice breath control.

garment. See skirt[2]; suit: bathing suit[1, 4]; tiny.

gas. They used to gas on the steps; now they step on the gas.
See congressman[2]; go-getter[1]; leather: shoe leather[1]; salesman[3]; suicide[3].

gas station. 1. It's a poor corner that has no gas station.
2. No matter how small your lot in life, there's always room on it for a gas station.

gate. See football[3].

gauge. See railroad[2].

genealogist. One who traces back your family as far as your money will go.

genealogy. The study through which you trace yourself back to people better than you are.

general. The man who has his men behind him before the battle and ahead of him during it.
See cover; store: general store.

generalization. All generalizations are false, including this one.
See candidate[3].

generation. The present generation raises the younger generation for the older generation to worry over.
See finance; gentleman[9]; regeneration.

next generation. It will be a generation before the next generation starts worrying about what's to become of the next generation.
See debt: government debt; statesman[6].

passing generation. So-called because it is passing its debts on to the next generation.

rising generation. 1. People who are fond of sitting. 2. The rising generation may be rising but it's mighty hard to get it out of bed. 3. Alarmists always regard the rising generation as a falling one.
See retire.

younger generation. 1. It stands on its own feet but it dances on other people's. 2. Give the younger generation enough rope and it will keep on skipping.
See disrespect.

generosity. Replacing a broken promise with another one.

generous. When a man is generous to a fault, it's usually his own fault he is generous to.

See credit[4]; writing[1].

generous men. Women take to generous men; also from.

genius. 1. The talent of a man who is dead. 2. One who can do almost anything except make a living. 3. One percent inspiration and ninety-nine percent perspiration. 4. The capacity for making somebody else take infinite pains. 5. The infinite faculty for not taking pains.

See hereditary; limit; slouch; song: song writer[3].

gentleman. 1. A man who wouldn't strike a woman with his hat on. 2. A man you don't know very well. 3. One who doesn't care whether he is one or not. 4. One who has never heard the story before. 5. A man who never strikes a woman without provocation. 6. One who is polite to you even when he has no favors to ask. 7. One who has no business in this world. 8. A man of high principle and no interest. 9. What it takes three generations to make, or one lucky guess on the stock market.

See blend; blonde[3, 4, 5]; brunette[2]; farmer: gentleman farmer; lady[1, 2]; mutual.

geometry. 1. It teaches one how to move in the best circles. 2. A branch of mathematics which shows us how to bisex lions and angels.

germs. 1. They are usually caught on the fly. 2. Doctors say exercise will kill germs, but how is one to get the germs to exercise?

See whiskey[5].

get. 1. Man wants all he can get; woman wants all she can't get. 2. Success is getting what you want; happiness is wanting what you get. 3. Disappointed men who say they are forgetting girls usually mean they are for getting girls. 4. The man who gets a lot of money usually lets a lot of money get him.

See afford; conservative; cry[2, 3]; diplomacy[6]; earn[2]; forget; gold: gold digger[8]; hold: holdup man; itch[2]; like[2, 4]; politician[3]; politics[14]; profiteer[1]; tragedy; voice[3]; wage: living wage[1]; want[1, 3].

get away. See fish[3].

get back. Money may not go as far as it used to, but we have just as much trouble getting it back.

get even. You can never get ahead of a person by trying to get even with him.

See cigar[3].

get off. See politeness[1].

get up. See bed; call; hit[1]; insomnia[2]; lark[2]; rise; sleep: sound sleep[2].

getaway. The way of the transgressor.

ghost. 1. A spirit everybody talks about but nobody has seen. 2. A girl with no spirit hasn't got a ghost of a chance.

See average: average man[4]; rap; scare.

gift. 1. A synonym for trade. 2. It is more blessed to give than to receive; it depends on the gift.

See binding; book[3]; husband: ideal husband; poetry[1]; politician: crooked politician.

gigolo. 1. A fee-male. 2. One who believes that the world owes him a loving.

giraffe. 1. An African skyscraper. 2. A rubberneck cow.

girdle. Everything in life eventually adjusts itself, except a girdle.

girdle manufacturer. Another fellow who lives off the fat of the land.

girl. 1. What every young man should know. 2. A vision in the evening and a sight in the morning. 3. Many a girl is the picture of her father and the talkie of her mother. 4. In the past, a girl was a little dear; now she's a little bare. 5. A girl is always one of three things: hungry, thirsty, or both. 6. There are four kinds of girls: the mental, temperamental, accidental, and experimental.

See boy[6]; child[4]; dimple; get[3]; showgirl; spring[5]; sucker[1]; three; toast; wink[1].

See also under different entries according to type. For example, see clever: clever girl; extravagant: extravagant girl; etc.

best girl. Often necks best too.

good-looking girl. She doesn't have far to look.

petite girl. One who gets that way because she would rather pet than eat.

shrewd girl. One who makes you feel she is taking dinner with you, not from you.

unpopular girl. The most unpopular girl among women is the girl who wins a popularity contest.

up-to-date girl. A pretty package wrapped to take out.

give. 1. During Christmas people complain about the high cost of giving.   2. It is better to give than to lend, and it costs about the same.

See Christmas: Christmas gift[1]; cigarette; cow; diplomacy[6]; forget[1]; kiss[17]; liberty[5]; marriage: happy marriage[1]; pain; philanthropist[1,2]; philanthropy[1]; problem: Christmas problem; wage: living wage[1]; word[1].

give & receive.   See advice[1]; gift[2]; judge[3].

give away.   One way to keep your friends is not to give them away.

See wedding[4]; will[1].

give in.   The man who gives in when he is wrong is wise, but he who gives in when he is right is married.

glacier.   A person whose job is putting glass in windows.

glad.   No two people are alike, and both of them are glad of it. See home[12].

gland.   The only thing secretive about women.

glass.   Many a man who doesn't wear glasses, empties them.

See beer; bottle[1]; glacier; mirror: woman's mirror; pessimist[15].

glasses.   Men seldom make passes at girls who wear glasses.

See eyesight.

sunglasses.   Some mothers think their children so bright, they ought to look at them through sunglasses.

globetrotter.   A person with a roamin' nose.

gloves.   Don't wear them when calling on your girl; you'll feel better without them.

gnu.   1. An animal whose most common habitat is in crossword puzzles.   2. Something gnu in the animal world.

go.   Some cause happiness wherever they go; others whenever they go.

See coal: coal dealers; college[3]; driver: reckless driver[2]; homely: homely girl; grouch[2]; modern: modern girl[6]; opportunity[2,4]; pet: petting[2]; relatives: poor relatives[1]; restroom; tongue: woman's tongue[2]; trousers: man's trousers; wait[5]; zoo.

go around.   Girls and golfers have the same ambition to go around in as little as possible.

See football: football player; golfer: woman golfer[2]; nudist[3]; revolution; round[1]; suit: bathing suit[4].

go back.   When a girl threatens to go back to her mother, the man can also threaten to go back—to his wife.

going concern. Many a going concern is going the wrong way.

See invest.

go out. There's no place like home—if you haven't got the money to go out.

See fire: forest fire; respect.

goat. 1. A lamb who has kidded himself into believing that he knows Wall Street. 2. In heaven the sheep and goats will be divided, but on earth the sheep are usually the goats.

goblet. A small sailor.

God. 1. The John Doe of religion. 2. God gets only those women that men do not want. 3. Man can't make a flea, but history shows that that doesn't prevent him from making gods. See agnostic[1]; asunder; atheist[2]; believe[4]; devil; dog[1]; effect; fee; friend[8]; historian; microbe; rest; sap[3]; talk: talking machine; worse[1].

godliness. Cleanliness is vexed by godliness.

See cleanliness.

go-getter. 1. One who runs out of gas a few miles from a station. 2. One who walks a few blocks to the place where he has parked his car.

gold. 1. The only thing that critics haven't panned. 2. It's often found in sand, but so is spinach.

See diamond[4]; heart: heart of gold; touch.

gold digger. 1. One who has the gift of grab. 2. One who uses the males to defraud. 3. One who loves a man for all he's worth. 4. One who insists upon picking her friends, and picking them clean. 5. One who purses her lips when she kisses. 6. A girl who knows a good thing when she sues it. 7. A girl may be able to make or break any man, but a gold digger does both. 8. The difference between a millionaire and a gold digger is that he's got what it takes, and she takes what he's got.

See good[2]; minor; pick[3].

gold-dust. Man is made of dust, but woman thinks it's gold-dust.

golden. The fact that silence is golden may explain why there's so little of it.

See silence.

golf. 1. The only thing that depreciates above par. 2. The game

that has turned the cows out of the pasture and let the bull in.
3. A game in which most of us stand too close to the ball—
after we have hit it. 4. An outdoor game played with the head
and hands; the head is on the club and the hands are on the
golfer. 5. Two can live as cheaply as one can play golf. 6. It's
a sin the way people play golf on Sunday—the way some people
play. 7. Ten percent of the people play golf, or rather, ten
percent of the golfers. 8. The only time you can be sure a
man plays a fair game of golf is to watch him.
See brassie; businessman[1]; fair; fairway; hit[2]; swear[4].

golf ball. 1. An object that has to be hard hit to get anywhere.
2. A small object which remains on the tee while a perspiring
citizen fans it vigorously with a long club.
See caddie[2].

golf club. See dig.

golf course. 1. The course of true golf never runs smooth.
2. It's a wise golf course that knows its own par.

golf links. 1. The best place for a woman to find a husband.
2. Not all wooden-headed drivers are on the golf links.
See businessman[1].

golf terms. The most common ones are unprintable.

golfer. 1. A man who hits and tells. 2. Golfers, roughly speaking, play golf roughly speaking. 3. Golfers must have endurance—and so must their listeners. 4. All golfers are entitled
to life, liberty, and the pursuit of golf balls. 5. A golfer has
one advantage over the fisherman: he doesn't have to show anything to prove it.
See downtown; go: go around; nudist[3]; spring[4]; tee; vice-
president[1].

woman golfer. 1. One who doesn't even know how to hold a
caddie. 2. She may go round in less and less every month,
but that doesn't mean her playing improves.

good. 1. What a man is when he is old; what a thing is when
it is new. 2. A wife does a man good, but a gold digger does
him better. 3. Some people are born good; others have to
make good. 4. Men are not good or bad; they are good and
bad.
See agree[3]; coquette; dare; die; divorcee; egg[2]; egotism; evil;
excuse[1]; faithful; husband[6]; individualism; justice[1]; lawsuit[5];
lawyer: good lawyer[2]; lonesome; longevity; marriage: before &

after[7]; nothing: good for nothing; opinion[2]; pessimist[10]; prompt; punishment: capital punishment[3]; resolution; sanitary; speech: good speech[2]; teeth: false teeth[2]; three; weather: bad weather; whale.

good-by. What money says when it talks.

goodness. Goodness only knows how it feels to be kind and virtuous.

good night. Many a girl won't let a man kiss her good night because, by the time he leaves her, it's morning.

goods. Censors would like to get the goods on the nudists.
See widow: wealthy widows.

    stolen goods. Men steal kisses in the hope that stolen goods will be returned.
    See fence[1].

gospel. The eternal gospel does not require an everlasting sermon.

gossip. 1. A person with a keen sense of rumor. 2. One who always talks about things that leave her speechless. 3. One who gets her best news from somebody who promised to keep it a secret. 4. One who never has tales too rumorous to mention. 5. One half the world doesn't know how the other half lives, but it's not the fault of the gossips. 6. Gossips are the spies of life. 7. Get a gossip wound up and she will run somebody down.
See public opinion[2].

    idle gossip. It's never idle.

govern. See man[7]; right: divine right.

government. 1. No system of government will work unless the people do. 2. Government generally needs much more pruning and much less grafting. 3. The government lives not only beyond its own income but also beyond ours.
See amendment; believe[1]; budget: balance the budget[2]; democracy[2, 4]; freedom[2]; hold: hold up; Nazism; nuisance; public utility; reins; republic; support[2]; tax[2]; underhand.

    representative government. One that elects six men in favor of one thing and six men against it, and wonders why something isn't done.

    stable government. It takes a lot of horse sense to maintain it.

gown. See dress: evening dress; penny.

evening gown. 1. Low and behold! 2. A dress that picks up everything including men.

See backbone[2].

low-cut gown. It shows that a woman's heart is in the right place.

See dress: coming-out dress.

night gown. It's not an evening gown.

grab. The way to fight a woman is with your hat; grab it and run.

See animal; driver: backseat driver[2]; gold: gold digger[1].

graceful. See dance: new dance; disgraceful.

grade crossing. See crossing: grade crossing.

graduate. See college: college graduate; hurry.

graduation. A ceremony that marks the end of college study and the beginning of education.

graft. Laws against graft will not carry conviction until their violations do.

See family: family tree[3]; government[3]; liberty: tree of liberty; plum.

grafter. One who chisels a career instead of carving it.

grain. About the only thing left in this world that can still be shocked.

See advice[5].

grammar. Money talks, but nobody notices what grammar it uses.

grand. See larceny[2].

Grand Canyon. It's gorges.

grandmother. 1. The person you bring the baby to for an overmauling. 2. Children are often spoiled because you can't spank their grandmothers.

See baseball: baseball season; wear[1].

grape. Wine in pill form.

See raisin.

sour grapes. They usually start rumors circulating through the grapevine.

grapefruit. 1. An orange with a swelled head. 2. The most frequently used American eyewash. 3. There's more in a grapefruit than meets the eye.

grass. The pedestrian who allows the grass to grow under his feet soon finds it growing over his head.

See sailor[3].

grasshopper. A cockroach that chews tobacco and camps out.

grate. Some men are born great, some achieve greatness, and some just grate upon you.

See grateful.

grateful. The more people grate on you, the less grateful you become.

gratitude. 1. The lively anticipation of future favors. 2. Next to ingratitude, the most painful thing to bear.

grave. The difference between a grave and a groove is only a matter of depth.

See mortician; restroom.

marital grave. It's usually made with a series of little digs.

gravedigger. It's wise to begin at the bottom and work your way up, unless you're a gravedigger.

graveyard. The man who wants a wife that can cook and sew and that doesn't smoke or drink, should go to the graveyard and dig one up.

See Wall Street[1].

gravity. The law of gravity is a serious thing.

See law: law of gravitation.

gravy. To most women potatoes and gravy are avoirdupoison.

See cannibal[1]; politics[3].

grease. He who burns his candle at both ends spills grease.

See justice: wheels of justice.

great. Some men are born great, some achieve greatness, and some thrust greatness upon themselves.

See grate; home[4].

Greece. Money talks turkey even in Greece.

Greek. See college: college courses; homer.

green. When a man sees red, he ought to stop and wait until he sees green, or else he's liable to get a ticket.

See blackberry; light[2], traffic light[2]; servant[2].

gremlin. An elf-made man.

grief. A widow's grief is very brief; when she loses her husband, she pines only for a second.

grin. In spite of criticism, nudists always grin and bare it.

grindstone. Many a man keeps his nose to the grindstone so that his wife can turn hers up at the neighbors.

grit. You can't clean up in this world with soft soap; it takes grit.

groan. See pun[1, 2].

grocer. See marriage[14].

groom. 1. A person associated with brides and bridles. 2. A new groom sweeps clean.

See bridegroom; honeymoon[4]; path: bridle path; wedding[4].

groove. See grave.

grouch. 1. A man who thinks the world is against him—and it is. 2. One who never goes where he is told until he dies.

See rise.

ground. Mud thrown is ground lost.

See camp: old campground; salesman[2]; top[3].

> **grounds.** At present prices, there are grounds for complaint in every coffee pot.
>
> See coffee[1]; insanity.

grow. Children grow by leaps and bounds—in the apartment overhead.

See adult[1, 2]; congressman[1]; disgraceful; dogmatism; ego; equal; fish[2]; grass; hair: bobbed hair; hoax; zoo: zoological garden.

grumble. 1. Gambling and grumbling go together. 2. Some grumble because they don't get what's coming to them; others, because they do.

See home[2].

guarantee. See pay.

guess. 1. Many a true word is spoken in guess. 2. There are millions of telephones in the United States, so when the operator makes it in two guesses she's not doing so badly.

See conjecture; guest: unwelcome guest[2]; vision; weather: weather bureau.

> **woman's guess.** It's much more accurate than a man's certainty.

guest. 1. A person that will happen in, in the best regulated families. 2. Like a fish, a guest begins to stink after three days. 3. There are two kinds of guests: those who come after dinner, and those who come after dinner. 4. The first week a guest, the second a pest.

See club: night club[1]; drop; fly: house flies; leave[1]; scare.

> **unwelcome guest.** 1. A person who takes everything but leave.
> 2. Unwelcome guests never guess they're unwelcome.

3. Your sins will find you out, but you'll have no such luck with unwelcome guests.

See hostess.

welcome guest. A person who knows when to leave and let live.

guide. See reformer[1].

guillotine. 1. The first real cure for dandruff. 2. One of the things that gave Louis XVI a pain in the neck.

guilty. When money talks, it frequently says: *Not guilty.* See defendant[3].

gum. See chewing gum.

gun. A weapon which gives people lead poisoning.

See elephant[2]; gangster; woman[6].

gunpowder. A black substance much employed in marking the boundary lines of nations.

See progress[4].

H

habit. 1. That which makes father, after working his way through college, work his son's way through. 2. Some men are regular in their habits, but we're not saying anything about their habits.

See ride: riding habit; tobacco: tobacco habit.

loose habits. The woman of loose habits often wears tight clothes.

hair. 1. Hair today and gone tomorrow. 2. A man's hair should be parted or departed. 3. A hair in the head is worth two in the brush.

See age: middle age[2]; bald: bald-headed man[1]; barber[4], barber trade; bleach; comedian[2]; education: college education[3]; elevator; extremist; face: face-lifting[1]; fall: fall out; irony; life[1]; lose; millennium; top[2]; woman[9].

bobbed hair. One of those things that grows on you.

golden hair. It's frequently the reflection of what's in the mind beneath it.

split hairs. When lawyers split hairs, you may be sure it's somebody else's hairs.

See razor.

straight hair. It can be a very beautiful thing in a woman provided she has legs to match.

haircut. A load taken off one's mind.

hair cutter. The man who always gets to the top.

hairdresser. One who does his head work with his hands.

half. One half the world doesn't know how the other half lives, and the other half wonders why it doesn't mind its own business.

See agriculture; bread; dachshund[2]; driver: woman driver[4]; fullback; gossip[5]; hear[1]; loafer; matrimony: state of matrimony; mind: half a mind; pedestrian[18]; politician[14]; voter[1]; wife[1]; wit[3], half-wit[1]; worm[2].

better half. 1. Usually the half that has not been told. 2. Many a better half is a better half-wit. 3. A husband often shows his worst side to his better half.

See mathematics; quarters.

halitosis. It's better to have halitosis than no breath at all. See lockjaw.

halter. See bride: bridal day; nature: human nature[1]; path: bridle path.

ham. The trouble with actors is that there are too many hams and not enough good roles.

See actor: ham actor.

hamburger. The last roundup.

hand. 1. Many a man who wins a girl's hand finds himself later under her thumb. 2. A diamond on the finger is worth more than a spade in the hand. 3. It's proper to hold a man's hand in the dark, and often necessary. 4. Many hands want light work. 5. Many a young man who asks for the daughter's hand gets the father's foot.

See bird[2]; blackout; bridge[4]; clock[1]; dentist[5]; dish: washing dishes; dollar: dollar bills; driver: woman driver[2, 3]; driving[3]; dye; eyes: black eyes[3]; golf[4]; hairdresser; itch[2]; jackpot[1]; manicuring; manicurist[1, 2]; manners: table manners[1]; marriage: before & after[4]; marry: married man[1]; money[10]; mosquito[4]; nail; politician[4]; psalmist; ring: engagement ring; swim; towel: paper towel; town: small town[2]; Venus[2]; woman[12]; work[4].

handbag. See puff.

hanging. The worst use a man can be put to.

hangman. It's noose to him.

hangover. 1. Two heads are better than one, except during a hangover. 2. The best way to avoid getting a hangover is not to stop drinking long enough to have one. 3. The liquor of today is the hangover of tomorrow. 4. When a man has a hangover, he needs an aspirin; when a woman has a hangover, she needs a brassiere.

See aspirin.

happen. See driver: bad driver[1]; expert: military expert; history[3]; news[1]; Occident; occurrence; optimist[2]; probable; unexpected.

happily. And then they were married and lived happily even after.

happiness. 1. Something that depends not on position but on disposition. 2. A man never knows what real happiness is until he gets married, and then it is too late. 3. Happiness has one great advantage over wealth: friends don't try to borrow it.

See comfort; get[2]; go; pursue; temptation[2].

pursuit of happiness. All that the Constitution guarantees is the pursuit of happiness; you have to catch up with it yourself.

secret of happiness. 1. It's liking what you do, not doing what you like. 2. The five secrets of happiness are: money, money, money, money, money.

happy. A man can be happy with any woman as long as he doesn't love her.

See alone[2]; bald: bald-headed man[2]; end[2]; hypochondriac[2]; imagination[3]; mother-in-law[6]; pessimist[8]; triumphant; want[5].

happy people. Those who have no particular reason for being so.

See bliss.

hard. Some girls are so hard, the only thing that will make an impression on them is a diamond.

See cider; diamond[5]; diet: soft diet; friend: real friend; heart: heart of gold; liquor[6]; writing: easy writing.

hardship. A condition helped by soft words.

hare. See light: traffic light[3]; rabbit[1].

harlot. A merry magdalene.

harmful. See drink: mixed drink.

harmony. If you want harmony in the orchestra of matrimony, don't keep harping.

See saxophone : saxophone player.

domestic harmony. 1. It's produced only if the husband plays second fiddle. 2. When the wife has her way when they agree, and the husband has her way when they disagree.

harness. 1. It usually breaks when a person hitches his wagon to a movie star. 2. A married man may be in harness without working like a horse.

harp. 1. Learning to play this instrument is no guarantee that you'll get to heaven. 2. The first thing the typical American asks when he gets to heaven, is the amount of the down payment on a harp.

See angel[5] ; harmony ; heaven[1] ; harpy.

harpy. A person who plays the harp.

hash. 1. The connecting link between the animal kingdom and the vegetable kingdom. 2. The substance of things hoped for and the evidence of things which have been. 3. Hash isn't made; it accumulates. 4. Like life, hash is what you make it. 5. When an enthusiastic cook puts all she has into her cooking, the result is usually hash. 6. There's only one thing worse than restaurant hash where you don't know what goes into it, and that's homemade hash where you do.

See divorce[1] ; faith[2].

haste. 1. The more haste, the less speed. 2. Marry in haste, and you'll never have any leisure to repent in.

See father-in-law ; minister : stuttering minister ; modern : modern girl[4] ; repeat[5] ; repent.

hastily. Nothing should be done hastily, except killing mosquitoes.

hat. 1. The best thing to put on a bald head. 2. A head covering which women buy because they can't get it for nothing. 3. Something the average man covers his head with, the beggar passes around, the statesman throws into the ring, and the politician talks through. 4. Men wear hats because it is easier to check a hat than a cold.

See artist : tonsorial artist ; bull : bull ring ; candidate[5] ; club : night club[5] ; crown ; elevator ; expose ; farmer : gentleman farmer ; gentleman[1] ; grab ; head[1] ; milliner ; purse[1] ; restaurant[2] ; straight[1] ; try : try on[2] ; Uncle Sam.

straw hat. It can hardly be felt.

woman's hat. Something that looks as if it had made a forced landing on her head.

hatch. See birth: births, marriages, deaths[1]; brood[2].

hatchet. See bury.

hate. The man who hasn't got an enemy, doesn't need one; all his friends hate him.

See censor[1]; woman[3].

haughtiness. Rectitude, platitude, high-hatitude.

hay. The trouble with a husband who works like a horse is that all he wants to do evenings is hit the hay.

See sunstroke.

hay fever. See fever: hay fever season.

head. 1. Most men lose their heads more often than their hats. 2. Early to bed and early to rise, and your head will never feel three times its size.

See ahead; backbone[1]; barber: barber shop[2]; bloc; bone[1]; brain: brains; breeding; cheek; coed[6]; cold[1, 2, 4]; column: spinal column; combination; conversation: thin conversation; crossroad[1]; dollar: dollar bills, silver dollar; drum[2]; face[5]; father[2]; figure[1]; fill[1]; fingernails[1]; flirt[2]; golf[4]; hair[3]; hairdresser; hangover[1]; hat: woman's hat; headache[2]; itch[2]; kiss[18]; lice; manufacturer: hat manufacturer; mob[2]; pin; rattle; reducing: reducing exercise; shirt: stuffed shirt; shoulder; success[2]; telephone: telephone operator[3]; uneasy.

hard-headed man. A person you can't soft-soap.

light-headed. See blonde[2].

swelled head. Nature's frantic effort to fill a vacuum.

See body; grapefruit[1]; writer: writer's cramp.

headache. 1. The best thing to take for a headache is whiskey the night before. 2. A person with a headache doesn't want to get rid of his head even though it hurts him to keep it.

See children[2]; father[2].

headless. The headless horseman was a myth, but the headless motorist is a stark reality.

heal. The doctor who heals a broken bone often leaves the patient broke.

See wrinkle[1].

health. 1. The only way to keep it is to eat what you don't want, drink what you don't like, and do what you'd rather not.

2. Health is wealth, but this is a good rule that won't work both ways. 3. If you drink to other people's health too often, you'll ruin your own.

See hypochondriac[1]; onion[5]; regain; sick: sick people; stretch: stretching; undertaker[1].

board of health. A proper diet.

good health. See doctor[2].

hear. 1. Believe only half of what you hear, but be sure it's the right half. 2. No one knows the anguish a heartbroken woman suffers; that is, no one outside of hearing distance. 3. It you've never heard a good word about some people it's because you've never heard them talking about themselves.

See believe[2]; gentleman[4]; nose[3]; obligation; parents[3]; repeat[1, 2]; town: small town[3]; whisper[2].

hearse. 1. Father Time's delivery van. 2. Everything comes to him who waits, especially the hearse.

hearse driver. The only man who never gets backseat driving.

heart. 1. An organ kept in a trunk, played by beats, and enjoyed only after it is lost or given away. 2. A girl may love you from the bottom of her heart, but there's always room for some other fellow at the top.

See absinthe; cash: cold cash[1]; church[2]; combination; flirt[2]; fond; gown: low-cut gown; love[1, 3]; muscle; present [1, 2]; stomach[3]; surgery.

big heart. The trouble with girls who have big hearts is that they usually have hips of the same size.

faint heart. Faint heart ne'er won fair lady, but a faint whisper often catches her.

See fur; jackpot[2]; purse[2].

hard-hearted man. One who was probably raised on rock candy, marble cake, and brick ice cream.

heart murmur. It's off the beatin' path.

heart of gold. It's sometimes yellow and hard.

heart trouble. Love.

See pretty: pretty girl.

soft-hearted woman. One who was probably raised on soft-boiled eggs and soft drinks.

heartache. See children[2].

heartburn. 1. It's as prevalent among cold-hearted as among warm-hearted people. 2. You can't swallow your pride without getting heartburn.

See love².

heat. Heat travels faster than cold because a person can catch cold.

See air: hot air¹; blonde⁴; contribute; janitor³; steam; stupidity.

dead heat. What the race to the crossing often ends in.

heaven. 1. The place where marriages are made, which explains why married people are always harping at each other. 2. The best way to get there is to turn to the right and then go straight forward. 3. Choose heaven for climate but hell for company. 4. Heaven only knows where heaven is.

See angel², ³; bald: bald head; bladder; cannibal⁴; cat²; church⁶; cigar: cigar-lighter; cook¹; despise; earth¹; goat²; harp; hell⁴; infancy; love¹⁵; match: matches; music: musical instrument; prayer¹; preacher¹; reformer⁶.

heavy. See match¹.

hedge. Many a politician finds when he comes to repair his political fences that a hedge will do better.

heel. The man without a soul.

See chiropodist²; detective; time².

high heels. They were invented by a woman who had been kissed on the forehead.

See lift¹.

height. The best way to rise to the heights is to stay on the level.
See depth.

heir. A man isn't necessarily bald because he has no heir.

See pregnant: pregnant woman; rain: rainy day¹; squander².

heiress. All heiresses are beautiful.

hell. 1. The place paved with good intentions—also asbestos. 2. If there isn't any hell, where has all the business gone to? 3. Cold-blooded people who want to warm up should go to hell. 4. Marriages are made in heaven; they don't need them in the other place; they've got enough hell without them.

See cannibal⁴; convention¹; driving²; heaven³; love¹⁵; preacher²; war³.

road to hell. It's paved with war inventions.

help. It's easy to pick out the best people; they'll help you do it.
See abet; altruism²; friend³; kleptomaniac; lie²; prison¹; squander¹; stretch: stretching; tip.

hen. 1. About the only one who can lay down on the job and still get results. 2. The only creature on earth that can sit still and produce dividends. 3. An egg's way of making another egg. 4. The only animal that can lay around and make money. See discourage; lay; set.

cackling hen. She's either laying or lying.

dead hen. 1. The hen that lays the longest. 2. She's better than a live one because she will lay wherever you put her.

henpeck. The man who cackles in his sleep is probably henpecked.

henpecked husband. A man whose nerve is in his wife's name. See catch[3].

hereditary. Many people believe genius to be hereditary; those who think otherwise have no children.

heredity. 1. An evil that ought to be prevented. 2. Something a father believes in until his son starts acting like a damn fool. See environment.

heresy. What the minority believe.

hero. 1. Every man is a hero until the company leaves. 2. Every hero becomes a bore at last. 3. No man is a hero to his own wife; no woman is a wife to her own hero. See collector: bill collector[1]; marriage[20]; wallet.

hero worshipper. The self-made man.

movie hero. The man who sits through it.

hesitate. 1. He who hesitates is bossed. 2. She who hesitates is lost; so is the man who doesn't. See last; vice versa[3].

hiccough. Many a hiccough is a message from departed spirits.

hiccup. There's many a slip 'twixt hiccup and lip.

hide. 1. Nowadays the last thing a girl bothers to hide is her hide. 2. Men no longer hide behind women's skirts; neither do women. See chair: high chair; embarrassment; newspaper; ocean: ocean liner; pants[4]; skin[3]; tan.

high. Some people get high when they take a drop. See politics[11]; shoes: low shoes; skirt: modern skirts[2]; thermometer[3]; toper.

highbrow. 1. A man who has found something more interesting than women. 2. A person you can't have a high time with. 3. One whose education exceeds his intelligence. 4. A lowbrow

who won't admit it.   5. Highbrows are not always high-minded.
6. Highbrows usually get low salaries.

See baldness.

highway.   1. Don't count your chickens if you live near a main
highway.   2. Along the highways, you can't see the scenery for
the signery.

See measure; nut.

hike.   See driving: driving dangers; hitchhiker.

hint.   Do your Christmas hinting early.

See suggestion.

hips.   See diet: dieting; free[2]; heart: big heart; potato: French
fried potatoes; weight[2].

hire.   1. Employers believe hire should be lower.   2. Hire should
be made worthy of the laborer.

See executive; lawyer[2].

historian.   God cannot alter the past, but historians can.

historical.   Some women, when they quarrel, become hysterical
while others become historical: they rake up the past.

See farce.

history.   1. A record of the evil that men do.   2. An account,
mostly false, of events, mostly unimportant.   3. Something that
never happened, written by a man who wasn't there.   4. A series
of lies agreed upon.   5. Anybody can make history, but only a
great man can write it.   6. We learn from history that we do
not learn from history.   7. History is not fiction agreed upon
but the truth disagreed upon.   8. If history repeated itself, learning history would be much easier.

See respect[3, 6]; stone: Stone Age.

personal history.   History repeats itself, but the neighbors
repeat it when it's your personal history.

hit.   1. Never hit a man when he's down—he may get up.   2. The
difference between learning to drive a car and learning to play
golf is that when you learn to play golf you don't hit anything.
See brakes[1]; break: even break; Cupid[1, 2]; golf: golf ball[1];
golfer[1]; homer[2]; matrimony[7]; nail; strike[1]; thumb: sore thumb.

hitch.   In love, the hitch comes when the knot is tied.

See harness[1]; press: press agent[2].

hitchhiker.   The only person who is completely incapacitated by
the loss of his thumb.

Hitler, Adolf.   A man who is positively naziating.

hoarse. See windbag.

hoax. Great hoax from little falsehoods grow.

hobby. People who have hobbies seldom go crazy, but those who have to live with them do.

detective's hobby. Collecting clues.

hobo. A road's scholar.

hog. See squeal.

hold. 1. The best way to hold a man is in your arms. 2. A woman thinks the only way to hold a man is down.

See conviction[1]; dance[2]; examination: bar examination; golfer: woman golfer[1]; idea[3]; intoxicate; marriage; before & after[3]; obstinacy: obstinate man; perfume: good perfume; present[3]; worst; youth[3].

hold up. Some patriots support the government; others hold it up.

holdup man. One who usually gets everything except what is coming to him.

See swim: swimming instructor.

hole. See bonanza; cheese; circle[4]; darn[1]; doughnut: doughnut hole; fullback; moth[1]; pessimist[1]; prosperity[6]; puncture; Santa Claus; spats[1]; subway[2].

holiday. See prohibition: Prohibition Era[1]; tongue: woman's tongue[1].

See also Christmas; Decoration Day; etc.

Hollywood. 1. The land of yes men and acqui-yes girls. 2. Hollywood may be thickly populated but to most people it's still a bewilderness. 3. The easiest way to clean up in Hollywood is to become a censor.

See retake; telescope.

Hollywood life. Mere sexistence.

Hollywood society. It moves in the best triangles.

holy. See marriage: common law marriage.

home. 1. The place where, when you go there, they have to take you in. 2. The place where we are treated the best, and grumble the most. 3. A place where you can take off your new shoes and put on your old manners. 4. Where the great are small, and the small are great. 5. Where you don't have to make reservations in advance. 6. Where part of the family waits until the rest of them bring back the car. 7. Where you can scratch any place that itches. 8. A home is not what you make it; neighbors make it noisy, friends mess it up, and the landlord makes it expensive. 9. There's no place like home, once in a while. 10. There's no place like home—thank God! 11. Home is where the mortgage is. 12. There's no place like home, and many a man is glad of it. 13. Be there ever so many payments, there's no place like home. 14. First a man buys a home, and then he buys a car to get away from it.

See build[1]; charity[1]; chic; college: college cheer; commuter[2]; damp; daughter[4]; economics: home economics; economist[4]; fill: filling station; garage; go: go out; hero[1]; hostess; man[9]; nation: civilized nation[2]; office; order; pie: homemade pies; reform[1]; relativity; schoolboy; select; son: prodigal son; spit[3]; squeak; switch; tact: social tact; trouble[5].

American home. It's as sound as ever, thanks to the radio.
See family[1].

homeless. All men are not homeless, but some men are home less than others.

homely. See face[1]; moralize; office[2].

homely girl. One who is all dressed up and no face to go.

homemade. See hash[6].

homemaker. As a homemaker, the modern wife simply isn't in it.

homer. 1. A term which shows that baseball must have been played by the ancient Greeks. 2. A four-base hit, proving that the Greeks had a word for it.

homesick. 1. To be sick of one's home. 2. Some people never get homesick because they never stay there long enough.

homework. 'Tis better to have loved and lost than to have to do the children's homework.

honest. See lawyer[5]; policemen; politician[5].

honest man. One who does business with people who are too smart to be fooled.

honesty. 1. Mostly fear of being caught. 2. The best policy because it has so little competition. 3. The best policy, but not the best foreign policy. 4. The best policy, but he who acts on that principle is not an honest man. 5. The best policy where there's danger of being caught. 6. Honesty is praised and starves.

honey. A fool and his honey are soon parted.
See busy[3].

honeymoon. 1. The period during which the bride trusts the

bridegroom's word of honor. 2. Something that happens only
once every few years. 3. The cooing stops with the honeymoon
but the billing goes on forever. 4. The honeymoon is over when
the bride serves hot tongue and cold shoulder to the groom.
See marriage[29]; plan[2].

honor. The honor among thieves is generally his Honor, the
judge.
See lawyer[5]; profit[1].

honor system. An educational plan in which the teachers have
the honor and the students have the system.

hope. The only universal liar who never loses his reputation for
veracity.
See diet: reducing diet[2]; disappoint[2]; marriage: second marriage; optimist[9]; pedestrian[24]; religion[3]; spinster[3]; success[1].

horn. The only part of an old car that doesn't make a noise.
See cowbell; driver.

hors d'oeuvres. A sandwich cut up into a hundred pieces.

horse. 1. An oatsmobile. 2. A curious animal: he eats best when
he hasn't a bit in his mouth. 3. The only way he can work is to
turn his back on it.
See advantage[1]; bareback; bet[3]; car[4]; centaur; driver: careless
driver; driving[1]; follow; harness[2]; hay; moral: morals[2]; shape[3];
street: street cleaner[2]; taxidermist[2]; wreck; zebra.

dark horse. Frequently the one who is willing to pony up.

horsepower. The unit of measurement which has put the horse
out of business.
See co-operation.

horse race. 1. It's difference of opinion that makes horse races.
2. We cannot expect to have an honest horse race until we
have an honest human race. 3. People pay to see a horse race,
but horses are more intelligent; they never pay to see the
human race.

horse sense. See sense: horse sense.

race horse. An animal that feels the cold acutely even though
many people's shirts are on him.

hose. A flexible water tube that plays when it works and works
when it plays.
See fireman; leg: shapely legs.

hospital. 1. Where many a man is put for beating his wife.
2. Where people who are run down generally wind up.

See birth[3] ; enema ; nurse[1] ; propose[1].

hostess. The hostess who is at home to unwelcome guests, wishes her guests were.

hot. See Chile ; climate : temperate climate ; coolness ; exterior ; hotel[2] ; scab ; tenderfoot ; velocity ; winter[2].

hotel. 1. A place where one gives up good dollars for poor quarters. 2. Many hotels which advertise hot and cold running water, really have it : hot in the summer and cold in the winter. See man[9] ; news[2] ; spoon[2].

hotel guest. A person who leaves his room only because he can't get it into his bags.

hotel register. The only place where some men can make a name for themselves.

summer hotel. See resort : summer resort.

hound. The favorite sport of fleas is to follow the hounds.

hour. See committee[1] ; liquor[3] ; optional ; potato : French fried potatoes ; public speaking[1] ; regular ; spare ; stay[1] ; travel[3] ; wake : wake up[2] ; word : few words[3].

house. 1. The people who live in the same house longest are those who get life sentences. 2. People who live in stone houses shouldn't throw glasses. 3. The best way to warm a house is to have the painter give it two coats. 4. Nothing annoys a woman like having her friends drop in unexpectedly to find the house looking as it usually does. See build[2] ; Samson ; screen : fly screen ; termite.

glass houses. 1. People who live in glass houses shouldn't. 2. People who live in glass houses shouldn't throw parties. 3. People who live in glass houses should pull down the blinds. 4. People who live in glass houses should undress in the dark. See window : window demonstrator.

household. Nowadays the only males who boss the household are less than three years old.

housekeeping. Light housekeeping is just one canned thing after another.

housewarming. 1. A last call for wedding presents. 2. A house swarming.

housewife. A married woman during ancient days. See servant : servant problem.

popular housewife. The kind of woman who hasn't any salesman resistance.

typical housewife. One who reaches for a chair when answering the telephone.

housework. 1. If you do it for wages, you're a servant; if you do it for nothing, you're a wife. 2. When it comes to housework, some women like to do nothing better. 3. The woman who is too proud to do housework for pay, will marry and do it for nothing. 4. The woman who is too weak for housework probably has a husband who is not too strong for it either.

howl. See winter[1].

hug. 1. Energy gone to waist. 2. A roundabout way of expressing affection.

See curve[2]; dance[2]; driving: driving dangers; wife: clever wife.

human. To err is human; therefore the mule can do no wrong.

See err; jitterbug.

human nature. See nature: human nature.

human race. See race: human race.

humbug. The political bee that buzzes in many a bonnet.

humility. One of the qualities left out of a self-made man.

humor. Like history, humor repeats itself.

See comedian[4]; crossroad[2]; indulge; joke[1]; pun[1]; serious[2].

radio humor. Stuff that has stood the test of time.

sense of humor. 1. The funniest thing about some people is their sense of humor. 2. Women have a keen sense of humor; the more you humor them, the better they like it. 3. The best sense of humor is that which tells you what it is not safe to laugh at. 4. God made women without a sense of humor so they could love men instead of laughing at them.

wholesome humor. Don't expect it from half-wits.

humorist. One who originates old jokes.

See optimist[5].

hungry. Never argue at the dinner table, for the one who is not hungry always gets the best of the argument.

See girl[6].

hunter. The lucky lion hunter is not the one who finds many lions but the one who doesn't find any.

big game hunter. 1. One who can spot a leopard. 2. Some men are big game hunters; others are merely big dame hunters.

wise hunter. During the hunting season the wise hunter disguises himself as a deer.

hunting. See bear; perfect: perfect man; shoot.

hurdle. People who jump at conclusions lose sight of the hurdles.

hurricane. Something that starts off with an inch paragraph and winds up on the front page with pictures.

hurry. The young man who worked so hard to graduate, later wonders what the hurry was.

See king; laziness[2]; next; preacher[1]; speeder; telegram[2]; wind[1].

hurt. See innocent: innocent bystander; pain; pedestrian[4].

husband. 1. The man of few words. 2. One who seems to be against marriage but is only up against it. 3. Some men are husbands merely because some women disliked being old maids. 4. Many a woman thinks she can do nothing without a husband, and when she gets one she finds she can do nothing with him. 5. A husband is like a car: if you take care of him you won't have to be getting a new one all the time. 6. A husband is never as good as his wife thought he was before marriage, and never as bad as she thinks him after marriage.

NOTE: This word has not been cross-referenced because it occurs very often in this dictionary.

average husband. One who lays down the law to his wife and then accepts all her amendments.

conceited husband. One who expects everything and suspects nothing.

considerate husband. One who, on his wife's night out, stays home with the maid.

educated husband. One who knows everything and suspects nothing.

ideal husband. The kind of man no other woman would have as a gift.

misunderstood husband. One whose wife understands him too well.

model husband. 1. He's all right if he is a working model. 2. A woman's idea of a model husband is the man she regrets having given up for the one she mistakenly married.

peaceful husband. No matter how long he's been married, a peaceful husband loves his wife still.

rich husband. A rich husband is always a rich man, but a rich man is often a poor husband.

second husband. 1. Most men would rather be the second

husband of a widow than the first.   2. A second cousin is a distant relative; so is a second husband sometimes.

See drown; grief.

tactful husband.   One who remembers his wife's birthday but forgets which one it is.

well-regulated husband.   One who can't pass a mailbox without feeling in his pockets.

hush.   Many a secret is hushed about from place to place.

hussy.   When a wife doesn't come home, the husband wonders; when a husband doesn't come home, the wife wonders—who the hussy is.

hustle.   It's love that makes the world go round, but it's marriage that keeps most of the inhabitants hustling.

hypochondriac.   1. One who enjoys poor health.   2. One who is happy being miserable.

hypocrite.   A man who sets a good example when he has an audience.

See actor[1]; American: one-hundred-percent American[2]; despise; modesty[1]; moralize.

hysterics.   A man doesn't look for a happy ending to a love affair; merely one without hysterics.

See historical.

I

I.   See columnist[2]; conceit[2], conceited man, conceited person; egotist[2].

ice.   One of the few things that really is what it's cracked up to be. See cherry.

icebox.   A good place to starve to death in.

ice cream.   See heart: hard-hearted man.

idea.   1. A funny little thing that won't work unless you do. 2. If you want to kill an idea, just get a committee to work on it.   3. An opinion is an idea that you hold; a conviction is an idea that holds you.   4. As soon as an idea is accepted, it is time to reject it.

See exchange; father[3]; mind: open mind[2]; oration; rung.

theoretical ideas. Those which a professor of economics has about money.

ideal. See disillusion; ordeal; political: political deal.

ideal man. 1. He's as numerous as there are women to describe him. 2. One who is clever enough to make money and foolish enough to spend it.

ideal woman. The creature a man spends most of his life looking for, but in the meantime gets married.

man's ideal. It's not what he stands for but what he falls for.

idealist. One who hopes to keep politics out of politics.

idle. Let the man who does not wish to be idle fall in love.

See gossip: idle gossip; idol; luck.

idleness. 1. Nothing to do and lots of time to do it in. 2. It's most enjoyed when there is plenty of work to do.

idol. It's always idle.

See luck.

ignorant. 1. What all people are, only on different subjects. 2. Blessed are the ignorant, for they are happy in thinking that they know everything.

See bliss; intelligence: intelligence test[2]; jury[2]; knowledge[2]; law[4]; lawyer[4, 8]; newspaper: newspaper's function; religion[3]; wisdom[1].

illegitimate. There are no illegitimate children, only illegitimate parents.

See child: illegitimate child.

illness. Patients worry over its beginning, but doctors worry over its end.

illusion. See age: middle age[2].

imagination. 1. Something that sits up with a woman when her husband comes home late. 2. What makes the average man think he can run the business so much better than the boss. 3. Were it not for imagination, a man would be just as happy with one girl as with any other. 4. When another person departs from the truth, it's a lie; when we do, it's imagination. 5. Some people are always indebted to their imagination for facts.

See asset; asterisks[1]; infant: infant prodigy[1]; nation[1]; poet[2]; run: run away; tax: income tax return[1]; truth[1]; wear: women's wear[1].

imagine. See fame: test of fame; try: try on[1].

imitate. Women who try to imitate men make perfect fools of themselves.

See counterfeiter; song: song writer[1].

imitation. See catskin; originality.

immigrant. The difficulty in turning immigrants into good citizens is to find a proper model.

See American: American melting pot.

immigration. The sincerest form of flattery.

See Mayflower[2].

import. See duty: painful duties.

important. At man's birth, his mother is the important character; at his marriage, the bride is; at his death, the widow.

See trousers: man's trousers.

importer. One who expects every man to pay his duty.

impose. Man proposes, then woman imposes.

impossible. Before the telephone was invented, people thought it was impossible; it still is.

impress. Many people live expensively to impress people who live expensively to impress them.

impression. Too much lipstick may be vulgar, but it leaves a good impression.

See hard[1].

improve. See golfer: woman golfer[2]; perfume[2]; race: human race; temper[2]; Ten Commandments[2].

impunity. Some people drink with impunity, or with anyone who invites them.

impure. To the pure all things are impure.

inattention. When a girl marries she gives up the attentions of several men for the inattention of one.

incense. See perfume: bad perfume.

inch. Give a girl an inch and she'll make a dress out of it.

See chiropodist[1]; fender[2].

inclined. People who are inclined to be fat are usually the least inclined to be so.

income. 1. Something you can't live without or within. 2. Many a girl is willing to live on her sweetheart's income, if he gets another for himself. 3. Where do the people who live beyond their incomes get the money to live beyond their incomes?

See capitalist; faith[6]; government[3]; incompatible; outcome; place[1]; poorhouse; support[2]; vacation[3].

fixed income. It's impossible to budget if you have a fixed income.

income tax. See tax: income tax.

incompatible. The lack of harmony due to income.

inconsistency. The only thing in which people are consistent.

inconvenient. It's no disgrace to be poor, but it's mighty inconvenient.

increase. See raise[1, 3].

index. The absence of an index is often the best index of a book.

India. See untouchable.

Indian. See America: history of America; communism; Thanksgiving[3].

indigestion. 1. The one thing that people who eat frankfurters have in common. 2. A distressing stomach trouble relieved temporarily by kicking the cat or whipping the children. 3. A condition sometimes caused by being forced to eat our own words. 4. The failure to adjust a square meal to a round stomach. See abdomen; drug store[1].

indiscreet. Questions are never indiscreet; answers sometimes are.
See tact: tactless people.

individual. See corporation[2]; debt: public debt; socialist.

individualism. The theory that one man is as good as another, and often a great deal better.

   rugged individualism. Rugged for the few and ragged for the many.

indulge. Any comedian who indulges his audience, humors them.
See wife: indulgent wife.

inevitable. Death and taxes are equally inevitable, but death is not a repeater.

inexperience. The reason so many marriages are failures is that so many inexperienced people go into it.
See young[1].

infancy. Heaven lies about us in our infancy, and everybody else when we grow up.
See jazz; radio[5].

infant. See nursery[1]; pregnant.

   infant prodigy. 1. A young child whose parents are highly imaginative. 2. One who usually remains an infant long after he ceases to be a prodigy.

infatuation. Blisskrieg.

inferior. Scientists are having a hard time proving that man descended from an inferior animal.

See man : present-day man ; mingle.

inferiority complex. It would be a fine thing if only the right people had it.

See meddler.

inflation. Congress consists of lawmakers who huff and puff and blow up inflation.

inform. See form ; year : formative years.

best-informed woman. The one who's on a party line.

information. See appendix[2] ; culture : cultured man.

ingratitude. See gratitude[2].

inherit. When the time comes for the meek to inherit the earth, taxes will be so high they won't want it.

See meek ; relatives[4].

injure. See pedestrian[24] ; stop : sudden stop ; twins[1].

injustice. See nation : civilized nation[2].

ink. See blotter.

in-law. 1. The only law you can't flout. 2. One of the disadvantages of marriage. 3. If married people had their way, in-laws would be outlaws.

See outlaw.

innocence. Innocence is never in a censor.

See murderer.

innocent bystander. The person who always gets hurt.

insane. One reason why the insane are happier than the sane is that they don't have to worry over doctor bills.

See murderer.

insane asylum. 1. Where the latest craze can always be found. 2. Persons are put there for no reason at all. 3. An institution whose inmates are simply crazy about it.

insanity. Grounds for divorce in some states but grounds for marriage in all.

insect. See jitterbug ; picnic ; screen : fly screen ; sexes.

See also ant ; bee ; fleas ; fly ; grasshopper ; etc.

inseparable. Beware of the married couple that's inseparable ; it may take a dozen people to pull them apart.

inside. There is a bright side to everything ; in politics it's the inside.

See skeleton[2].

inside information. Many surgeons get by because they have inside information.

insomnia. 1. The triumph of mind over mattress. 2. The inability to sleep even when it's time to get up. 3. The girl who looks like a dream always gives a fellow insomnia. 4. Insomnia keeps a lot of innocent sheep jumping over a fence all night because one man can't sleep. 5. People who have insomnia lie awake all night for an hour.

See content.

inspiration. See genius[3].

installment. 1. What the Lord giveth, the installment man taketh away. 2. Half the world doesn't know how many things the other half is paying installments on. 3. Some people's idea of thrift is to take care of the down payments and let the installments take care of themselves.

See diamond: diamond jubilee; prosperous; stall.

installment buying. 1. A system where you pay a few dollars down, and the rest when they catch you. 2. The only system by which you can doll up on a dollar down. 3. A system that consists of easy payments and difficult collections. 4. A system that makes the months shorter and the years longer. 5. Installment buying has come to stay, but a lot of things bought that way haven't.

installment collector. 1. One who meets some of our best people. 2. Many marriages crack up when the installment collector cracks down. 3. Your sins will find you out but the installment collector will find you in.

See collector: bill collector.

installment plan. 1. The only method known to get some people to do things on time. 2. The woman who buys her clothes this way will always be dressed on time. 3. You don't have to buy on the installment plan to pay your bills on time. 4. The woman pays and pays, if she buys on the installment plan.

See furs[4]; polygamy[3].

instep. The woman who concealed her instep now has a daughter that shows her step-ins.

instinct. The power which tells a woman whether a man needs inducement or discouragement.

See intuition.

institution.   See marriage; matrimony[5, 6].

instrument.   See music: musical instrument; revolver; telephone[2].

insult.   1. It used to be an insult to offer a girl a drink of liquor, but nowadays she just swallows the insult.   2. Think twice before you speak, and then you may be able to say something more insulting than if you spoke right out at once.

See repartee[2]; twins[1].

insurance.   See religion[1].

  accident insurance.   One person in every eight has an accident; the other seven have accident insurance.

  automobile insurance.   It's not the car but the pedestrian who needs automobile insurance.

  insurance company.   An institution which you can't convince that life begins at forty.

  life insurance.   1. It provides for the widows and orphans— of the company's officers and directors.   2. It keeps you poor all your life so you can die rich.

  See fun[2].

intellectual.   1. One who is seldom intelligent.   2. One who should never marry because he won't enjoy it; and besides he shouldn't reproduce himself.

intelligence.   Intelligence consists of having enough wit to talk well or enough judgment to be silent.

  See education[1]; highbrow[3]; intellectual; man[7]; virtue[3]; wreck.

  adult intelligence.   It's not the intelligence of a dolt.

  human intelligence.   It's millions of years old but it doesn't seem to act its age.

  intelligence test.   1. So far no one has invented an intelligence test to equal matrimony.   2. Where ignorance is bliss, 'tis foolish to take an intelligence test.

intention.   See hell[1]; wedding[5].

inter.   At the undertaker's, you pay as you inter.

  See internationalism.

interest.   1. What a woman without principle draws.   2. Some girls live on the interest men have in them.   3. Interest has neither rest nor religion; it works day and night, Sundays and holidays.

  See busy[2]; collection[1]; doings; gentleman[8]; highbrow[1]; matrimony: bonds of matrimony; pawnbroker[4]; percent; politics[5]; slouch; women[3]; worry[1].

vested interests. The invested interests.

interesting. See favor.

interesting people. Men with a future and women with a past. See taxi: taxi driver[2].

interfere. See resolution: good resolution.

interior. See exterior.

international. See pact: international pacts; peace[3].

internationalism. Its aim is to inter nationalism.

interrupt. A word to the wise interrupts a monologue. See coma; prisoner.

interval. The shortest interval of time is between the change of the traffic light and the honk from the car behind you.

intervention. See necessity[1].

interview. You seldom learn a person's views from his interviews.

intoxicate. No man is intoxicated so long as he can lie on the floor without holding on.

intoxicated woman. A tight skirt.

introducer. From our traducers and introducers, may the Lord deliver us.

intrude. People who hope they don't intrude usually do.

intuition. The instinct that tells a woman she is right whether she is or not. See see: see through.

invent. See saxophone[4]; scientist; swing.

invention. The mother of necessities. See hell: road to hell; laziness[1]; necessity[2]; success: road to success.

inventor. The greatest inventors are not scientists but newspaper reporters.

inventory. If you watch some women shop, you'd think they were taking inventory of the store.

invest. Those anxious to invest in a going concern should make sure which way it's going. See evening; interest: vested interests; investigate; stock.

investigate. In the dictionary invest comes before investigate; but in practice reverse the order. See faith[3]; paint: fresh paint.

investor. The man who refuses to believe in Santa Claus but who is convinced he can beat Wall Street.

Ireland. A great copper-producing country.

Irish. An English-piquing people.

irk. Nothing irks the college boy more than shaking out the envelope from home and finding nothing in it but news and love.

iron. See maid: old maid[3].

irony. The comb that experience hands us after we have lost our hair.

See laundry: Chinese laundry ticket.

irrigate. Drinking doesn't drown your sorrows; it only irrigates them.

island. 1. A place where the bottom of the sea sticks up through the water. 2. On certain islands in the South Pacific there are no taxes, crime, beggars, radios—or inhabitants.

Italy. See billboard[1].

itch. 1. That's where the rub comes in. 2. If your left hand itches, it's a sign you're going to get something; if your head itches, it's a sign you've already got something.

See home[7]; man: marked man; niche; scratch[2], scratch pad.

J

jack. 1. Another name for money because it lifts such a load off a person. 2. All work and no play makes jack. 3. All work and no play makes jack the dull way. 4. One small jack can lift a car, but it takes a lot of jack to keep it up.

See car: used car[3]; dollar[1]; dull; specialist: nerve specialist; uplift: uplift movement; whoopee; work[3].

jackass. Kisses bring out the beast in some men—usually the jackass.

See sense: horse sense[4].

jackpot. 1. Many hands make light work; also a good jackpot. 2. A faint heart may never win a fair lady, but five of them have won many a jackpot.

jail. 1. The only place where they won't raise your rent. 2. You can't put a man in jail because he owes money; and you can't put him there if he has money. 3. It is easier for a camel to pass through the eye of a needle than for a rich man to enter jail. See poorhouse; prison; regular; speeder.

jam. When some men get into a jam they shake like jelly.
See bus: bus motto.

janitor. 1. One of the chief causes of dust. 2. The man who never puts out any excess hot air. 3. The man who would rather sleep than heat. 4. The only man who can make a quick clean-up in Wall Street and get away with it.

January. See resolution: New Year's resolution[1].

jaw. See chewing gum[3].

jazz. Either a passing fancy or a lingering infancy.

jealous. See lover[1].

jealous people. Those who suffer from poison envy.

jealousy. The friendship one woman has for another.

jelly. See jam.

jest. See comedian[2]; joker; whisper[1].

jeweler. See ring: wedding ring[1].

jitterbug. Not an insect, but a human being acting like one.

jittery. N-n-nervous.

job. 'Tis love that makes the world go round—looking for a job.
See designers; hen[1]; leather: shoe leather[2]; look: look for; radical[2]; self-made: self-made man[7]; telephone: telephone operator[2]; wage: wage slave.

joint. See rheumatism[3].

joke. 1. A form of humor enjoyed by some and misunderstood by most. 2. The only things Adam would recognize if he came back to earth are the jokes.
See album: family album[2]; bridegroom[3]; comedian: radio comedians; laugh[2], laugh last[2]; old[1]; pun[2]; radio[5]; repeat[4]; respectable.

broad jokes. You must be broad-minded to enjoy them.

old jokes. See comedian[1]; corn: corn borer; diplomat[4]; humorist.

joker. A jestnut.

Jonah. See whale.

journalism. Journalism is unreadable and literature is unread.

yellow journalism. The trouble with it is that it's read.

journalist. A person who works harder than any other lazy person in the world.

joy. See boy[3]; marriage[6]; tariff: tariff supporter.

judge. 1. When a judge makes a mistake, it becomes the law of the land. 2. Judges and criminals are the only persons who take the law into their own hands. 3. Judges hand out sentences on the theory that it is more blessed to give than to receive.
See book[1]; company[4]; conviction[3]; defendant[3]; honor; judgment; lay: lay down; misdeed; writer[2].

judgment. What this country needs is not more judges but more judgment.
See endurance; son: favorite son.

wife's judgment. Don't question your wife's judgment; look whom she married.

jump. 1. The last word in airplanes. 2. Never hit a man when he's down; jump on him. 3. The flyer whose parachute doesn't open jumps at a conclusion.
See hurdle; kangaroo[3]; pedestrian[21]; politician[2]; tree[1].

June. The month of brides; the other eleven are devoted to divorces.

junk. One man's junk is another man's antique.

jury. 1. Twelve men chosen to decide who has the better lawyer. 2. A group of twelve people of average ignorance. 3. The only thing that doesn't work right when it's fixed. 4. A group of persons that should have the courage of its convictions.
See acquit; America[2]; appeal; bathing: bathing beauty contest; defendant[1, 3]; letter: love letter[3]; peer; thief.

fix a jury. A common attempt to repair the system of criminal justice.

justice. 1. Something that is too good for some people and not good enough for the rest. 2. It is well that justice is blind; she would not like most of the things done in her name if she could see.
See cell; courtroom; defendant[2]; disarmament; jury: fix a jury; power: balance of power; scales[1]; sex: fair sex[2].

wheels of justice. Generally they don't turn unless they are well greased.

K

kangaroo. 1. One of nature's abortive methods to produce a safe pedestrian. 2. Nature's initial effort to produce a cheer leader. 3. A very jumpy animal because it is usually left holding the bag.

keep. 1. The best way to keep a man's love is not to return it. 2. Some men are known by the money they keep. 3. A girl who keeps her figure generally finds it easy to find a keeper to keep her while she keeps it.

See cartel; cash: cold cash[2]; compact; company[2, 4]; complexion: schoolgirl complexion; give: give away; headache[2]; letter: love letter[1]; love[28]; money[13]; producer: theatrical producer; resolution: New Year's resolution[2]; secret; servants[1]; temper; word[1].

keep away. See collector: bill collector[3]; fruit; onion[3].

keep on. When all is said and done, too many people keep on saying and doing.

See unlucky[1].

keep up. It's hard to keep up with the neighbors without falling behind with the creditors.

See down[2]; matrimony: bonds of matrimony.

keeper. Keeping up appearances and keeping down expenses are seldom done by the same keeper.

Kentucky. The state where they have poor feud laws.

key. See typewriter.

keyhole. 1. It shows everything but good taste. 2. It's easier to keep the wolf from the door than the columnist from the keyhole. 3. The only way to stop some men from peeking through a keyhole is to leave the door open. 4. People who look through keyholes don't see much to speak of.

See mind: narrow-minded man; music: true musician.

kibitzer. See bridge: bridge expert.

kick. 1. When a chorus girl marries, she continues to do a lot of kicking. 2. Some people will kick anywhere, except in a football game.

See chair; chorine; lazy: lazy people; leg[1]; liberty[3]; mule[4, 5]; opportunity[6]; sick: sick people; skirt: modern skirts[1].

Kidd, Captain. See finance: finance company.

kidney. Many a man gives up drinking on account of the wife and kidneys.

See modesty[3].

kill. The reason why worry kills more people than work is that more people worry than work.

See birth: birth rate; care; cure; death: natural death; doctor[1, 4]; germs[2]; lion; measure; pessimist[11]; song: popular song[3]; swimmer; time[4]; whiskey[4, 5].

kind. See goodness; tax: tax cut.

kindle. A girl doesn't have to be a good match to kindle a flame in the heart of a young man.

kindness. See college: college boy[2]; pessimist[9].

kindred. People who are afraid of their family or relatives.

king. 1. A cat may look at a king, but it will have to hurry. 2. History shows that most kings deserve to be crowned. 3. If a king can do no wrong, how can he get any fun out of life? See crown; frown; right: divine right.

kiss. 1. Nothing divided by two. 2. A trick of nature to stop speech when words become superfluous. 3. Of no use to one, yet absolute bliss to two. 4. The only agreeable two-faced action. 5. A report at headquarters. 6. The baby's right, the lover's privilege, and the hypocrite's mask. 7. To a young girl it is faith; to a married woman, hope; to an old maid, charity. 8. Not enough for one, just enough for two, and too much for three. 9. Irritation in infancy, ecstasy in youth, a sign of fidelity in the middle-aged, and homage to the old. 10. What the child receives free, the young man steals, and the old man buys. 11. The anatomical juxtaposition of two orbicularis oris muscles in a state of contraction. 12. He who kisses and runs away will live to kiss another. 13. Never let a fool kiss you or a kiss fool you. 14. Kiss her first, then argue about it. 15. It takes a little experience to kiss like a professional but a lot of experience to kiss like an amateur. 16. The man who never kisses his wife resents when another man kisses her. 17. You cannot give a kiss without taking it and cannot take it without giving it. 18. In kissing, two heads are better than one. 19. There's nothing in kissing a girl once; it's the second time that counts.

See appetite[4]; ceremony; clever: clever girl; devour; doubt[2]; eyes[2]; first[2]; gold: gold digger[5]; goods: stolen goods; heel:

high heels; jackass; larceny; lips; maid; make-up[2, 3, 4]; male[2]; marriage: before & after[1, 3]; old: old-fashioned girl[2]; olive; promiscuous; shorten; swear[3]; telephone: telephone booth[3]; willing.

before & after. All women act alike after they're kissed; the difference lies in their actions before.

first kiss. 1. It comes only once in a lifetime. 2. Women still remember the first kiss after men have forgotten the last.

kitchen. The place where you go to take things out of cans and put them on plates.

kitchenette. Polygamy would never work in this country: think of four wives in a kitchenette.

kite. Men are like kites because they rise with wind and pull.

kittenish. Pity the man who comes home dog-tired only to find his wife feeling kittenish.

kleptomaniac. One who helps himself because he can't help himself.

knee. 1. Girls nowadays seem to think that beauty is knee-deep. 2. It's an ill wind that shows no pretty knees. 3. Water on the knee is now a common occurrence for those girls who are out in the rain.

See dictaphone; man: self-conscious man; Pilgrims; skirt[3]; slip; wind[2].

knife. See cabbage; company[5]; conscience[2]; day: daily dozen[1]; exercise: strenuous exercise; temper[5].

knit. 1. Something a man can't do but which his broken bones can. 2. It doesn't mean a man can sew if, after an accident, his bones begin to knit.

knitting. An occupation that gives women something to think about while talking.

knock. Autos are generally like their drivers; the older they become, the more knocking they do.

See America[3]; neighbor[4]; opportunity[5, 6]; ring[1].

knocker. Opportunity never knocks at the door of a knocker. See brass.

knot. It's not a knot when it's not a knot.

See censor[6]; hitch; marriage: marriage tie; matrimony[4]; sailor: sailor's life.

know. 1. It's better to know nothing than to know what isn't so. 2. As soon as people are old enough to know better, they don't know anything at all. 3. A man thinks he knows; his wife knows better. 4. A man who wants to get married should know either everything or nothing. 5. There are two good reasons why we don't trust people: one, because we don't know them, and the other because we do.

See agnostic[2]; censor[2]; education: educated person; etc.; expert[2]; father: wise father; fatherland; flunk; fool[2]; friend[5]; gentleman[2]; girl[1]; gold: gold digger[6]; heaven[4]; husband: educated husband; ignorant[2]; old[3]; philosopher; prude[1]; psychology; shut[1]; taxi: taxi driver[3]; taxidermist[1]; teaching: secret of teaching; wait[2].

knowledge. 1. Knowledge is power, if you know it about the right person. 2. Knowledge begins when you acknowledge ignorance.

See college[1]; experience[2].

L

label. See libel.

labor. It's always within striking distance of capital.

See art[3]; baby[4]; class; collective bargaining; self-made: self-made man[1].

> **labor union.** An association of workers who believe that wage reduction is a capital offense.

laborer. When it comes to wages, the laborer is worthy of his higher.

See hire[2]; philanthropist[4].

lack. Many a man creates his own lack of opportunities.

See relatives[2].

ladder. The only thing that stands between the college graduate and the top of the ladder.

See rung; success: ladder of success; unlucky[2].

lady. 1. A person who is never a gentleman. 2. A woman who makes it easy for a man to be a gentleman. 3. One who never shows her underwear unintentionally. 4. A woman who always remembers others and never forgets herself. 5. When a lady says *no,* she means *perhaps;* when she says *perhaps,* she means *yes;* when she says *yes,* she's no lady.

See fur; outwit.

lady in waiting. The feminine of bachelor.

See maid: old maid[2].

lamb. See goat[1]; millennium; pool: stock pool.

land. If a man owns land, the land owns him.

See country[2]; drunk; farm[2]; find; missionary[2]; Pilgrims; Plymouth Rock; real estate agent; restroom: ladies' restroom; sailor[1]; spiritualism.

landing. See hat: woman's hat; rumor: flying rumor.

landlord. See air: hot air; home[8]; rent.

lane. It's a short lane that has no road hog.

language. 1. The art of concealing thought. 2. Money talks in all languages.

See Chinese; psychology; rhetoric; Spanish.

colloquial language. Slanguage.

dead languages. The ones that have lived longest.

See Latin.

romance languages. What coeds generally sign up for.

sign language. Money talks, but credit uses the sign language: people who buy on credit sign for everything.

lap. A girl in the mind is more dangerous than a girl in the lap.

See fast: fast woman.

larceny. 1. Stealing a kiss is only petting larceny. 2. Stealing a kiss may be petty larceny, but sometimes it's grand.

large. See tooth: tooth cavity.

lark. 1. You can't rise with the lark if you've been on one the night before. 2. Some men get up with the lark, but others want a swallow the first thing in the morning.

laryngitis. The rich man has acute laryngitis but the poor man has a cold.

lass. A good-looking lass seldom passes a good looking glass.

last. He who hesitates is last.

See cemetery[1]; early[2]; future[1]; laugh: laugh last; love: first love[2]; marriage: long marriage; mint; pants[3]; passion; ring: wedding ring[2]; romance[6]; see[1]; souse; suicide[1].

late. Women are their own excuse for being—late.

See appointment; early[2]; experience[3]; happiness[2]; imagination[1];

mother[2]; punctuality[2]; repartee[3]; spend; swamp; wait[5]; wake: wake up[3].

Latin. It's still used on tombstones because it's a dead language. See status quo.

laugh. 1. It's better to be laughed at for not being married than to be unable to laugh because you are. 2. If you want a girl to laugh at your jokes, tell her she has a musical laugh.

See Bible[4]; comedian[3], radio comedian; humor: sense of humor[3, 4]; man[2]; mind: broad-minded, serious-minded people; piano; raise[2]; repeat[4]; vegetable; weep.

belly laugh. A mirthquake.

laugh last. 1. He who laughs, lasts. 2. He who laughs last, didn't see the joke at first. 3. He who laughs last may laugh best, but he soon gets a reputation for being dumb. 4. He who laughs last sits in the last row. 5. He who laughs last lacks spontaneity. 6. His laugh lasts who laughs best. 7. He who laughs last seldom gets the point anyway. 8. He who laughs last is probably the one who intended to tell the story himself a little later.

laughter. The sensation of feeling good all over, and showing it principally in one spot.

See maid: old maid's laughter.

laundress. In the old days she was the only one who knew what the ladies wore underneath.

laundry. A place where clothes are mangled.

See soil.

Chinese laundry ticket. A mark of irony.

law. 1. A system that protects everybody who can afford to hire a good lawyer. 2. Like frankfurters, laws cease to inspire respect in proportion as we know how they are made. 3. The law is supposed to speak for itself; if it did, it would complain against the lawyers. 4. Ignorance of the law is no excuse; neither is the ignorance of lawmakers. 5. Everybody says this country has too many laws, but everybody knows of another law that ought to be passed.

See child: child labor; confession; Congress[1]; custom; damage; equity; graft; husband: average husband; in-law[1]; judge[1, 2]; Kentucky; lawyer: woman lawyer; lay: lay down; necessity[3]; nuisance; politician[14]; production: mass production; prohibition;

repeal; resolution: good resolution; self-possession; **Ten Commandments**; today[2].

blue laws. Great yokes from little blue laws grow.

blue sky law. A law intended to protect what we **have saved** for a rainy day.

lawbreaker. The more lawbreakers, the more laws; the more laws, the more lawbreakers.

law of gravitation. The only law that everybody observes. See gravity; tax[1].

law of Medes & Persians. One man's Mede is another **man's** Persian.

majesty of the law. It seems to be going the way of other majesties.

lawsuit. 1. A matter of expense and suspense. 2. A garment worn by a policeman. 3. A matter of dollars and suspense. 4. Something which nobody likes to have, and nobody likes to lose. 5. The way to win a lawsuit is to have a good case, a good lawyer, and good luck. 6. Truth is stranger than fiction—in lawsuits.

See will[2].

lawyer. 1. A learned gentleman who rescues your estate from your enemies—for himself. 2. A man who hires out his words and anger. 3. One who is willing to go to court and spend your last cent to prove he's right. 4. The only man in whom ignorance of the law is not punished. 5. One who must first get on, then get honor, and then get honest. 6. One whose greatest asset is his lie-ability. 7. One who earns his living by the sweat of his browbeating. 8. Ignorance of the law does not prevent the losing lawyer from collecting his bill. 9. Where there's no will there's no way—for the lawyers.

See advice[7]; award; bulk; businessman: ethical businessman; confuse; defendant[1]; hair: split hairs; jury[1]; law[3]; mistake[1]; necessity[3]; principle; talk[1]; white[1]; will[3].

good lawyer. 1. A person who makes a bad neighbor. 2. If there were no bad people, there would be no good lawyers. See law[1].

persistent lawyer. One who will not hesitate to spend a whole evening trying to break a girl's will.

right lawyer. She loved and lost, because she didn't have the right lawyer.

women lawyers. The reason there are so few of them is because women prefer to lay down the law rather than take it up.

lay. 1. Egg prices have gone up: the hen lays for the dealer and the dealer lays for the public. 2. Even when a hen is a bad layer, she lays good eggs.

See discourage; hen[4], cackling hen, dead hen.

lay down. Judges should lay down the law, not lay down on the law.

See hen[1]; lawyer: women lawyers; patriot[1]; repeal.

layman. One who can't understand why efficiency experts don't go into business for themselves and monopolize the world.

laziness. 1. The mother of invention. 2. There's no cure for laziness, but a second wife will hurry it somewhat.

lazy. Automobiles make us lazy, but not if we are pedestrians. See enemy[2]; journalist; osteopathy[1]; sailor[3]; truth[1].

lazy people. What they need is a kick in the seat of their can'ts.

See steps.

lead. Man leads woman to the altar and there his leadership ends.

See bride: bridal day; college[4]; marry: married life[1]; usher.

leader. Nearly all born leaders of men are women.

See follower; political: political leader.

lean. Fat people should rest against objects in a standing position; this will make them lean.

See slim: slim girl; year: lean years.

leap. Look before you leap; but if you're a pedestrian, leap before you look.

learn. Nothing grieves a child more than to study the wrong lesson and learn something he wasn't required to learn.

See classic; coed[2]; college[6]; education: college education[1]; fender[1]; history[6, 8]; hit[2]; live[1, 3]; philosopher[2]; teaching[1], secret of teaching.

least. To say the least—is not a woman's way of doing it.

See wife: small wives.

leather. Birds of leather sock together.

shoe leather. 1. In getting a job, it's more important to the college graduate than his sheepskin. 2. The more you step on the gas, the less shoe leather you wear out.

leave. 1. It's what the guests say after they leave that really counts.   2. When a group of women get together, God help the one who leaves first.   3. Some wives leave their husbands and take everything; others take everything and don't leave. 4. Some men don't leave their wives much when they die, at least not so much as when they were alive.

See alimony[7]; alone[1, 2]; audience; bulk; good night; guest: unwelcome guest[1], welcome guest; hotel: hotel guest; millionaire; orphanage; party: life of the party[2]; pessimist[6]; racketeer[3]; sleep: sleepwalking; son: prodigal son; stay[2]; successful: successful man[3]; threaten.

lecture.   A talk by which the notes of the professor become the notes of the students, without passing through the minds of either.

See explorer.

lecturer.   The lecturer who speaks straight from the shoulder would be more interesting if his remarks started a little higher up.

left.   1. Some nations fight for the right, but others fight for what is left.   2. The girl who thinks no man is good enough for her may be right, but she is more often left.

See fighter; politics[12]; socks[3].

leg.   1. The woman who is always kicking seldom has a leg to stand on.   2. Fashion predicts girls will be wearing their legs longer next season.

See bow; count[1]; hair: straight hair; neck[3]; rheumatism[2]; skirt: short skirt; stockings: stocking run; triangle: domestic triangle.

bowlegs.   1. They are few and far between.   2. Beautiful legs are sometimes without equal, but bowlegs are always without parallel.

See cellist.

shapely legs.   Girls with shapely legs often proclaim the fact from the hose-tops.

legacy.   The best way to secure one is to go at it with a will.

legal.   See alibi; dishonest; law; liquor[2]; trial.

legislation.   See law.

class legislation.   Any law that protects your enemies.

leisure.   The real problem of your leisure is how to keep other people from using it.

See haste[2]; modern: modern girl[4]; progress[3].

lend. 1. If you lend a friend five dollars and you never see him again, it's worth it. 2. The man who never lends money never has many friends, but he doesn't need them.

See acquaintance; friend: good friend; give[2].

length. See dimension; public speaker[1]; skirt[2]; travel[2].

leopard. An animal that can change his spots by going from one spot to another.

See hunter: big game hunter[1].

less. 1. Man wants but little here below, but he usually gets along on less. 2. The less you have to do with some people, the less you are worse off.

See friendship[5]; homeless; marriage: late marriage; more: more or less; philosopher[2]; rationing[3]; think[3].

lesson. See learn.

letter. 1. If you want a woman to read your letter, send it to her husband and write *Personal* on the envelope. 2. The only kind of letters a woman likes to receive from a man are the ones that should never have been sent.

See A B C; college: college boy[1]; co-respondent; female; P.S.; R; rich[1]; soup: alphabet soup.

love letter. 1. Some girls keep their love letters; others let their love letters keep them. 2. When writing one to your girl, it's a wise precaution to begin: *My dear sweetheart and gentlemen of the jury.*

lettuce. Sometimes a vegetable, but more often a proposition.

level. The best way for business to keep on the upgrade is to stay on the level.

See height.

level-headed. Many a man who prides himself on being level-headed doesn't know how low the level is.

level-headed man. One who is unconcerned when others are worried because he doesn't understand the situation.

levity. The soul of wit.

liability. The inability to tell the truth.

See lawyer[6].

liar. 1. A person who should have a good memory. 2. A person who, when he dies, lies still. 3. Figures don't lie, but liars figure. 4. A liar can always get another liar to swear he's telling the truth.

See bonanza; diplomacy[5]; diplomat[2]; hope; mustache[3]; unless.

clever liar. Clever liars give details, but the cleverest don't.

monumental liar. The writer of epitaphs.

libel. Some books sell by their label; others by their libel.

libelous. The only kind of talk that's not cheap.

liberal. One who is considered radical by conservatives, and conservative by radicals.

See conservative[4]; education: liberal education[1]; radical[4].

liberalism. It is beginning to be recognized in the churches but it has not reached the contribution boxes yet.

liberty. 1. What a man exchanges for a wife. 2. The power to mind everyone else's business. 3. The freedom to kick about the lack of it. 4. The privilege of being free from the things we don't like in order to be slaves of the things we do like. 5. The one thing you can't have unless you give it to others. 6. In some countries liberty is preserved; in others, it's canned. See golfer[4]; pursue.

tree of liberty. The most wonderful thing about it is the amount of grafting it is able to survive.

library. Many a person visits his book-borrowing friends just to look over his own library.

public library. Where only low conversation is permitted.

lice. The only thing some people have in their heads.

license number. The best thing to take when you are run down.

lie. 1. A very poor substitute for the truth, but the only one so far discovered. 2. An abomination unto the Lord and an ever present help in time of trouble. 3. If a man lies, and says that he lies, does he lie or tell the truth? 4. There are three kinds of lies: lies, damn lies, and statistics. 5. The light that lies in woman's eyes—lies. 6. A lie in time saves nine. 7. Many a husband lies awake at night, and also lies in his sleep. 8. It is wiser to tell a lie that sounds like the truth than to tell the truth that sounds like a lie. 9. There are two types of people through whose lips lies never pass: those who tell the truth, and those who talk through their noses.

See ambassador[1]; beach; circumstance; country[2]; diplomacy[1, 4]; epitaph; figure[2, 3]; fisherman[2]; flowers: flower bed; history[4]; imagination[4]; infancy; lawyer[6]; liar[1]; lying; mirror[4]; newspaperman; opportunity[3]; politician[11]; praise[4]; prevaricate; real estate agent; recognize; romance[5]; shield; sleep[3]; truth[7, 9], truthful woman; uneasy; well; witness: witness stand[1]; yellow.

lie-detector. The first one was made out of the rib of a man, and there has been no improvement since the original machine.

life. 1. An everlasting struggle to keep money coming in and teeth and hair from coming out. 2. A fatal complaint and a contagious one. 3. It can only be understood backwards but it must be lived forwards. 4. It's what you make it, until someone comes along and makes it worse. 5. A continuous process of getting used to things we hadn't expected. 6. It consists of ups and downs: keeping appearances up and expenses down. 7. For most of us, life is what we make it, but for the pedestrian, it's *if* he makes it. 8. The first half of our lives are usually ruined by our parents, the second half by our children. 9. At about the time one learns to make the most of life, the most of it is gone.

See accident: auto accident[4]; alive; coach; consolation; debt[6]; difficulty[2]; fool[5]; golfer[4]; hash[4]; house[1]; murderer: pleasant murderer; patriot[1]; pessimist[6]; polygamy[1]; pursue; read: reading[2]; sleep[2]; spinster[3]; suicide[2]; taxi[1]; waiter[2].

double life. Most wives lead double lives—their husbands' and their own.

See suit: two-pants suit[2].

rural life. It's found mostly in the country.

wild life. It's not disappearing; it's just moving to the city. See zoo.

lifetime. Any car will last a lifetime, if the driver is reckless enough.

See ring: wedding ring[2]; song: song writer[6]; undo.

lift. 1. New clothes always give women a lift, especially high heels and brassieres. 2. Many a woman gets a lift when her face does.

See disillusion: disillusioned people; jack[1, 4]; song: song writer[5]; sycophant; town: small town[2].

light. 1. Something that travels inconceivably fast until it encounters a human mind. 2. If you want to live to be a hundred, all you have to know nowadays is a green light from a red light. 3. If you have matches and no cigarettes, just make light of the situation.

See blonde[4]; cake: birthday cake[1]; clear; contribute; crossroad[1]; dancer; dark; date: heavy date; fire[1]; literature: current literature; match[1]; reflection; trifle; work[4].

dim lights. Bright lights have the most candle power but dim lights the most scandal power.

headlight. See crossroad[1].

traffic light. 1. Where the speedy and the slow meet. 2. A little green light that changes to red as your car approaches. 3. Today the leisurely tortoise will frequently overtake the speeding hare at the next traffic light.
See interval.

lightning. It never strikes twice in the same place; it doesn't have to.
See electricity[1].

like. 1. All the things men like to do are either immoral, illegal, or fattening. 2. Some girls can get all the men they like, and others like all the men they can get. 3. Take care to get what you like, or you will end by liking what you get.
See company[3]; critic[3]; dislike; friend[2]; happiness: secret of happiness[1]; liberty[4]; reason[2].

lily. Once in a while you see a man who doesn't want any more money; he's holding a lily.

limb. See diamond[6].

Limburger cheese. See cheese: Limburger cheese.

limit. Genius may have its limits, but stupidity is not thus handicapped.
See live: live long; thigh.

speed limit. Whatever the car can do.

line. The most eloquent lines are neither written nor spoken; they are worn.
See art[1]; circle; lipstick[3]; masculine; streamline.

curved line. The loveliest distance between two points.

good line. The shortest distance between two dates.

straight line. The shortest distance between two points—when you're sober.

lingerie. 1. Brevity is the soul of it. 2. As long as women wear lingerie, they support the undie world.

lion. When a man wants to kill a lion, he calls it sport; when the lion wants to kill him, he calls it ferocity.
See equator; geometry[2]; hunter; millennium.

lionize. What the Romans did to the early Christians.
See Daniel.

lips. The only way a man is convinced that a girl can kiss, is when he has it from her own lips.

See bottle[2]; bow; cup; free[2]; gold: gold digger[5]; hiccup; lie[9]; rose; sailor[2]; sip.

lipstick. 1. It's not the kind the girls like that sells; it's the kind the men like. 2. Too much lipstick is unrefined; it leaves a bad taste in one's mouth. 3. The only line the modern girl draws is the one made with lipstick.

See courtship[3]; impression; taste[1].

liquid. See water[3]; whiskey[1].

liquidate. Men who spend their money like water find it difficult to liquidate their debts.

liquor. 1. A liquid that talks mighty loud when it leaves the bottle. 2. It's merely legal, but some people seem to think it's compulsory. 3. It makes one feel like a new person, but makes one look like an old one. 4. Liquor is what makes a drunkard's mouth water. 5. If all the students in this country were laid end to end, it would take a lot of liquor. 6. Some men like their liquor hard and their women soft; others like their liquor straight and their women curved. 7. The reason some people drink liquor is that they don't know what else to do with it.

See best[1]; hangover[3]; insult[1]; modesty[3].

liquor tax. The only tax that provides its own anesthetic.

lisp. To uthe the thound of *th* inthtead of the thound of *eth* in thpeaking.

listen. 1. The only time some women listen is when money talks. 2. Women can do almost anything men can, except listen. 3. Some men talk by the hour but listen by the minute.

See bore[1]; conversationalist; democracy[3]; golfer[3]; marriage[29]; money[5]; philosophy[5]; quarrel[1]; set: smart set; silent: silent man[1]; sleep: sleeptalking; speaker: speaking terms[2]; stop: stop, look & listen; talk[4]; windbag.

literature. There are three types: erotic, neurotic, tommyrotic. See journalism; writer[1].

current literature. It does not always make light reading.

little. See golden; mustache: young man's mustache; same[1]; satisfy; strong[1]; think[6].

little woman. A little woman is a dangerous thing.

live. 1. Some live and learn; others just live. 2. Some people live on love, some live on food, and some just live on. 3. If you can spend a perfectly useless afternoon in a perfectly useless manner, you have learned how to live.

See brave; Columbus[2]; garden; hobby; income; means; operation; relatives[3, 5].

live long. 1. The best way to live long is by not exceeding the feed limit. 2. You can live longer if you cut out all the things that make you want to live longer.

See do[2]; language: dead language; marry; married man[5]; paint[2]; relative: rich relatives[2]; scientist; spinster.

liver. Whether life is worth living depends on the liver.
See colorful.

living. 1. The world owes us a living, but it's sometimes hard to collect it. 2. Some men never go to work for a living until they have given everything else a fair trial.

See genius[2]; sailor[1]; soil; statistics: traffic statistics; warden[2]; weather: weather bureau.

cost of living. 1. It's highest after midnight. 2. The only way to beat it is to stop living. 3. It's always about the same—all a person has. 4. It has gone up but life is still worth it. 5. Whatever goes up, must come down—except the cost of living. 6. The cost of living doesn't seem to have much effect on its popularity. 7. Speaking of the high cost of living, the only thing nowadays that comes down is the rain, and even that soaks you.

loaf. 1. It's bred in the oven. 2. An attempt to make both weekends meet.

See actor[4]; bake; bread; college: college-bred; loafer; panhandler.

loafer. Half a loaf is better than a whole loafer.
See panhandler.

loan. The man who asks for a loan is left alone.
See close; memory; raise[2].

loan shark. One who never attacks those who do not go out beyond their financial depth.

lockjaw. The best thing for halitosis.

lockout. Capital's preference to lock horns with labor rather than to lock arms with it.

log. See sawmill.

logrolling. An aye for an aye.

lonesome. Be good and you will be lonesome.

See city.

long. See artist; centenarian; farmer: good farmer; hen: dead hen[1]; socks[1, 2]; spaghetti; speech[3], good speech[1]; stay[1]; tongue: fool's tongue; traffic: rotary traffic.

longevity. It's due to the fact that the good die young.

See live: live long.

look. A woman is as old as she looks; a man is old when he quits looking.

See breakfast; dirty; dress[3]; eat[2]; girl: good-looking girl; house[4]; king[1]; leap; liquor[3]; million[1]; mind: narrow-minded man; nudist: nudist camp[2]; overlook; poison; see[3]; sense: sensible girl; sight; soap: soft soap; span; stop: stop, look & listen; towel: guest towel.

look after. Look after your wife; never mind yourself, she'll look after you.

look for. The man whose wife makes him go out and look for a job, ends up by looking for a new wife.

See experience[2].

look up. See family: family tree[4].

loose. When a young man is on the loose, he is likely to get tight.

See accident: auto accidents[1]; censor[8]; screw; tight[1].

loose woman. One who often finds herself in a tight squeeze.

Lord. See installment[1]; introducer; lie[2].

lose. Many a man loses his hair through worrying—about losing his hair.

See beauty[2]; caddie[2]; character[1]; friend: real friend; friendly; head[1]; hesitate[2]; lawsuit[4]; love[10]; offer; race; stock; temper.

loser. Women are poor losers, especially when trying to reduce.

See pretend[2].

loss. One man's loss is another man's umbrella.

See hitchhiker; reputation; steer; taxi[1]; thought[2].

lot. 1. When a man asks a woman to share his lot, he shouldn't be surprised if she wants to know the size of it. 2. Man wants but little here below, but when he dies he gets a lot.

See build[2]; corner; gas: gas station[2]; problem: girl's problem.

lottery. See charity[3]; marriage[18, 19, 25, 26].

loud. See money[11], hush money[2]; party: life of the party[1]; senator[1]; snore: snoring[3]; speaker: loud speaker.

love. 1. A heart attack. 2. A heartburn. 3. A heart stroke.

4. Perpetual emotion. 5. The greatest indoor sport. 6. The delusion that one girl differs from another. 7. The last word in a telegram. 8. The comedy of Eros. 9. An island of emotions entirely surrounded by expenses. 10. The only game in which two can play and both lose. 11. The feeling that makes a man think almost as much of a girl as he thinks of himself. 12. A little sighing, a little crying, a little dying, and a great deal of lying. 13. The feeling that makes a woman make a man make a fool of himself. 14. The conflict between reflexes and reflection. 15. A season pass on the shuttle between heaven and hell. 16. The softening of the hearteries. 17. The greatest thing in the world because it's all-embracing. 18. Something any man can buy, and any woman get for nothing. 19. The form of insanity which makes a girl marry her boss and work for him the rest of her life without salary. 20. A game in which one doesn't always play for keeps. 21. A disease like the measles; it's all the worse when it comes late in life. 22. Calf-love, half-love; old love, cold love. 23. Man begins by loving love and ends by loving a woman; woman begins by loving a man and ends by loving love. 24. We always pay for love but we cannot buy it. 25. A woman knows the value of love, but a man knows its cost. 26. 'Tis better to have loved and lost—much better. 27. It is just as hard to live with a person you love as it is to love the person you live with. 28. As soon as you cannot keep anything from a woman, you love her. 29. One should always be in love; that's why one should never marry.

NOTE: This word has not been cross-referenced because it occurs very often throughout this dictionary.

art of love. See art[3].

first love. 1. A little foolishness and a lot of curiosity. 2. It is romantic to be a man's first love, but it is safer to be his last. 3. When a man's first love is himself he never finds a satisfactory successor.

See cynic[2]; romance[6].

maternal love. Smotherly love.

Platonic love. It's no play for the man and no tonic for the woman.

puppy love. 1. The beginning of a dog's life. 2. The only thing that can reconcile a boy to washing his neck and ears.

lover. 1. If all the world loves a lover, a lover's lover should be jealous. 2. The reason why lovers never tire of being together is because they are always talking about themselves.
See brood[1]; feeling[2]; flirt[1]; male[2]; parking[1]; place[2]; touch: sense of touch.

fickle lover. A passing fiancé.

low. God made man a little lower than the angels, and man has been getting lower ever since.
See contralto; dollar[3]; gown: evening gown[1]; highbrow[6]; hire[1]; level: level-headed; library: public library; politics[11]; toper; voice[3].

lowbrow. See browse; highbrow[4].

luck. The idol of the idle.
See deal[2]; pluck; royalty.

bad luck. See thirteen[2].

good luck. See lawsuit[5].

hard luck. It often results from waiting for a soft snap.

lucky. The man who is lucky in love is not the one who gets his woman, but the one who doesn't.
See cat: black cat; engage; wage: wage slave.

lunch. Base ingratitude to breakfast, and premeditated insult to dinner.

lungs. Oxygen tanks.

luxury. 1. It becomes a necessity if you can make the down payment on it. 2. There, little luxury, don't you cry; you'll be a necessity by and by.
See economy[2]; necessary.

lye. See flattery[3].

lying. 1. It always keeps a man down. 2. A little lying is a dangerous thing.
See ask; diplomacy[1]; etiquette[1]; exaggerate[2]; hen: cackling hen; lie; love[12]; tact[1].

M

M.A. Some girls go to college to get an M.A.; others go to get an M.R.S.

machine. See lie: lie detector; progress[3]; reducing: reducing machine.

machine-made. In this mechanized age, even public officials are machine-made.

mad. To be angr-r-ry or enr-r-raged.

See acquit; fat: fat people; insane; pregnant; prejudice[3]; temper: even-tempered person.

magazine. See date[3]; dentist[3]; editor; room: waiting room; sin: wages of sin[3]; subscription; trite.

magazine publisher. One who lives off the fatuous of the land.

magician. The man who hides behind a woman's skirts nowadays is no coward; he's a magician.

See argument[3].

magistrate. This word should not be accented on the last syllable.

maid. It's dangerous to awaken your wife with kisses—if you're giving them to the maid.

See divorce: ideal divorce; husband: considerate husband; path: primrose path.

old maid. 1. A singular being. 2. A lady in waiting. 3. A girl who failed to strike while the iron was hot. 4. A reflection on every unmarried man. 5. A girl who knows all the answers, but no one ever asks her the question.

See count[1]; date[1]; husband[3]; perfect: perfect people; unmarried: unmarried woman; widow[5].

old maid's laughter. He! he! he!

mail. On the first of the month there is no female more deadly than the mail.

See husband: well-regulated husband.

mail-order. See male[1].

maintain. What maintains one vice would bring up two children.

Main Street. A commonplace.

majority. 1. The best repartee. 2. The best way to get a majority is to get all the fools on your side. 3. One way to get a majority is to size up a minority. 4. Most people feel better after an election because the majority have their candidate in.

See minority, intelligent minority; political: political machine[2]; politician: average politician; republic.

make. A mother takes twenty years to make a man of her boy, and another woman makes a fool of him in twenty minutes.

See break[1]; gold: gold digger[7]; hash[4]; home[8]; love[13]; million[1]; mint; money[9]; nation[2]; self-made: self-made man[10]; world[3].

make-up. 1. Most girls make up their faces more easily than their minds. 2. The best way to make up is to kiss your sweetheart and say you're sorry. 3. In the old days they used to kiss and make up; nowadays the make-up comes first. 4. When a fellow and girl kiss and make up, she gets the kiss and he gets the make-up.

See mind[4]; quarrel[2]; weep.

male. 1. The only thing a woman can't order from a mail-order house. 2. A human being who is of no account from the time women stop kissing him as a baby until they start kissing him as a lover.

See blackmail; gigolo; gold: gold digger[2]; household; speech[2].

mammal. Mammals are classified thus: man and the lower animals; man does the classifying.

man. 1. Creation's masterpiece—so says man. 2. The only animal that laughs; also the only animal that has a Congress. 3. Nature's sole mistake. 4. Woman's last domestic animal. 5. The only animal that can be skinned more than once. 6. The only animal that can be skinned and still live. 7. A creature of superior intelligence who elects creatures of inferior intelligence to govern him. 8. An animal split halfway up that walks on the split end. 9. An irrational creature who is always looking for home atmosphere in a hotel and hotel service at home. 10. A kind of worm; he comes along, wriggles a bit, and then some chicken gets him. 11. Science should spend less time studying the origin of man, and more time on what his finish is to be.

See under different entries according to type. For example, see average: average man; breeding: well-bred man; etc.

abstemious man. One who never drinks at home.

man about town. A fool about women.

man higher up. He doesn't mean much if he's in the theater.
  See aviation[2].

marked man. One who starts from scratch and itches all over.

present-day man. He's physically inferior to prehistoric man, but it's better to be inferior than prehistoric.

second-story man. One who always has a second story ready if you don't believe his first.

self-conscious man. One who can't look a pretty girl in the knees.

self-made man. See self-made: self-made man.

small man. The one who usually talks big.
See fight[1].

stingy man. One who can drink any given amount.

suspicious man. One who counts his fingers after shaking hands with you.

tall man. Even a tall man is often short at the end of the month.

manage. 1. Every man knows how a wife should be managed, but few seem able to act on their knowledge. 2. The most foolish woman can manage a clever man but it takes a very clever woman to manage a fool.

manager. See fault: fault-finding woman.

management. See capital: capital & labor; priest.

manicuring. A handy profession.

manicurist. 1. A person who makes money hand over fist. 2. A person who always has her hands full. 3. Some men visit manicurists to have their nails trimmed.

mankind. Since the advent of the car, mankind is being rapidly divided into two classes: the quick and the dead.

manners. Customs invented by wise men to keep fools at a distance.
See children: ill-bred children; expose; home[3]; savage; truck.

good manners. The ability to put up with bad ones pleasantly.
See elevator; mimic.

table manners. 1. A bird in the hand is bad table manners. 2. All children face the hard problem of learning good table manners without seeing any.
See etiquette[2].

manufacturer. The manufacturer who makes the best of things usually succeeds.

hat manufacturer. Another man who insists that two heads are better than one.

pretzel manufacturer. The man who makes crooked dough and still remains within the law.

manure. See propaganda[1].

many. See individualism: rugged individualism; measles; mind[5]; monogamy[2].

map. See cut: short cut.

    road map. 1. A map that tells you everything except how to fold it up again. 2. The man who crosses his bridges before he gets to them is probably following a road map.

    See fold.

mark. See gunpowder; laundry: Chinese laundry ticket; Nazism.

market. See crop.

marriage. 1. It's an institution, but not every man is ready for an institution. 2. It's not a word; it's a sentence. 3. A rest period between romances. 4. The association of two persons for the benefit of one. 5. A miss-mating institution. 6. An institution where your joys are divided and your troubles multiplied. 7. The foreclosure of a mortgage on a man's future happiness. 8. There's more than one kind: trial, companionate, or fight-to-the-finish. 9. A great institution; no family should be without it. 10. A business in which the husband is a silent partner. 11. A union based on the principle that it takes two to make a quarrel. 12. The test of love at first sight. 13. It makes two people one—but which one? 14. The process by which the grocer gets an account the haberdasher once had. 15. An investment, with the mother-in-law putting her two cents in. 16. The condition that most women aspire to and most men submit to. 17. The only life sentence that is suspended by bad behavior. 18. A lottery in which you can't tear up your ticket if you lose. 19. The only lottery licensed by the state and supported by the clergy. 20. A romantic story in which the hero dies in the first chapter. 21. An institution which gives a man double duties and half the rights. 22. An institution where a man faces the music constantly, and the wedding march is where he faces it for the first time. 23. The condition of a community consisting of a master, a mistress, and two slaves, making in all —two. 24. A beautiful custom in which two people share all the troubles which their marriage created. 25. Marriage is a lottery: every wife does not become a widow. 26. Marriage isn't a lottery because in a lottery a man has at least a slight chance. 27. Girls expect money with marriage because they seldom find anything else in a man worth having. 28. Men who respect the institution of marriage believe that every woman should marry, and no man.   *29.* Before marriage he talks and she listens; during the honeymoon, she talks and he listens; later they both talk and the neighbors listen.   *30.* It takes two to make a marriage: a young girl and an anxious mother.

NOTE: This word has not been cross-referenced because it occurs very often throughout this dictionary.

before & after.   1. Before marriage, bushels of kisses; after marriage, a few little pecks.   2. Before marriage, when two people talk about each other, it's love; after marriage, it's an argument.   3. Before marriage, a girl has to kiss her man to hold him; after marriage, she has to hold him to kiss him.   4. Before marriage, when a man holds a girl's hand, it's love; after marriage, it's self-defense.   5. Before marriage, a woman waits up hours for her sweetheart to go home; after marriage, she waits up hours for him to come home.   6. Before marriage, a man catches a woman in his arms; after marriage, he catches her in his pockets.   7. Before marriage, a man thinks nothing is good enough for his wife; after marriage, he still thinks nothing is good enough for her.   8. In some Oriental countries a woman never sees her husband before marriage; in America she doesn't see him very much afterwards.   9. Before marriage, men swear to love; after marriage, they love to swear.

See husband[6]; yearn[2].

common law marriage.   Holy bedlock.

happy marriage.   1. Where the husband gives and the wife forgives.   2. One in which things go fine until the wife comes home from the country and spoils it all.   3. Where the wife makes allowances for her husband's shortcomings, and the husband for his wife's outgoings.

late marriage.   Its advantage is that there is less of it.

long marriage.   One that has lasted at least twenty awed years.

marriage proposal.   See proposal.

marriage ritual.   Many things are easier said than done, including the marriage ritual.

marriage tie.   It's only a slip knot.

marriage vows.   They would be more accurate if the phrase read: *Until debt do us part.*

model marriage.   One in which the wife is a treasure and the husband a treasury.

second marriage. The triumph of hope over experience.

successful marriage. 1. One in which the wife is the boss but the husband doesn't know it. 2. Successful marriages are based on two books: the cookbook and the checkbook.

marry. 1. Some people marry for love, some for money, but most people marry for a short time. 2. A woman marries a man for better or for worse, better for her and worse for him. 3. Pity the man who marries for love and then finds out that his wife has no money. 4. Nowadays a couple marries and the first thing you know they have a little divorce. 5. Nowadays people don't marry as early as they used to, but they marry oftener. 6. Men and women marry because both of them don't know what to do with themselves. 7. Women are fools to marry, but what else can a man marry?

married couple. Two minds with but a single thought—hers. See use.

married life. 1. A nice life for a man to lead if his wife would only let him do a little leading. 2. It's just one undarned thing after another. 3. The period when you make progress if you break even. 4. Praise married life but remain single. 5. The man who says he's satisfied with married life means he's had all he wants of it.

married man. 1. One who has two hands with which to steer a car. 2. A bachelor who has weakened. 3. One who never knows when he is well off because he never is. 4. One who makes a good salesman because he is used to taking orders. 5. A married man lives longer than a single man, or maybe it only seems longer.

See floor: dance floor²; give: give in; pedestrian²; skirt²; sign; yes².

married woman. One who believes there are two sides to every question—her husband's side and the right side.

unhappy married man. One whose first wife divorced him and whose second wife won't.

Marx, Karl. See communist; Nazism.

masculine. The best line to hook a woman with. See patrimony.

masculine woman. A female who has gender but not sex.

Mason & Dixon's line. The boundary between "you all" and "youse guys".

masses, the. The upper classes have always considered the masses as them asses.

See elevate.

masterpiece. See man[1].

match. 1. Its heavy end is the light end. 2. The best finishing touch to most stories.

See birth: births, marriages, deaths[1]; hair: straight hair; kindle; light[3]; nudist[2].

good match. Any marriage where the bridegroom is a man with money to burn.

matches. 1. Matches may be made in heaven, but they are sold down here. 2. Matches may be made in heaven, but they are usually dipped in the other place.

See cigar: cigar-lighter, five-cent cigar[3].

mate. It's never a happy marriage unless both get better mates than they deserve.

See divorce[3]; marriage[5]; shellfish.

material. See explorer; shadow[2]; silk.

mathematician. A mathemagician.

mathematics. Mathematics doesn't explain what happens to a man if his wife is his better half and he marries twice.

See geometry[2].

matrimony. 1. Often a matter-o'-money. 2. The root of all evil. 3. An insane idea on the part of a man to pay for some woman's board. 4. A knot tied by a preacher and untied by a lawyer. 5. Just another coeducational institution, but the most difficult one to get through. 6. An institution of learning in which a man loses his bachelor's degree and his wife acquires a master's. 7. A hit-or-miss proposition; if you don't make a hit, you remain a Miss.

NOTE: This word has not been cross-referenced because it occurs very often in this dictionary.

bonds of matrimony. They are worthless unless the interest is kept up.

matrimonial bark. It's often wrecked by the matrimonial barking.

matrimonial bureau. One with drawers packed full of a woman's clothes and a man's necktie.

sea of matrimony. So-called because husbands have such a hard time keeping their heads above water.

state of matrimony. The only state that can endure half slave and half free.

matter. 1. Never mind. 2. There's no difference between mind and matter; mind is matter—gray matter.

See comedian[1]; dirt; mind[1]; slush.

laughing matter. See Bible[4]; tax: amusement tax.

mattress. See insomnia[1].

Mayflower. 1. A small ship on which several million Pilgrims came to America in 1620.

mayor. Money makes the mayor go.

meal. The sign of a good meal is a good burp.

See indigestion[4]; soup[2]; umbrella[2].

hearty meal. Never go into the water after a hearty meal because you'll never find it there.

mealtime. Marry in haste, repent at mealtime.

mean. See sponger.

mean people. They are generally people of means.

meaning. See critic: literary critic.

means. 1. We should all live within our means even if we have to borrow the money to do so. 2. The person who lives beyond his means would like to be able to live the way he does.

See mean: mean people; prosperity[5].

measles. Everyone has had the measles, but no one knows how many he's had.

See love[21].

measure. Instead of measuring our highways in miles, we should measure them in killometers.

See breakfast: breakfast nook; horse: horsepower; tailor[3].

meat. 1. The real purpose of meat is to flavor vegetables. 2. One man's meat is another man's croquette.

See actor: ham actor; cook[1].

medal. See cover.

meddler. One who suffers from an interferiority complex.

medicine. The art of fooling the patient while nature cures the disease.

See umbrella[2].

medicine cabinet. A home drug store without sandwiches.

patent medicine. It's not what it's quacked up to be.

medium. Dead men tell no tales, except where there are mediums.

meek. It's going to be fun to watch and see now long the meek can keep the earth after they inherit it.

See inherit.

meet. See creditor[3]; expense; sandwich

member. See church[1]; triangle[3].

memorize. To rememberize.

memory. Nothing will destroy a man's memory so quickly as a loan of money.

See comedian[4]; conscience: clear conscience; spanking[3]; zeal.

> **good memory.** 1. Some people have a very good memory for forgetting. 2. Some people have good memories, but they're too short.
>
> See liar[1].

men. See man.

menace. Riches are no menace if we do not divorce dollars from sense.

See outlaw.

mental. See fog; girl[6]; statement; temper: temperamental person.

mention. Girls used to wear unmentionables; now they wear hardly anything worth mentioning.

See gossip[4]; unmentionables.

merger. In ordinary life it's darkest just before the dawn; in business life it's darkest just before the merger.

merry. See diet[1]; harlot.

mice. See oil[1].

microbe. In the last century men lost their fear of God and acquired a fear of microbes.

See pessimist[9].

microphone. See radio: radio announcer.

middle. See adult[2]; prisoner.

middleman. A gardener raises a few things, a farmer raises many things, and the middleman raises everything.

See price[1].

midnight. See oil[2].

might. See fighter; truck: truckdriver.

mile. See measure; minute; square; Texas.

milk. 1. Cows give all the milk they can, and farmers can all the milk they give. 2. All is not milk that comes from the cow.

See cow; cream; farmer: good farmer; sour[2].

evaporated milk.   Milk from a dry cow.

spilt milk.   1. Never cry over spilt milk; there's enough water in it already.   2. People who never cry over spilt milk probably never drink it.

millennium.   The millennium will be here when the lion will lie down with the lamb, and the hair will lie down without vaseline.

milliner.   One who works on the principle that a hat designed to look like a hat, would never sell.

million.   1. The girl who looks like a million dollars is often just as hard to make.   2. In national affairs, a million is only a drop in the budget.

See word: few words[2].

millionaire.   A person who leaves much to be desired when he dies.

See gold: gold digger[8]; troublesome.

scared millionaire.   The best kind of client.

mimic.   Children are natural mimics; they act like their parents in spite of every effort to teach them good manners.

mind.   1. No matter.   2. The man who doesn't know his own mind hasn't missed much.   3. The woman who is constantly giving others a piece of her mind usually has none to spare. 4. A man who cannot make up his mind probably has no mind to make up.   5. Many men have many minds, but one woman has more than all of them.

See brat; bridge: bad bridge partner, good bridge game; business[3]; change[2]; dietetics; dirty; hair: golden hair; half; insomnia[1]; lap; light[1]; make-up[1]; marry: married couple; matter: plow; prude[4]; resistance: sales resistance; verse: free verse[1]; weight[2]; wisdom[3].

best minds.   They are not those who mind best.

broad-minded.   If both sides make you laugh, you are broad-minded.

See joke: broad jokes.

broad-mindedness.   The result of flattening out high-mindedness.

half a mind.   Bachelors who have half a mind to get married don't realize that that's all it requires.

narrow-minded man.   One who can look through a keyhole with both eyes.

See narrow.

one-track mind. Lots of people who have one-track minds don't even have that in the right direction.

open mind. 1. One that is too porous to hold a conviction. 2. One where ideas come out as fast as they go in. 3. Some so-called open minds should be closed for repairs. 4. The person with an open mind is probably rearranging his prejudices. 5. Many a man thinks he has an open mind when it's merely vacant.

See wise: wise man[1].

peace of mind. A husband gets no peace of mind when his wife gives him a piece of hers.

presence of mind. See accident[1].

serious-minded people. Those who laugh at the comics.

woman's mind. It's cleaner than a man's mind because she changes it more often.

mingle. People who detest mingling with their inferiors probably haven't any.

minister. One who takes a text and preaches from it, usually very far from it.

See sinister.

stuttering minister. The one man who never marries in haste.

mink. It's the mink in the closet that's often responsible for the wolf at the door.

See rabbit[1].

minor. All women are minors before twenty-one, and many of them remain gold diggers thereafter.

See minority: political minority; parents[1].

minority. It often proves to be the majority because it turns out and votes.

See committee: committee-of-five; heresy; majority[3]; political: political machine[2]; republic.

intelligent minority. It never stays that way after it becomes a majority.

political minority. It never consists of minors.

mint. 1. The only business that makes money without advertising. 2. The mint makes it first, and it's up to us to make it last.

minute. You can still do fifty miles an hour even if you drive only ten minutes.

See committee[1]; listen[3]; potato: French fried potatoes; public speaking[1]; railroad: railroad crossing[2]; sucker[2].

miracle. An event described by those to whom it was told by men who did not see it.

See ass; critic[1].

mirage. The frequency of divorce proves that marriage is usually a mirage.

mirror. 1. Where your best friend is. 2. It reflects without speaking, while women speak without reflecting. 3. Women were made before mirrors and have been before them ever since. 4. Your mirror doesn't lie to you, so why should I?

See lass; reflect; road[3]; straight[1].

woman's mirror. The glass that cheers.

misdeed. Man is judged by his deeds, woman by her misdeeds.

miser. 1. A dough nut. 2. The first to put his hand in his pocket and the last to take it out. 3. Misers may be close but you can't touch them. 4. The only time a miser puts his hand in his pocket is during cold weather.

See wizard.

miserable. See hypochondriac[2]; pessimist[8].

miserable woman. A woman with no troubles to speak of.

misery. Misery loves company, but company doesn't reciprocate.
See rheumatism[2].

misfortune. 1. Bad luck that never comes singly; sometimes it comes married. 2. Take it like a man: blame it on your wife. 3. All of us have sufficient courage to bear the misfortune of others.

See optimist[7]; philosophy[4]; singly; together.

miss. 1. The closer the miss, the bigger the thrill. 2. A miss is as good as her smile. 3. Early to bed and early to rise, and you'll miss a good deal that doesn't go on in the daytime.

See company[5]; Cupid[1]; marriage[5]; matrimony[7]; mind[2]; taxi: taxi driver[4]; train.

junior miss. A young girl who, when she tells her mother she will wear short dresses no longer, means she will wear them longer.

missing link. What scientists can never find because, if found, it would no longer be the missing link.

missionary. 1. It's holy smoke when a cannibal cooks one. 2. A land that's unfit for white men is usually full of missionaries.

See cannibal[4]; taste[3].

misstep. A girl's first misstep often starts with a little trip.

mistake. 1. What a lawyer gets paid for, and a doctor buries. 2. If a husband hasn't the right to make mistakes, why did his wife permit him to marry in the first place?

See age[3]; alimony[4]; bachelor[6]; bigamist[2]; blanket: baby blanket; create; err; experience[1]; judge[1]; man[3]; positive; preacher[3]; victim.

misunderstanding. See dictator; husband: misunderstood husband; train: train announcer.

mutual misunderstanding. The proper basis for marriage.

mob. 1. A crowd in which the scum is equal to all of its parts. 2. A crowd with too many heads and too little brains. 3. Those who follow the crowd are quickly lost in it.

mode. See designer: style designer.

model. A model woman is a bare possibility but a woman model is a naked fact.

See copy; immigrant.

artist's model. 1. A girl who doesn't always feel in the nude for work. 2. A girl who is not as bad as she's painted.

moderate. Be moderate in all things, including moderation.

modern. See fiction[1].

modern girl. 1. One who is afraid of nothing except a stack of dirty dishes. 2. She's been tried and found wanting— everything under the sun. 3. A girl who has visible means of support. 4. One who rouges in haste and repaints at leisure. 5. One who is willing to get married if her father disapproves. 6. The girl who wants to go with every Tom, Dick, and marry.

See affected; clothes[5]; embarrassment; lipstick[3]; see[2]; upset; wear[1]; year[2].

modern man. He will stand for anything, except a woman in a bus.

modest. Nowadays even the price of a dress isn't modest.

See prude[4].

modesty. 1. The delicate form of hypocrisy. 2. Modesty is the best policy. 3. It has ruined more kidneys than bad liquor.

moist. See oyster[3].

molasses. A sweet syrup, often compared to trousers, because both are thinner in hot weather and thicker in cold weather.

mold. All people's faces come from the same mold, but some are moldier.

mole. An animal that makes molehills out of mountains.

molehill. Some women expect brassieres to make mountains out of molehills.

See mole.

monarch. A person who should be laying something aside for a reignless day.

money. 1. The fruit of all evil as well as the root of it. 2. The root of most family trees. 3. The only thing that talks without giving itself away. 4. The main prop in propaganda. 5. When money talks, everybody listens. 6. Money works two ways: it talks, and it stops talk. 7. Many a girl marries for money in order to make her dream come through. 8. Don't marry for money; you can borrow it cheaper. 9. Some people make money, others earn it. 10. You have to be dead to get your face on money, but very much alive to get your hands on it. 11. Like men, the tighter money gets, the louder it talks. 12. Money isn't everything in this world, but only the man with money thinks so. 13. Any fool can make money, but it takes a wise man to keep it.

NOTE: This word has not been cross-referenced because it occurs very often throughout this dictionary.

hush money. 1. Money talks, especially hush money. 2. No money talks louder than hush money when it finally gets its voice back.

See saxophone: saxophone player.

pin money. It doesn't amount to much unless the pin is a diamond brooch.

stage money. All the world's a stage, which is why our bankroll has about the same buying power as stage money.

tainted money. Money which 'taint yours and 'taint mine.

monkey. 1. The old folks. 2. The Bible proves that men made monkeys of themselves, but science proves that monkeys made men of themselves. 3. Many a wife makes a monkey out of her husband; it's just like her.

See descent[2]; evolution[1, 3].

monogamy. 1. What most men believe in because enough is enough. 2. Bigamy is having one wife too many; monogamy is often the same thing.

monologue. 1. A conversation between a man and his wife. 2. Very often a moanalogue. 3. A conversation between a realtor and a prospect. 4. A conversation between the man who went abroad and the man who remained behind.

See catalogue ; interrupt.

monopolize. The man who monopolizes the conversation usually monotonizes it.

See layman ; speaker : after-dinner speaker.

monotony. Marriage with two wives is bigamy ; with one wife, monotony.

month. See day[2] ; installment : installment buying[4] ; June ; mail ; man : tall man ; resort : summer resort[1] ; tax : income tax[2].

moon. It affects the tide and the untied.

moonshine. 1. If you drink enough moonshine, you won't see the sun shine. 2. Where moonshine comes from is a secret still.

See nose : red nose.

moonshiner. One who makes rye while the moon shines.

moral. People think they are moral when they are merely uncomfortable.

See sermon[1].

morals. 1. The movies have ruined many more evenings than they have morals. 2. The car has had great influence on public morals ; it has completely stopped horse stealing.

See censor[3].

moralize. A man who moralizes is usually a hypocrite, and a woman who moralizes is always homely.

more. See earn[2] ; friendship[5] ; nature : human nature[2] ; philosopher[2] ; progress[3] ; publicity[2] ; rationing[3] ; rum ; think[3].

more or less. A girl no longer marries a man for better or for worse ; she marries him for more or less.

morning. It's better to have your wedding in the morning because, if it isn't a success, you have the rest of the day to get a divorce.

See daylight : daylight saving time ; girl[2] ; good night ; lark[2] ; toper ; wake : wake up[2].

mortal. What fools these fools think other mortals be.

mortgage. 1. One-quarter of the United States is covered by forests and the rest by mortgages. 2. Some men are known by their deeds, others by their mortgages.

See cover : covered wagon ; farm[1] ; home[11] ; marriage[7] ; railroad[2].

mortician. One whose life is a grave undertaking.

mosquito. 1. A small insect designed by God to make us think

better of the fly. 2. The only one who never complains of
women's short skirts. 3. He rarely gets a slap on the back until
he goes to work. 4. He always bites the hand that feeds him.
5. The animal that approaches nearest to man. 6. Unlike the
doctor, he presents his bill before he works on you. 7. The
insect that always leaves a person up to scratch. 8. Have patience, mosquitoes, the night is long. 9. Science doesn't explain
how a mosquito can get along without any sleep.

See camp: camp life[2]; camper; hastily; Noah; nudist[6]; picnic;
resort: ideal summer resort.

smart mosquito. One that can pass a screen test.

moth. 1. An economical insect because he eats nothing but holes.
2. People who live in fur houses shouldn't throw moths. 3. Give
feminine fashions time enough and they will starve all the moths
to death.

mother. 1. The necessity of convention. 2. A boy's best friend,
and if he comes home late enough he may find her there. 3. The
man who boasts that all he is he owes to his mother, can probably settle the account for a few cents.

See advice: fatherly advice; economics: home economics; extravagant: extravagant girl; fact: facts of life; girl[3]; go: go
back; marriage[30]; necessity[2]; responsible; trust[2]; wedding: wedding dress.

modern mother. One who can hold safety pins and a cigarette
in her mouth at the same time.

Mother's Day. See day: Mother's Day.

unwed mother. One who has obeyed the boyological urge.

mother-in-law. 1. Another mouth to heed. 2. One who should
be careful not to go too far, unless she stays there. 3. It's not
how often your mother-in-law visits you that counts, it's how
long she stays. 4. Love is blind, but your mother-in-law isn't.
5. A man's mother-in-law is a relative, and always on his wife's
side. 6. Of all men, Adam was the happiest; he had no mother-
in-law. 7. An outspoken mother-in-law is never outspoken.

See advice[7]; bigamy[2]; marriage[15].

motion. See promotion.

perpetual motion. The one thing that proves its existence is
the family upstairs.

See emotion; love[4].

motion pictures. See movies.

motor. When a driver stops, looks, and listens, there's something wrong with his motor.

    electric motor. People said the electric motor would never work; today the electric motor works and the people don't.

motorist. One who pays in the long run.

    See collision; driver; headless; pedestrian[15]; road: road hog[1]; tourist[1].

mountain. See mole; molehill.

mouth. 1. At the end of the evening some women are so tired they can hardly keep their mouths open. 2. If a woman could talk out of both corners of her mouth, there would be a great deal said on both sides. 3. It is better for a man to keep his mouth shut and be thought a fool than to open it and remove all doubt.

    See boaster; cold[3]; dentist[4, 5, 6]; down[1]; films; horse[2]; lipstick[2]; liquor[4]; mother-in-law[1]; nose[2]; open; shut; tapeworm; wise: wise man[1]; yawn[3].

    gum chewer's mouth. It goes without saying that a gum chewer's mouth goes without saying.

move. See performance; Reno.

movement. The back-to-the-farm movement would be all right if it didn't break the back.

    See nudism[3].

movies. 1. Reel life. 2. Where love passeth all understanding. 3. Seeing is believing, except in the movies. 4. Some people love to go to the movies, and some people go to the movies to love. 5. The trouble with the movies is that they publicize actors and shoot movies instead of vice versa.

    See applaud; book[1]; brutal; censorship; church[4]; difficulty[2]; dummy; encore[2]; end[2]; moral: morals[1]; newsreel; production: super-production.

    movie star. A girl who never knows where her next husband is coming from.

        See angel[1]; harness[1]; publicity[2].

    retired movie star. One who isn't her old sylph any more.

    movie titles. Some people who attend the movies are so stupid, they can't read the titles; and others are so stupid, they do.

Mrs. A title which brings with it heavy duties and light earnings.

    See Cupid[2]; M.A.

much. See satisfy.

mud. Mud is thicker than water.

See dust[1] ; ground ; football[4] ; ground.

mugwump. An animal that sits on the fence, with its mug on one side and its wump on the other.

mule. 1. An animule. 2. An animal without pride of ancestry or hope of posterity. 3. A stubborn animal that is backward about going forward. 4. An animal that can't pull while kicking, and can't kick while pulling. 5. An animal that lives only about forty years, but every year has a kick in it. 6. It's a poor mule that won't work both ways.

See human ; zebra[2].

mumble. You have only to mumble a few words in church to get married, and a few in your sleep to get divorced.

murder. In murder crimes, there is usually no clue as to the whereabouts of the police.

See Christmas[3] ; commit ; obituary ; story : detective stories[2] ; tabloid[7] ; theory : beautiful theory.

murderer. One who is presumed to be innocent until he is proved insane.

pleasant murderer. One who takes life cheerfully.

muscle. The two most important muscles which operate without the direction of the brain are the heart and the tongue.

See athlete.

music. See contralto[2] ; dance[2] ; dreamer : practical dreamer ; restaurant[5] ; snore : snoring[2] ; soup[2] ; ukulele ; violinist.

bad music. If one hears bad music, it is one's duty to drown it in conversation.

modern music. It's played so fast and hot, you can't tell what song is being played, much less what song it was stolen from.

musical instrument. Thank heaven it selected its musical instruments before the uke and the sax were invented.

See beat ; harp ; oboe ; saxophone.

sour music. A malady.

musician. 1. A person who earns his living just by playing around. 2. Many a musician who plays Beethoven, should play bridge.

See deft ; swing, swing band.

true musician. One who, when he hears a lady singing in her bath, puts his ear to the keyhole.

mustache.   1. A soup strainer.   2. A misplaced eyebrow.   3. The only thing that keeps many a man from being a bare-faced liar. 4. Most people can't see what's right under their noses; if they could, a lot of mustaches would be shaved off.

> **young man's mustache.**   A little down and then a little more each week.

mutter.   A girl's best friend is her mutter.

mutual.   Gentlemen prefer blondes, but it isn't always mutual.

mystery.   When a man has solved the mystery of a woman, there is nothing left—except another woman.

myth.   See evil; headless.

N

nag.   A woman with no horse sense.

nail.   Some men hit the nail on the hand every time.
>   See file: fingernails; manicurist[3]; thumb: sore thumb.

naked.   Not all nudists go naked: some dress their wounds, and others have coats on their tongues.
>   See college: college graduate[2]; model; silk.

name.   When a girl begins calling you by your first name, it's really your last name she's after.
>   See Broadway[4]; effect; forgery; hcnpeck: henpecked husband; hotel: hotel register; spoon[2]; tour: all-expense tour.

> **maiden name.**   As long as a woman has her maiden name, her maiden aim is to change it.

> **pen name.**   A penitentiary name.

napkin.   See fast: fast woman.

narrow.   The narrower the mind, the broader the statement.

nasty.   See censor[1].

nation.   1. The conflicts within a nation are always between stagnation and imagination.   2. When nations are not trying to make up with each other, they are trying to make off with each other. See bust; gunpowder; left[1]; pact; square; statesman[5].

> **Christian nations.**   Where reducing nostrums are sold while the rest of the world is starving.

See Christianity[1].

civilized nation. 1. One that is horrified by other civilized nations. 2. One that can't tolerate injustice or oppression except at home.

native. See Spanish; weather[2].

nature. See alcohol: denatured alcohol; California: California climate; create; disposition; fault; medicine; perfume[2]; shut; spectacles[2].

human nature. 1. It can't be altered by being haltered. 2. Human nature will never work as hard for money as for more money.

possessive nature. What a girl has when she knows how to keep her youth—away from other girls.

navy. The race is not always to the swift, but the navy is always willing to put its money on the fleet.

Nazi. A hot Aryan.

Nazi youth. One who follows in his father's goose steps.

Nazism. A system of government which uses German marks to convince easy marks that Karl Marx is their supreme enemy. See Nazi; fascism.

near. See flyer: stunt flyer; relatives[3]; trust[3].

neatness. The one good thing about being bald.

necessary. Nowadays our necessities are too luxurious and our luxuries too necessary.
See success: husband's success.

necessity. 1. The mother of intervention. 2. The mother of invention, but nobody has found out who the father is. 3. Necessity knows no law, and neither does the average lawyer.
See economy[2]; invention; luxury; necessary.

neck. 1. The favorite piece of chicken among men. 2. The quickest way for a girl to become popular is to get necks to herself. 3. Love is a funny thing: a man bites a girl's neck because she has beautiful legs.
See boil; bride: bridesmaid; charm; coeducation; dalliance; dense; face: face-lifting[3]; girl: best girl; guillotine[2]; love: puppy love[2]; politics[14]; remember.

necking. 1. A form of embrace in which the neck is unimportant. 2. It may not be fatal but it has put an end to many a bachelor. 3. The best thing to do with a fellow who thinks of nothing but necking is—to neck.

necktie. See tie.

need. See buy[2]; country[1]; fraud; friend[6].

needle. See jail[3].

negative. See darkroom.

neighbor. 1. A person who borrows things. 2. One who knows more about your affairs than you do. 3. A person who wonders when that damned party will end. 4. Opportunity knocks but once, and the neighbors the rest of the time. 5. Love your neighbor, but not your neighbor's wife.

See blind[1]; claptrap; enemy[6]; freedom[2]; grindstone; history: personal history; home[8]; keep: keep up; lawyer: good lawyer[1]; marriage[29]; percent; realize; Rip Van Winkle; wealth[2]; weeds[2].

    quarreling neighbors. They never agree because they argue from different premises.

nerve. A man who talks in his sleep may ruin his wife's nerves —if he doesn't talk distinctly.

See henpeck: henpecked husband; price[4].

nervous. The reason some people work so hard is that they're too nervous to steal.

See jittery.

    nervous breakdown. See option.

neurotic. A woman who calls a doctor when all she wants is an audience.

See literature.

never. 1. The 30th of February. 2. When cows give beer.

new. See gnu[2]; good[1]; quarrel[4].

newlywed. One who tells his wife everything.

See rice.

news. 1. The same old thing, only happening to different people. 2. When a man bites a dog, or robs a hotel, that's news. 3. When a man bites a dog or a bull throws a congressman, that's news.

See editor: newspaper editor; gossip[3]; newsprint; noose; publicity[3]; scarce; spread; useless.

newspaper. A portable screen behind which a man hides from the woman who is standing up in a bus.

See doings; inventor; President[1]; puff; swat; tabloid[2]; town: small town[2].

    newspaper's duty. To comfort the afflicted and afflict the comfortable.

newspaper's function. To make the ignorant more ignorant and the crazy crazier.

newspaperman. An ambassador is sent abroad to lie for his country; a newspaperman stays at home and lies for himself.

newsprint. A kind of paper which is neither news nor print.

newsreel. A moving picture that shows real news.

New Year. See resolution: New Year's resolution.

next. Some drivers are in such a hurry to get into the next state that they often get into the next world.

See brassiere[3]; cleanliness; religion[1, 2]; wedding: wedding dress.

niche. An itch for office seldom leads to a niche in the hall of fame.

nickel. 1. The only thing it's good for nowadays is to get the wrong number on the telephone. 2. It may not be as good as a dollar, but it goes to church more often. 3. The best buy for a nickel is a telephone call to the right man.

See cigar: five-cent cigar[1]; number: wrong number; trust[2].

night. Proper dress for night clubs does not include nightgowns or nightshirts.

See cat[1]; chair; daylight: daylight saving time; dissipation; lark[1]; mosquito[8]; prayer[1]; sheep.

nightcap. 1. It used to be something you put on top; now it's something you put down. 2. At night clubs people don't wear their nightcaps; they drink them.

night club. See club: night club.

night owl. One that doesn't give a hoot.

nightmare. What the girl of a man's dreams often turns out to be.

no. Men prefer girls who don't "no" too much.

See diplomacy: business diplomacy; diplomat[5]; lady[5]; petition; quick; sense: horse sense[2]; wise: wise man[2]; yes: yes man[2].

Noah. How much happier we should be during summer evenings if Noah had stepped on the male mosquito before he left the ark.

nobody. See everybody.

noise. 1. Noise annoys an oyster and makes a clam clamor. 2. The best way to get rid of the noise in the back of the car, is to make her sit up front.

See beat; boy[2, 3, 4]; horn; sound; squeak; still; ukulele; voice[1].

noose. No noose is good news.

See hangman.

North Pole. It proves that there's no one sitting on top of the world.

nose. 1. The leading article. 2. What a woman will talk through if you shut her mouth. 3. An organ that should be seen and not heard. 4. Some say through the nose, others pay through the nose. 5. If a man has his nose broken in two places, he ought to keep out of those places. 6. You've got a very good nose, as noses run.

See censor[7]; cold[5]; colorful; curious[2]; dreamer: practical dreamer; exercise[2]; flu; globetrotter; grindstone; lie[9]; mustache[4]; pick[1]; plain[1]; smell[3]; uplift; wedding[3].

red nose. A condition caused by sunshine or moonshine.

unpowdered nose. A shining example of old-fashioned simplicity.

note. See lecture; winter[5].

nothing. 1. Something many people are good for. 2. Women seem to dress on the theory that nothing succeeds like nothing. See courtship[2]; criticism[1]; expect; fame[2]; gamble: gambling[2]; kiss[1]; marriage: before & after[7]; persuade; philosopher[2]; story; tell[1]; theater[1]; wear[2].

do nothing. 1. The man who does nothing usually does somebody. 2. The easiest way of doing nothing is to do it. 3. Some people do nothing in particular but they do it very well. 4. Nothing is so difficult as doing nothing.

See busy[1]; committee[2]; do; housework[2]; husband[4]; idleness[1]; receivership; weather[1].

good for nothing. Some people are so good, they are good for nothing.

say nothing. See say; subject[2]; when; wise: wise man[8].

notorious. Some men wake up and find themselves famous; others stay up all night and become notorious.

noun. See can: garbage can; skirt[1].

novel. Many a writer takes a year off to do a novel when he could buy one for a couple of dollars.

See asterisks[1, 2]; bustle; novelist.

great American novel. It has not only been written already, but it has been rejected.

novelist. People in every walk of life think they can write novels, including novelists.

nowadays. A generation ago the girls never thought of doing the things they do nowadays; that's why they didn't do them.

nude. See model: artist's model[1]; woman[4].

nudism. 1. The Nude Deal. 2. It's only a skin game. 3. A back-to-the-form movement. 4. The only cult which gives you the bare facts.

nudist. 1. A person you can't pin anything on. 2. A person who goes coatless and vestless and wears trousers to match. 3. One who should make an excellent golf player because he goes around the whole course in nothing. 4. A person who is wrapped up only in himself. 5. A person who loves to run around in his silhouette. 6. Nudists must be right: they have millions of followers—mosquitoes. 7. Don't blame a person for being a nudist; he was born that way.

See bareback; cushion; goods; grin; naked; tie: home ties.

nudist camp. 1. Where every morning brings the dawn of a nude day. 2. The one place where you don't look a person in the face.

nudist colony. A dnude ranch.

nuisance. The government issues bulletins on the eradication of all kinds of nuisances except foolish laws.

See progress[1].

number. Everybody agrees that there are too many crimes, but nobody knows what the ideal number should be.

See safety; telephone: telephone operator[5]; thirteen[1]; two.

wrong number. Getting the wrong number on the telephone has its advantages: think of all the people you can get for a nickel.

See nickel[1]; telephone[5], telephone booth[4]; youth[1].

nurse. 1. Many a hospital patient takes a turn for the nurse. 2. Sick men go from bad to worse, or from bed to nurse.

nursery. 1. The infantry. 2. The bawlroom.

nut. It takes hundreds of nuts to hold a car together, but it takes only one of them to scatter it all over the highway.

See oyster[1]; peanut; tree[2]; wheel.

O

oats. See alimony[9]; horse[1].

obesity. A surplus gone to waist.

obey. See citizen: law-abiding citizen; wife: obedient wife.

obituary. Some people commit murder; others get their satisfaction from reading obituary notices.
See pudding.

object. No one objects to how much you say if you say it in a few words.

obligation. When some men discharge an obligation, you can hear the report for miles around.
See report.

obligatory. Under fascism, everything that isn't forbidden is obligatory.

oboe. A cockney tramp.

obscene. Children should be seen and not obscene.
See art: work of art; epicene.

obstetrician. The only thing he has in common with the stork is the size of his bill.

obstinacy. Perseverance is the result of a strong will; obstinacy is the result of a strong won't.

obstinate man. A person who does not hold opinions; they hold him.

occasion. A woman may not always be equal to the occasion, but she is always equal to the occasional.
See sit: sit down.

Occident. Where occidents happen.

occupation. See collector[1]; pulse.

occurrence. Something which happens to happen.

ocean. 1. A large body of water entirely surrounded by trouble.
2. The only power on earth that can make a woman indifferent to her personal appearance.
See promoter.

ocean liner. A ship whose passengers usually play hide and sick.

octopus. See rumor[3].

oculist. A man with an eye for business.

odd. How strange!

Odd Fellow. The odds are that he is not odd.

odds. Dollars to doughnuts are no longer the big odds they used to be.

See odd: Odd Fellow.

odor. See cheese: Limburger cheese[1]; unmelodious.

off. The apparel off proclaims the woman.

See birthday[1]; day: day off; dress: silk dress; water: water wagon.

offense. See fence[3].

offer. When a man loses his wife, everybody offers him another; but when he loses his dog, nobody offers to replace it.

See throat.

office. 1. The place where you can relax from your strenuous home life. 2. A place that needs either one homely stenographer or a dictionary.

See brain; businessman[2]; commuter[2]; niche; politician[8, 13], conservative politician; squeak.

officer. See soldier[2]; vice-president[2].

offspring. See redistribute; respectability.

often. 1. A child whose parents are dead. 2. Many a wife is a woman of few words, but often.

See marry[5]; once.

oil. 1. A greasy liquid which is good for squeaks, except when they are in mice. 2. Burning the midnight oil doesn't help much if it's in the car.

See burn; public speaker[3].

old. 1. No person ever lives to be as old as his jokes. 2. One great advantage of being old is that one is beyond being told that he is getting old. 3. If the young knew; if the old could. 4. It's not how old you are but how you are old. 5. The worst thing about growing old is to have to listen to a lot of advice from one's children. 6. A man is as old as he feels; and a woman is as old as she feels—like admitting.

See breakfast; die; everything; fifty; forty; furniture; good[1]; look; quarrel[4]; waitress[1]; yearn[1]; young.

old age. See age: old age.

old maid. See maid: old maid.

old man. A person who likes babies, especially those born about twenty years ago.

See advice: good advice; faithless.

old-timer. The person who remembers when a bureau was a piece of furniture.

old woman. There are three kinds: the dear old soul, the old woman, and the old witch.

old-fashioned. See nose: unpowdered nose; ring: wedding ring[2].

old-fashioned girl. 1. One who used to stay at home when she had nothing to wear. 2. One who has never been kissed, and admits it. 3. One who doesn't drink old-fashioneds. 4. What's become of the old-fashioned girl, thank God!

See upset.

oleomargarine. A food bought by people who have seen butter days.

olive. Kissing a girl is just like opening a bottle of olives: the first may come hard, but it's easy to get the rest.

on. See lawyer[5].

once. Some people will try anything once; others, once too often.

See kiss[19]; opportunity[6].

one. If husband and wife are one, the husband when seated with his wife must be beside himself.

See cheap[1]; drum[2]; expensive[1]; golf[5]; hangover[1]; kiss[3, 8, 18]; manufacturer: hat manufacturer; marriage[13].

oneself. The easiest person to deceive.

onion. 1. In onion there is strength. 2. An onion a day gives your diet away. 3. An apple a day keeps the doctor away, but an onion a day keeps everyone away. 4. A girl doesn't mind a fellow knowing his onions so long as he doesn't eat them. 5. Some people think the secret of health lies in eating onions, but the difficulty is in keeping it a secret.

See vegetable.

open. Open air, open hands, and open minds are all desirable, but there's too much open mouth.

See burglar; detour[2, 4]; eyes[1]; mouth[1, 3]; parachute; Pullman: Pullman window.

opening. See burglar; parking: parking space.

operation. Before undergoing an operation, arrange your business affairs; you may live.

See ether.

surgical operation. No man ever got so much conversation out of a surgical operation as Adam did.

opinion. 1. A belief that should be sound, but not all sound. 2. The only good thing about some people is their opinion of themselves. 3. Most people never have their own opinions; they just wear whatever happens to be in style. 4. Fools and the dead are the only ones who never change their opinions.

See change[1]; conscience[3]; fanatic[3]; fascist; idea[3]; obstinacy: obstinate man; prejudice[2]; public opinion[3]; radical[1]; soldier[2].

candid opinion. It's never a candied opinion.

opportunist. 1. A person who meets the wolf at the door, and appears the next day in a fur coat. 2. A person who, finding himself in hot water, decides he needs a bath anyway.

opportunity. 1. A favorable occasion for grasping a disappointment. 2. It always looks bigger going than coming. 3. Opportunities lie on every hand, and so do a lot of people. 4. If opportunity is seized when it comes, it will not have to be chased when it goes. 5. The person who doesn't grasp opportunity when it knocks, usually ends up by knocking opportunity. 6. The difference between opportunity and the kicker is that opportunity knocks but once.

See America[3]; chastity[1]; door; knocker; lack; neighbor[4]; optimist[10]; pessimist[16]; ring[1].

optimist. 1. A proponent of the doctrine that black is white. 2. A person who doesn't care what happens so long as it happens to somebody else. 3. A man who sees only the down payment. 4. One who makes the best of it when he gets the worst of it. 5. One who thinks humorists will eventually run out of definitions of an optimist. 6. The fellow who doesn't know what's coming to him. 7. One who always sees the bright side of the other fellow's misfortune. 8. A woman who marries a pessimist. 9. A pessimist thinks all women are bad; an optimist hopes so. 10. The pessimist thinks he is taking a chance, but the optimist thinks he is grasping an opportunity.

See pessimist.

option. A nervous breakdown on paper.

optional. Crime doesn't pay, but the hours are optional.

orange. See grapefruit[1].

oration. Usually a flood of words and a drought of ideas.

orator. 1. One who misses many fine opportunities for keeping quiet. 2. The orator who deals largely in quotations speaks volumes.

ordeal. Marriage often changes an ideal into an ordeal.

order. Women like to have husbands to order and homes in order. See physic; salesman[2, 3]; taxpayer.

out of order. See vocabulary.

organ. See heart[1]; stomach[1].

abdominal organs. The department of the interior. See abdomen.

hand organ. It takes a musical crank to play it.

organ recital. A patient's complaint to his doctor.

Oriental. A person who never salaams the door. See face[1]; marriage: before & after[8].

origin. See man[11].

originality. Undetected imitation. See eccentricity.

originate. Marriage originates when a man meets the only woman who really understands him; so does divorce. See humorist.

orphan. See insurance: life insurance[1].

orphanage. When some men die they leave all they have to the orphanage—their children.

osteopath. 1. One who makes no bones about his profession. 2. A doctor who works his fingers to your bones. 3. A person who has a bone to pick with other types of doctors.

osteopathy. 1. A lazy man's gymnastics. 2. Osteopathy appeals to people who feel in their bones that it's the best treatment of disease.

otherwise. Some men are wise, some otherwise. See bird[2].

ounce. See perfume[3].

out. See cigar[1]; pedestrian[6]; stock: stock market[3].

outcome. The outcome of the income depends on the outgo for the upkeep.

outing. Every man has his innings as well as his outings.

outlaw. A menace to society, but not so bad as an in-law. See in-law[8].

outlive. The best way to avoid having enemies is to outlive them.

outspoken. Women are generally not outspoken—at least, not by their husbands.
See mother-in-law[7].

outstrip. In burlesque the girls all try to outstrip one another. See equality[2].

outwit. Who was that lady I saw you outwit last night?

oven. See loaf[1].

overlook. When a woman looks her age, she tries to overlook it. See resort: summer resort[2].

overtime. The disadvantage of practising what you preach is that you have to put in so much overtime.

overweight. Physicians say one million women are overweight; these of course are round figures.

owe. 1. A man is out of debt when he owes no one but the doctor and dad. 2. Maybe the man who boasts that he doesn't owe a dollar in the world, couldn't if he tried.
See America[4]; bank[5]; break: break even; mother[3].

own. See land.

oyster. 1. A fish that's built like a nut. 2. An animal that's not so dumb; it gets four months' vacation every year. 3. There's nothing moister than an oyster.
See noise[1]; pearl.

P

Pacific Ocean. See island[2].

pacifist. 1. One who cannot argue in favor of peace without using his fists. 2. The only person who can attend a peace conference without getting into a fight.

package. See girl: up-to-date girl.

small package. A man wrapped up in himself.

pact. The deal the little nations get from the big ones is from the bottom of the pact.

international pacts. Agreements made to avert international impacts.

paddle. Like canoes, children behave better if paddled from the rear.

padlock. As the world becomes more and more civilized, we keep on improving padlocks.

page. It's a long page that has no turning.
See farce; hurricane.

pain. It has been discovered that, in giving till it hurts, some people are extremely sensitive to pain.
See child[2]; extraction; guillotine[2]; Thanksgiving[2].
pains. See genius[4, 5].

painless. Another difference between death and taxes is that death is frequently painless.

painstaking. When dentists are not, their patients are.

paint. 1. Women paint what they used to be. 2. Women live longer than men because paint is a great preservative. 3. It's sometimes difficult for a man to know if he's stepping out with a new girl or just with the old one painted over.
See model: artist's model[2]; reformer[8]; ship[2]; smoke[2]; white[1].
fresh paint. The only sign no one will believe without personal investigation.

painting. Unlike steaks, well done paintings are rare.

pair. See pants[6].

pajamas. A man ought to divorce his wife when he finds her company wearing—his pajamas.
See dormitory.

pallbearer. One who gets his exercise at the funerals of his friends who exercise.

pan. If you want to keep dishes clean, eat out of pans.
See dish: chafing dish; father[1]; gold[1].

panhandler. A beggar that loafs or a loafer that begs.

pantomime. Where people talk but say nothing—as usual.

pantry. See coterie.

pants. 1. The country cousin of trousers. 2. Whenever you wear your pants out, be sure to wear them back home again. 3. If you want to make pants last, make the coat first. 4. The man who never hides behind a woman's skirts is the one whose wife wears the pants in the family. 5. Pants may be singular or plural: when men wear pants, it's plural; when they don't, it's singular. 6. When a woman pants for a man and a man pants for a woman, that makes a pair of pants.

See buttocks; censor[5]; dog[2]; resturant[2]; slacks[1]; suit; suspenders.

paper. See newsprint; option.

paper hanger. A person whose business is a put-up job.

paperweight. The best way to keep down bills is to use one.

par. See fortune hunter; golf[1], golf course[2].

parachute. Nobody has ever complained of a parachute not opening.

See jump[3].

parade. See Elks[2].

parallel. See leg: bowlegs[2].

parenthetically. Father-like and mother-like.

parents. 1. One of the hardships of a minor's life. 2. People who spend half their time wondering how their children will turn out, and the rest of the time when they'll turn in. 3. Parents think children should be seen, not heard; children think parents should be neither seen nor heard.

See blood[1]; child: child labor; children[3]; college: college boy[2]; depression[1]; diet: soft diet; illegitimate; infant: infant prodigy[1]; life[8]; mimic; often[1]; psychologist: child psychologist; son: favorite son; spanking[2]; tell[5]; vanity: extreme vanity.

doting parent. One who is never a don'ting parent.

male parent. See daddy.

rich parents. They usually make poor parents.

well-behaved parent. One who has learned to keep still when the children are talking.

parking. 1. All the world loves a lover, until he complicates the parking problem. 2. What this country needs is a place to park a car. 3. If you think the automobile has come to stay, try to park your car for an hour.

See go-getter[2]; pedestrian[13].

parking lot. A place where you leave your car to have dents made in the fenders.

parking space. 1. The space in which another car is parked. 2. An unfilled opening in an unending line of cars near an unapproachable fire plug.

parole. A cell-out.

part. A fool and his wife are soon parted.

See bald: bald-head; doughnut[1]; hair[2]; honey; marriage: marriage vows; mob[1]; usher.

partial. Women are partial to those men whom they can't love wholly.

partner. See dancer, toe dancer; dollar[4]; floor: dance floor[1]; marriage[10].

   life partners. Men and women can get along nicely as life partners if they can avoid being bridge partners.

party. 1. Hear no evil, see no evil, speak no evil—and you'll never be a success at a party. 2. A fool and his money are some party. 3. Some women tell their secrets to only two parties: the Democrats and the Republicans.

   See apartment[1]; fool[4]; formal; house: glass houses[2]; neighbor[3]; politician[1]; rum.

   dull party. Its advantage is that you can get to bed at a decent hour.

   hen party. A gathering of women where there isn't much to talk about until after some of the guests have gone.

   informal party. A gathering at which you wear your own clothes.

   life of the party. 1. The person who can talk louder than the radio. 2. Some people, as soon as they leave, become the life of the party.

   See story: risqué storyteller.

   third party. This country doesn't need a third party; it was a third party that spoiled things in the Garden of Eden.

   two-party system. A system consisting of the appointed and the disappointed.

pass. Love makes time pass, and time makes love pass.

   See beauty: beauty parlor[2]; car: second-hand car[1]; cold[4]; collection; glasses; lass; law; mosquito: smart mosquito; tracks; Uncle Sam.

   pass the buck. See buck: pass the buck.

passenger. See ferryboat; taxi[1].

passion. The only difference between a flirtation and a life-long passion is that the flirtation lasts a little longer.

past. 1. The past is often forgotten for a present. 2. You can always tell a girl's past by her presents. 3. You can sometimes tell by looking at a girl what kind of a past she is going to have. 4. When a woman talks about her past, she's confessing; when a man does, he's boasting.

See Christmas[4, 5]; future[3]; historian; historical; interesting: interesting people; politics[13]; sinner[2].

pasture. See golf[2].

pat. See back: pat on the back; dachshund[4].

path. See Broadway[4]; claptrap; driver: bad driver[2], woman driver[1].

> **bridle path.** Something that is associated with halters, not altars, and with grooms, not brides.

> **primrose path.** The way of a man with a maid.

patience. A virtue, though it is usually a case of not knowing what to do.

See mosquito[8].

patient. The more patient pedestrians, the fewer pedestrian patients.

See convalescent; cure; dermatology; enema; heal; illness; medicine; nurse[1]; organ: organ recital; painstaking; quit; recover; specialist.

patrimony. Masculine of matrimony.

patriot. 1. A fellow who is always ready to lay down your life for his country. 2. A man who loves his country, and wants to make as much out of it as possible.

See hold: hold up.

> **patriotic people.** They feel they should owe something to their country; that's why they don't like to pay income taxes.

patriotism. The willingness to make any sacrifice so long as it won't hurt business.

patter. See standpatter.

paunch. Food gone to waist.

pave. See hell[1], road to hell; success: road to success.

pawn. It's darkest just before the pawn.

pawnbroker. 1. One who lives on the flat of the land. 2. One that prefers customers who have no redeeming qualities. 3. A mercenary man to whom money is the one redeeming quality. 4. One who takes more interest in his business than most other men. 5. The person who hopes you will see him at your earliest inconvenience. 6. A man who is always ready to make advances to women regardless of their age or appearance.

See radio[8]; stockbroker.

pax. 1. The less pax, the more tax. 2. Pax is not always insured by pacts.

pay. A person who can't pay usually gets another person who can't pay to guarantee that he can pay.

See charge; chiropractor; deposit[1]; dull; educator; electricity[1]; horse: horse race[3]; installment: installment plan[4]; love[24]; motorist; nose[4]; optional; poet[3]; prosperity[1]; raise[1]; syntax; tailor[3, 4]; tax: income tax[3]; tip; train: train pass; vote; war[4].

payday. No matter how far money goes, it still can't go as far as next payday.

pay envelope. The worm turns—he turns over his pay envelope.

pay off. War starts by paying off old scores and ends by paying off new debts.

pay roll. See country: uncivilized country.

payment. The easiest way for a driver to lose control of a car is to forget to make the payments.

See diamonds[5]; harp[2]; home[13]; installment: installment buying[3]; pedestrian[11]; reducing: reducing machine; thanks.

down payment. See installment[1, 3]; luxury[1]; optimist[3].

easy payment plan. The man who first called it the easy payment plan was mighty careless with his adjectives.

easy payments. They are easier said than done.

peace. 1. The brief lull before the storm. 2. What we are all fighting for. 3. In international affairs, a period of cheating between two periods of fighting.

See Christmas[3]; enduring; pacifist; pax; wave: permanent wave[1].

peace conference. See pacifist[2].

peanut. It's not a nut but the fruit of a vegetable.

See will: will power[2].

pearl. A man can sometimes get a pearl out of an oyster but it takes a pretty girl to get a diamond out of an old crab.

pebble. When a girl learns that she's not the only pebble on the beach, she becomes a little bolder.

peck. See fat: fat woman[2]; marriage: before & after[1].

pedestrian. 1. A case of the survival of the flittest. 2. A married man who owns a car. 3. The vanishing American. 4. A person who should be seen and not hurt. 5. A street-walking object, invisible to the motorist. 6. A man who is down but never out—of danger. 7. The man who falls by the wayside. 8. A man whose wife has gone off with his car. 9. A person who has bought a second-hand car.   10. A man with a family of grown-up children and only one car.   11. The man who has failed to keep up his payments on the car.   12. The man who has learned that it doesn't pay to go straight.   13. The man who is looking for the place where he parked his car.   14. The only thing in the way of further automobile progress.   15. One who usually knows what the motorist is driving at.   16. The most approachable chap in the world.   17. One who has rights, but usually they are only the last rites.   18. One half the world's pedestrians doesn't know how the other half lives. 19. The wisest thing for a pedestrian to do is to get a suit of armor, insure his life, and then stay home.   20. It is only a question of time until every pedestrian will have a car or wings. 21. If evolution works, nature will produce a pedestrian who can jump three ways at once.   22. When a pedestrian crosses the street, he hopes to get the brakes.   23. Pity the poor pedestrian: he doesn't know where his next car is coming from.   24. About all a pedestrian can hope for nowadays is to be injured only slightly.

See ambulance; automobile; car[2, 5], streamlined car; collision; co-operation; dodge; grass; insurance: automobile insurance; kangaroo[1]; lazy; leap; life[7]; patient; provision; reach; run: run down[1]; safe; spare: spare parts; street: one-way street[2]; think[7]; way: right of way; whiz; wing[2].

peep. As she shows, so shall we peep.

peer. 1. A man never knows how stupid he is until he is tried by a jury of his peers.   2. Only knaves and fools are ever tried by a court and jury of their peers.

pen. The pen is mightier than the sword, or would be if we could get the criminals inside it.

See warden[2].

fountain pen. Even if it won't write, it will keep the cigars in your pocket from being broken.

See blot; crossword puzzle[1].

penny. Penny wise, gowned foolish.

See squander[2].

pennypincher. A man with one-way pockets.

pension. The pension is mightier than the sword.

people. The only thing wrong with the world.

See city; civilization[3]; democracy[1, 4]; dreams[1]; Eskimos; flowers[1]; freight; genealogy; glad; government[1]; motor: electric motor; public opinion[1]; race: human race; square; swim: swimming pool; tabloid[5]; tax[3].

See also under different entries according to type. For example, see best: best people; conscience: conscience-stricken people; etc.

tiresome people. They tire everybody but themselves.

percent. Don't take too much interest in the affairs of your neighbors; six percent will do.

See golf[7]; statistics[4]; temperamental: temperamental person.

perfect. See brute; Utopia.

perfect man. Even if a woman never expects to find the perfect man, it still is lots of fun hunting.

perfect people. Bachelors' wives and old maids' children.

perfection. Trifles make perfection, but perfection is no trifle.

performance. A moving performance by an actor leads to fame; a moving performance by the audience leads to the nearest exit.

perfume. 1. Any smell which is used to drown a worse one. 2. Perfume proves that art can improve on nature. 3. The more per ounce, the better perfume.

See flattery[1].

bad perfume. Rankincense.

expensive perfume. A matter of dollars and scents.

good perfume. The kind that holds you smell bound.

perhaps. See diplomat[5]; lady[5].

period. A comma that has curled up and gone to sleep.

permanent. What this world needs is less permanent waves and more permanent wives.

See tariff: permanent tariff.

perseverance. The ability to stick to something you are not stuck on.

person. See under different entries according to type. For example, see agree: agreeable person; clever: clever person; etc.

personal. See letter[1]; paint: fresh paint.

personality. 1. The best substitute for personal ability. 2. A quality that's important only to those people who haven't got any.

See charm; darkroom; window: bay window.

perspire. See dog[2]; genius[3].

persuade. Blessed are they who have nothing to say, and who cannot be persuaded to say it.

pessimist. 1. One who sees only the hole in the doughnut. 2. The man who wears a belt as well as suspenders. 3. The fellow who backed an optimist. 4. Anyone who lives with an optimist. 5. An optimist who once tried to practice what he preached. 6. A person who thinks life isn't worth leaving. 7. One who, when he has the choice of two evils, takes both. 8. One who is never happy unless he's miserable. 9. One who always sees microbes in the milk of human kindness. 10. One who feels bad when he feels good for fear he'll feel worse when he feels better. 11. One who would commit suicide if he could do it without killing himself. 12. One who not only expects the worst but makes the worst of it when it happens. 13. Always borrow from a pessimist; he never expects it back anyhow. 14. The optimist proclaims that we live in the best of all possible worlds, and the pessimist fears this is true. 15. The optimist says his glass is half full while the pessimist says his is half empty. 16. An optimist sees an opportunity in every calamity while a pessimist sees a calamity in every opportunity. See optimist[8, 9, 10].

pest. See children: ill-bred children; endurance: endurance test; guest[4].

pet. A fool and his money are soon petted.
See chow; girl: petite girl.
> **mother's little pet.** She is now mother's little petter.
> **pet method.** Many a man's pet method of winning a girl is the pet method.
> **petting.** 1. A ticklish proposition. 2. Some girls go in for petting while others go out for it.

petition. A list of persons who did not have the backbone to say *no*.

petrify. See stone: Stone Age; tree: petrified trees.

philanthropist. 1. One who gives away what he should be giving back. 2. A man who takes it from one set of people and gives it to another. 3, One who returns to the people publicly a small percentage of the wealth he steals from them privately. 4. An employer who pays low wages so he can make enough money to provide charity for needy workingmen.

philanthropy. 1. The business of giving it back to the people you took it from. 2. Giving away your money to strangers who appreciate it rather than leaving it to your relatives.

philosopher. 1. A person who always knows what to do until it happens to him. 2. One who keeps learning more and more about less and less, until he finally knows everything about nothing. 3. A person who writes about something he doesn't understand and makes you think it's your fault.

philosophy. 1. Nonsense in a dress suit. 2. A route of many roads leading from nowhere to nothing. 3. Something which enables the rich to say there is no disgrace in being poor. 4. What enables us to view misfortune more calmly, thereby enabling us to be unhappy more intelligently. 5. A system where both the speaker and the listeners to whom he speaks do not understand.

phone. See coed[4]; dial; telephone.

phonograph. See run: run down[1].

photograph. Taking a photograph is like love: you never know how it will come out.

    passport photograph. The only way you can see yourself as others see you.

photographer. One who can make an ugly girl as pretty as a picture.

photography. It's easy; taking pictures is usually a snap.

phrase. See tongue: tongue twister.

physic. Following the doctor's orders to take a physic and stay in bed can't be done.

physician. After forty, a man is either a fool or a physician, or both.

See doctor; double: double jeopardy; recover.

piano. They laughed when he sat down to play the piano—and they're still laughing.

pick. 1. A person can't choose his face but he can always pick his nose. 2. Some people choose their friends; others also pick them—to pieces. 3. There are lots of rich old fools, which explains why the gold digger has her pick. 4. As a rule, a man doesn't pick a quarrel with his wife because she picks much better ones.

See banjo: banjo player; gold: gold digger[4]; osteopath[3]; ripe; select; wallflower.

    pick up. The easier girls are to pick up, the harder they are to drop.

See auction; bowling alley; fingers; gown: evening gown[2]; shoplifter.

pickpocket. One who generally lives alone, but occasionally goes out in a crowd for a little change.

picnic. The more the mosquitoes, the better the picnic grounds; fifty million insects can't be wrong.

See ant[1].

picture. The girl who's as pretty as a picture often has a nice frame too.

See album: family album[2]; girl[3]; hurricane; photographer; photography; pose.

pie. See reformer: professional reformer.

homemade pies. Nobody knows what kind of homes the homemade pies you buy in restaurants come from.

political pie. It's made of applesauce and plums.

pigskin. 1. The skin a college man loves to touch. 2. Too much attention to the pigskin doesn't help the sheepskin.

pile. The world is full of a number of things, and they all seem piled on our desk.

See reactionary[2].

Pilgrims. They landed on the shores of America, and fell upon their knees; then they fell upon the aborigines.

See Mayflower[1]; Plymouth Rock.

pill. See grape.

pin. 1. Like a person, it becomes useless when it loses its head. 2. Consider the pin: its head keeps it from going too far. 3. Nobody knows where pins disappear to because they are always pointed in one direction and headed in another.

See bowling alley; cautious: cautious man; nudist[1].

pin money. See money: pin money.

rolling pin. 1. Just another form of night club. 2. A rolling pin gathers no moss.

safety pin. See mother: modern mother.

pinch. See police: police station.

ping-pong. A game invented for the benefit of furniture and crockery dealers.

pinochle. Rarely does a card player reach the pinochle of fame.

pint. Two pints make one cavort.

See quartet[1].

pioneer. One who blazed a trail; his descendants now burn up the road.

pipe. A thing that makes a man think: he thinks it's lit when it isn't.

place. 1. Another very annoying place to live in is just beyond your income. 2. To a lover there are only two places in the world: one, where his sweetheart is, and the other, where she isn't.

See critic[7]; gown: low-cut gown; hush; lightning; Main Street; nose[5]; parking[2]; telegram[1]; toilet[2]; tongue[2]; trouble[5]; trousers: man's trousers; war[3]; woman: woman's place.

placenta. To judge from some children, you'd think the mother threw away the child and raised the placenta.

plagiarism. See preacher: dull preacher; research.

plagiarist. A writer of plays.

plain. 1. Never tell a woman a thing is as plain as the nose on her face. 2. It is hard to understand a woman because she never wants to make herself plain.
See tears.

plaintiff. The person whom a lawyer abuses when he has no basis for an argument.

plan. 1. Something either abandoned or unfinished. 2. Many an architect has discovered after the honeymoon that his wife could make plans too.
See architect[1]; calendar[3]; economist[1]; success[5].

plane. Thanks to aviation, the country is now going plane crazy.
See walk: walk on air.

plant. See bulb; tobacco.

plaster. It has its drawbacks.

plaster cast. After the season, most of the football teams are put away in plaster casts.

plate. See kitchen.

platform. It's usually a platforum.
See political: political platform.

platitude. An old saw that has lost its teeth.
See applause[1]; candidate[3]; haughtiness.

play. Most plays require our faith, hope and charity: faith in the first act, hope in the second, and charity in the last.
See actor[3]; Christmas[1]; dramatist; farce; golf[6]; hose; jack[2, 3];

love: Platonic love; musician; organ: hand organ; plagiarist; specialist; tune[2]; work[3].

modern plays. They have to be sin to be appreciated.

pleasant. 1. Pleasant company is always accepted. 2. The most pleasant things in life are either wicked or indigestible.

See enjoyment; manners: good manners; remorse.

please. 1. Persons who do as they please, never please. 2. A girl dresses to please herself, and nowadays it doesn't take much to please her.

See displease; fascism[1, 3]; surgeon: plastic surgeon; weigh; wife: obedient wife.

pleasure. 1. No one has ever proved which gives a woman more pleasure: to hear herself praised or another woman criticized. 2. Combining business and pleasure is easy but combining vacation and pleasure is almost impossible.

See professional; repeat[5]; snore: snoring[4].

plenty. A man sometimes marries so he'll have someone to tell his troubles to, and then he certainly has plenty to talk about.

See rag; weight[1].

plodder. Everybody has faith in a plodder, and nobody in a plotter.

plow. You can't plow a field by turning it over in your mind.

See spring[4].

pluck. Success in life depends on two things: luck and pluck; luck in finding someone to pluck.

plum. A fruit that ripens and falls from the political tree, but only after careful grafting.

See pie: political pie; prune.

plural. See pants[5]; trousers.

Plymouth Rock. It would have been much better if Plymouth Rock had landed on the Pilgrims.

pneumonia. The difference between ammonia and pneumonia is that one comes in bottles and the other in chests.

poach. Children are always poaching on their mother's preserves.

pocket. 1. There'll be little change in men's pockets this year. 2. Even when a wife doesn't select her husband's clothes, she picks his pockets.

See change[3]; double; husband: well-regulated husband; marriage: before & after[6]; miser[2, 4]; pen: fountain pen; penny-pincher; Venus[2].

pocketbook. The book whose contents rule the world.

See Santa Claus; vacation[2].

poem. See check: bad check.

poet. 1. One who either puts fire into his verses or his verses into the fire. 2. A person who has a great imagination; he imagines people will read his poems. 3. Poets are born, not paid. 4. The best reason why so many poets are poor is that there are so many poor poets. 5. Poets are born; that's the trouble.

poetry. 1. It's a gift, but most editors won't take it even at that. 2. It's not what poets create but what creates poets. 3. The trouble with most poetry is that it's not published on the same terms as advertising.

See spring[1, 3]; verse: free verse[2].

point. See laugh: laugh last[7]; line: curved line, straight line; pin[3]; rationing[2].

    decimal point. Many a girl loves a man chiefly for himself, and only for his money up to a certain point—the decimal point.

poise. One woman's poise is another woman's poison.

poison. The only way a wife can keep her husband from looking at other women is to give him some poison.

See divorce[3]; gun; jealous: jealous people; poise.

poker. A game in which it's darkest just before you've drawn.

pole. See fishing[4]; North Pole; sit: flagpole sitter; telephone: telephone pole.

police. They usually work on the theory that if a burglar is left alone, he'll soon become rich enough to quit.

See conscience[4]; cop; freedom[2]; murder; separate.

    police force. Often a police farce.

    police station. Sleeping there is all right in a pinch.

policeman. If it takes a thief to catch a thief, all our policemen must be very honest.

See cop; lawsuit[2].

policy. See modesty[2].

polish. All the polish some girls have they wear on their fingernails.

See dull: dull people; education: college education[3].

politeness. 1. Offering a lady your seat when you get off the bus. 2. A form of behavior that looks well in every man except an undertaker. 3. Nothing is ever lost by politeness, except your seat in the bus.

See gentleman[6].

political. See roast.

political deal. Something that quickly destroys a political ideal.

political leader. One whose task is to keep ahead of several crowds, each going in a different direction.

political machine. 1. A machine that developed out of man's aversion to work. 2. A united minority working against a divided majority. 3. The only well-oiled machine that develops friction.

political platform. 1. Something not to stand on but to get in on. 2. What a candidate stands on before election, and falls down on after election. 3. A politician's principle that, since his rival has been robbing the public for years, he should now be given a chance.

political troubles. They are always multiplied by division.

politician. 1. One who belongs to the opposite party. 2. One who doesn't stand on his own record but jumps on the other fellow's. 3. The fellow who's got what it takes to take what you've got. 4. A man who refuses a bribe but sticks out his hand. 5. A person so busy, he has no time to be honest. 6. An animal that can sit on the fence and yet keep both ears to the ground. 7. One who shakes your hand before election and your acquaintanceship afterwards. 8. A man who divides his time between running for office and running for cover. 9. A man who usually talks himself red, white and blue in the face. 10. One who has to back down when the public gets its back up. 11. One who does not make up his bed and lie in it but makes up his bunk and lies out of it. 12. One who talks about public opinion until he's defeated and then talks about herd ignorance. 13. One who will find an excuse to get out of anything except office. 14. One who spends half his time making laws and the other half helping his friends evade them. 15 A word that should be accented on the last syllable.

See ambassador[2]; exposure; fence[1]; hedge; prosperity[3]; recount; side: two sides[1]; spoon[2]; statesman; straddle; turkey.

active politician. One who stumps the state both before and after election.

average politician. You can't fool all the people all the time, but the average politician is contented with a majority.

cheap politician. There's no such thing.

conservative politician. One who is in office.

crooked politician. One who fears those baring gifts.
    See try.

honest politician. One who, when bought, will stay bought.

politician's son. He isn't much good either.

politics. 1. The most promising of all careers. 2. Two sides and a fence. 3. Where the path of glory leads but to the gravy. 4. The conduct of public affairs for private advantage. 5. A strife of interests masquerading as a contest of principles. 6. The only profession which requires no preparation. 7. A matter of passing the buck or passing the dough. 8. The art of obtaining money from the rich and votes from the poor on the pretext of protecting each from the other. 9. Politics makes strange bedfellows, but they soon get used to the same bunk. 10. In politics, be sure you're in right, then go ahead. 11. The lower politics goes, the higher it comes. 12. What's right and left in politics is not right and wrong in life. 13. Many a man has gone into politics with a fine future and come out with a terrible past. 14. Politics is where a man gets it: sometimes in the neck, sometimes in the bank. 15. If you think politics easy, try sitting on a fence while keeping one ear to the ground. 16. The man who goes into politics as a business has no business to go into politics.
    See fence[3]; idealist; inside.

polls. 1. Voting places where you stand in line for a chance to decide who will spend your money. 2. Many politicians, like the earth, are flattened at the polls.

polygamy. 1. The attempt to get more out of life than there is in it. 2. The proof that there can be too much of a good thing. 3. One of the things now operated on the installment plan in America. 4. The advantage of polygamy is that wives fight each other instead of their husbands.
    See kitchenette; strain.

poodle. What you step into when it rains cats and dogs.

pool. Never shoot pool with an actor; he's too sure of his cues.
    See shoot.

stock pool. Where many an innocent lamb is drowned.

poor. 1. Remember the poor—it costs nothing. 2. The only class that thinks more about money than the rich. 3. A man never realizes the blessing of being born poor until he gets over it.

See acquaintanceship; appetite[1]; children[1]; democracy[2]; disgrace; feeling[1]; husband: rich husband; inconvenient; insurance: life insurance[2]; laryngitis; parents: rich parents; philosophy[3]; poet[4]; pretend[1]; relation; self-denial; shekels; stork[2]; virtuous; wrong[3].

poorhouse. If you make out your income tax correctly, you go to the poorhouse; if you don't, you go to jail.

pop. Young men usually have more trouble in popping the question than in questioning the pop.

See propose[2].

popular. If you want to be popular, you must endure being taught many things which you know already.

See neck[2]; truth[4].

popular girl. One who lives a date-to-date existence.

popular people. People who are not known, not people who are.

popular song. See song: popular song.

popularity. No man ever achieved popularity by telling the truth about anyone other than himself.

See girl: unpopular girl.

population. See birth: birth control[1]; census: census taker; dense; white[2].

porcupine. Animated cactus.

pose. The secret of posing for pictures is to know how to let go of your face.

position. See disposition; happiness[1]; stenographer.

positive. There's no one so positive as he who's mistaken at the top of his voice.

posterity. 1. What the Founding Fathers would not have talked about so glowingly if they had known we were going to be it. 2. Some people believe we should not do anything for posterity because posterity has never done anything for us.

See birth: birth control[3]; mule[2]; prosperity[7]; speech[3].

postgraduate. All men make a study of women, but some take up postgraduate work.

posterior. The hereafter.

pot. See boil; stew.

potato. See gravy.

French fried potatoes. They stay in your mouth a few minutes, in your stomach a few hours, and on your hips the rest of your life.

potato bug. An insect that plays on the tuber.

potent. Beauty is potent but money is omnipotent.

pour. Many a woman looks as if she had been poured into a dress and forgot to say when.

See puritan.

poverty. 1. A state of mind sometimes induced by a neighbor's new car. 2. If poverty is a blessing in disguise, the disguise is perfect. 3. Poverty is no disgrace, but that's about all one can say in its favor.

See poor; wealth: wealthy people.

powder. 1. Some powder goes off with a bang, while some goes on with a puff. 2. It's harmless on a woman but on a man who comes home late, it may be the cause of an explosion.

See bathing: bathing beauty[2]; progress[4]; ship[2].

sleeping powder. When a husband requires absolute quiet, the wife should take a sleeping powder.

power. The powers that be usually take orders from the power companies that be.

See bore[5]; knowledge[1]; light: dim lights; queen; will: will power.

balance of power. It's not adjusted for weighing justice.

See bank: bank balance.

power companies. They are always more careful not to overcharge their batteries than their customers.

water power. In spite of all the talk about water power, it doesn't taste as if it had any.

See tears: woman's tears.

practice. 1. Except for the censor, we could preach what we practice. 2. No matter how long a doctor has been treating patients, he is still practicing.

See fool: old fool; overtime; prudence; righteousness; sin: original sin.

praise. 1. What you get after you're dead. 2. Faint praise ne'er won fair lady. 3. Try praising your wife even if it does frighten her at first. 4. The only reason some wives lie is because they think it's their duty to praise their husbands.

See fault: woman's faults; honesty[6]; pleasure[1]; virtue[1].

pray. Many a man who prays on his knees on Sunday, preys on his friends the rest of the week.

See Congress: chaplain of Congress; preacher[5].

prayer. 1. A message to heaven, usually sent at night to get the low rate. 2. When the gods wish to punish us, they answer our prayers.

preach. See ant[2]; clergyman; minister; overtime; pessimist[5]; practice[1].

preacher. 1. One who looks forward to the wonders of heaven but is never in a hurry to get there. 2. One who doesn't expect to go to hell but spends most of his time talking about it. 3. When a preacher makes a mistake, nobody knows the difference. 4. Preachers don't talk in their sleep; they talk in other people's sleep. 5. When preachers pray, they shut their eyes; when they preach, they shut the eyes of others.

See experience[7].

dull preacher. All work and no plagiarism makes a dull preacher.

predict. See forecast; radio: radio commentator[2].

pregnant. 1. Stork-mad. 2. To infanticipate.

pregnant woman. One who is heir-conditioned.

prejudice. 1. Being down on anything you are not up on. 2. A vagrant opinion without visible means of support. 3. The difference between a prejudice and a conviction is that you can explain a conviction without getting mad.

See mind: open mind[4].

preposition. A bad word to end a sentence with.

prescribe. 1. Doctors always prescribe rest and change—the rest for those who have the change. 2. The doctor who prescribes pleasant thoughts while eating should edit the food prices.

present. 1. Presents make the heart grow fonder. 2. Absence makes the heart grow fonder, but presents make for better results. 3. Absence conquers love, but it takes presents to hold it. 4. There's no time like the present for a present.

See Christmas[4, 5]; housewarming[1]; past[1, 2].

preserve. See alcohol[2]; dignity; fruit; liberty[6]; paint[2]; poach.

president. See advancement; dean.

President. 1. It's strange the President doesn't do better, what with all the advice from the newspapers. 2. What this country

needs is a man who can be right and President at the same time.
See senator[2]; tippler.

press. See newspaper; magazines; suit: divorce suit; serenade.

press agent. 1. A man who gives you the benefit of the dirt.
2. One who has hitched his braggin' to a star.
See telescope.

pressure. Gentlemen who prefer blondes are apt to suffer from
high blonde pressure.

pretend. 1. Pretending to be rich keeps many people poor.
2. Some players are good losers, but others can't pretend.

pretty. See photographer; picture; wise: worldly-wise man.

pretty girl. A pretty girl is like a malady; she gives a young
man heart trouble.
See unlucky[2]; weak[2]; wool[2].

prevaricate. Some people lie, while others merely prevaricate.

preventive. Statistics prove that marriage is a preventive of
suicide, and vice versa.

price. 1. The only part of the nation's food supply raised by the
middleman. 2. Every man has his price, but some hold bargain
sales. 3. Oh for the spirit of '76 and the prices of '36. 4. Once
price was an indication of value but now it's an indication of
nerve.
See amend; antique[3]; break[2]; cigar: five-cent cigar[2]; coal: coal
dealer; cynic[5]; fall: early fall; farm[3]; modest; prescribe[2];
profiteer[2]; prohibitionist[5]; prohibitive; soar; supply: supply &
demand[2]; top[1]; uncanny; widow: wealthy widows; year: leap
year[2].

falling prices. No one has ever been able to hear the sound of
falling prices.
See consumer.

high prices. When prices are high, money doesn't talk; it
whispers.
See decline; wages[1].

present prices. Present prices discourage buying at present
prices.
See coal[2].

rising prices. There is never a peak to rising prices but
always a pique.

pride. 1. It has two seasons: a forward spring and an early fall.
2. After a man swallows his pride, his appetite improves.

3. Pride goeth before a fall—and then comes winter. 4. Pride goeth before destruction, except in the dictionary.

See heartburn[2].

priest. One who undertakes the management of our spiritual affairs in order to better his temporal ones.

primitive. See Christianity[1].

principal. It's not the school that schoolteachers dislike; it's the principal of the thing.

principle. Of all professional people, it is the lawyer who has the highest-priced principles.

See gentleman[8]; interest[1]; politics[5].

print. See together.

prison. 1. Stone walls do not a prison make, nor iron bars a cage, but they do help. 2. The only place where a man gets a jailbird's-eye view of life.

See jail; warden[1].

prisoner. The only person who doesn't mind being interrupted in the middle of a sentence.

See suspend.

private. See debt: public debt; public opinion[2, 3, 4]; snob[3]; telephone: telephone booth[5]; wedding[5].

prize. There are three kinds of husbands: prizes, surprises, and consolation prizes.

See virtue: old virtues.

prize fight. See fight.

probable. It is probable that many things will happen contrary to probability.

problem. See clever: clever person; eat[1]; schoolboy; science; stall; statesman[2].

  Christmas problem. What to give the girl who doesn't smoke.

  girl's problem. How to show a lot of herself and a lot of pretty clothes at the same time.

procure. It is easier to procure a wife than to cure one.

produce. See hen[2].

producer. One who is always a consumer.

  movie producer. The man who thanks his lucky stars.

  theatrical producer. One who is known by the company he keeps.

production. Fathers of triplets make good production men.

  mass production. It cheapens everything, including laws.

  super-production. A superficial movie produced by a super.

profession. See osteopath[1]; telephone: telephone operator[2].

  medical profession. Its purpose is to prevent people from dying natural deaths.

    See appendix[4].

professional. A person who does the same things for a livelihood which others do for pleasure.

  See kiss[15]; principle; tennis.

professor. 1. A textbook wired for sound. 2. One who is paid to study the sleeping conditions among students. 3. One who goes to college and never gets out.

  See ability[1]; coed[6]; dean; lecture.

  absent-minded professor. A person with a dream-lined brain.

profit. 1. A profit is without honor unless it is small. 2. Profits, not prophets, foretell the future.

  See competition[2]; corporation[2]; cotton[2]; farmer[3]; stock: stock market[1]; tennis.

profiteer. 1. One who should get what's coming to him instead of getting what's coming to us. 2. One way to send prices down is to send profiteers up.

  See supply: supply & demand[2].

  profiteering. It can be stopped by profit-airing.

progeny. The progeny of a single fly runs into the millions; it's a good thing flies don't marry.

progress. 1. Merely the exchange of one nuisance for another. 2. Making bigger and better circles to run around in. 3. The development of more machines to provide more people with more leisure in which to be more bored. 4. What we will have when the world spends more for face powder than gunpowder. See marry: married life[3]; pedestrian[14]; turn[2].

prohibition. An enforcement of the laws.

  Prohibition Era. 1. Alcoholiday. 2. The period when America had been dried and found wanting. 3. The Prohibition Error.

prohibitionist. 1. A spigot bigot. 2. A leerbeer. 3. A cellar smeller. 4. A pro-inhibitionist. 5. One who has no objection to prices taking a drop.

prohibitive. What some prices are called because they never take a drop.

promiscuous. Men are hard to please: if you kiss them when they ask you, you're promiscuous; if you don't, you're a prude.

promise. See candidate : hopeless candidate ; generosity ; politics[1] ;
wait[1].

  breach of promise. 1. What's wrong with this country is that
you can't sue a congressman for breach of promise. 2. Breach
of promise suits are declining because it is much easier nowadays to go through with marriage and divorce.

  See autopsy ; court[1].

  promising people. Those who are always borrowing.

promoter. A man who will furnish the ocean if you will furnish
the ships.

promotion. It's two-thirds motion.

prompt. Some husbands can pay their debts promptly, but most
men are good to their wives.

proof. The proof of the wedding is in the alimony.

  See alibi.

propaganda. 1. Like manure, it is of no use unless it can be
spread. 2. Propaganda is seldom proper.

  See money[4] ; source[2].

proper. See hand[3] ; propaganda[2] ; twenty-five.

property. Some widows have so much trouble over the property
that they wish their husbands hadn't died.

  See corpse ; suit : bathing suit[8].

prophesy. If you prophesy wrong, nobody will forget it ; but if
you prophesy right, nobody will remember.

prophet. A wise one makes sure of the event first.

  See America[1] ; profit[2].

proposal. 1. An attempt to acquire a huge vocabulary. 2. A
sentence ending with a proposition.

  See antique : romantic antique.

propose. 1. The man who proposes in the car will probably be
accepted in the hospital. 2. Men propose like corks : some will
pop the question while others have to be drawn out.

  See disclose ; impose.

proposition. See lettuce ; matrimony[7] ; pet : petting[1] ; proposal[2].

prose. No matter how bad prose is, it might be verse.

prosecutor. Usually a persecuter.

prosperity. 1. Being able to pay a little more for things we
shouldn't buy anyway. 2. A buy-product. 3. Something business creates for the politicians to take credit for. 4. An era

when people go into debt for things they don't need.   5. The
time when you can always get enough credit to live beyond your
means.   6. Prosperity is being in a rut, while depression is being
in a hole.   7. To most people prosperity is a matter for posterity.
See farm[2]; friend[5]; return; shop: shopping[1].

prosperous.   In prosperous times you pay installments on ten
things instead of one.
See chiropodist[2].

prostitute.   A woman who has been tried and found wanton.

protect.   See legislation: class legislation; politics[8]; suit: bathing
suit[8]; tariff.

proud.   Many a man's ambition is to marry a rich girl who is too
proud to have her husband work.

prove.   Evolution claims that the fittest survive, and we are all
here to prove it.
See golfer[5]; rule: golden rule; statistics[1]; understand[1].

providence.   The most popular scapegoat for our sins.

provision.   The law gives the pedestrian the right of way, but
makes no provision for flowers.

prude.   1. A girl who always knows a lot of things she shouldn't
know.   2. One who always thinks below the belt.   3. A good
woman in the worst sense of the word.   4. A girl who is so
modest that she pulls down the shade when she changes her mind.
See bath; promiscuous.

prudence.   The three most precious things are freedom of speech,
freedom of conscience, and the prudence never to practice either.
See driver: woman driver[7].

prune.   A plum that has seen better days.

P.S.   The most important part of a woman's letter.

psalmist.   A person who tells fortunes by reading hands.

psychoanalysis.   A disease whose symptoms psychoanalysis tries
to cure.

psychologist.   A person trained to cure the obscure.

   child psychologist.   A person who would be better off if he
   were a parent.

psychology.   The science which tells us what everybody knows in
language that nobody understands.

puberty.   See adolescence[1].

public.   See character[3]; lay[1]; political: political platform[3]; snob[3];
bus: bus motto.

publicity. 1. What you get when you're already successful and don't need it. 2. What some movie stars say they don't want in order to get more of it. 3. If an actor bites a dog, it's not news but publicity. 4. 'Tis better to have loved and divorced than never to have had any publicity at all. 5. Truth is stranger than fiction, and publicity is stranger than both of them.
See candidate[2].

public opinion. 1. What people think other people think. 2. Private gossip which has reached the proportions of an epidemic. 3. Private opinion that makes noise enough to attract converts. 4. The weakness of public opinion is that so many people express it only in private.
See politician[12].

public speaker. 1. One who generally makes up in length what he lacks in depth. 2. One who is rarely so well inspired as when he talks about himself. 3. One who, if he does not strike oil in ten minutes, should stop boring. 4. A person who should stand up, speak up, and shut up.

public speaking. 1. The art of diluting a two-minute idea with a two-hour vocabulary. 2. The three secrets of success in public speaking are: be sincere, be brief, be seated.

public utility. People advocate government control of public utilities to do away with government control by public utilities.

publish. See poetry[3].

publisher. See date[3]; verse: free verse[2].

pudding. The proof of the pudding is sometimes in the obituary notices.

puff. A puff in the newspaper is worth two in the handbag.
See powder[1].

pull. It takes a lot of pull to get a job milking cows.
See kite; mule[4]; push.

Pullman. See berth.

Pullman window. It takes jacks or better to open one.
See air: air-condition.

pull-over. A traffic violation.

pulse. There are worse occupations than feeling a woman's pulse.

pun. 1. A form of humor that goes over with a groan. 2. A joke at which everybody groans because they didn't think of it first. 3. A little less than p-u-n-k and more than p-u. 4. The pun

is mightier than the sword. 5. A pun is meant as punishment.
See pundit.

punctuality. 1. The thief of time. 2. The art of guessing how
late the other person is going to be.

puncture. A little hole found in tires at long distances from
phones and garages.

pundit. A person fond of making puns.

punishment. See prayer[2]; pun[5].

    capital punishment. 1. The anxiety that a person feels for
lack of funds. 2. A method by which people are put to death
by elocution. 3. As to capital punishment, if it was good
enough for my father, it's good enough for me. 4. People
who don't believe in capital punishment have probably never
tried it.

    See socialism.

pure. Blessed are the pure, for they shall inhibit the earth.

    See drink: mixed drink; impure; story: detective stories[1];
theater[2]; truth[8].

puritan. A person who pours righteous indignation into the
wrong things.

    See Thanksgiving[3].

purple. See blackberry.

purse. 1. The way to tell a woman's hat from her purse is, if it
has money in it, it's her purse. 2. Faint heart ne'er won fair
lady, but a full purse can always pull the trick.

    See doctor: grasping doctor; gold: gold digger[5].

pursue. Nowadays every man is entitled to life, liberty, and a
car in which to pursue happiness.

    See coed[2].

pursuit. See collector[1]; golfer[4]; reformer[2].

push. It will get a person everywhere—except through a door
marked *pull*.

Q

quack. Quacks are stubborn things.

quarrel. 1. Something which results from a wife's talking when she should be listening. 2. When husband and wife stop quarreling, they make up—another quarrel. 3. Some men quarrel with their wives and others have learned to say *Yes, dear*. 4. Many married couples manage to patch up their old quarrels until they are as good as new ones.

See blame; budget[1]; evolution[5]; flail; historical; marriage[11]; pick[4]; ripe; select; two; way[3].

quarterback. Many a father spends thousands of dollars on his son's college education and gets only a quarterback.

See requirement.

quarters. Sometimes a man marries his better half in order to get better quarters.

See board: boarding house[1]; hotel[1].

quartet. 1. It usually contains a couple of pints. 2. Where all four think the other three can't sing.

queen. The power behind the drone.

queer. All the world is queer but me and thee, dear, and sometimes I think thee is a little queer.

See question[2].

quest. Love is the quest, marriage the conquest, divorce the inquest.

question. 1. Every question has two sides so long as it doesn't concern us personally. 2. A question may be queer, but the questioner is always the querist. 3. The most annoying questions of the day are those children ask.

See ask; bottom[1]; coed[4]; indiscreet; maid: old maid[5]; pop; propose[2]; return; side: two sides; yes[1].

quick. Half the world's troubles can be traced to saying *yes* too quickly, and half to saying *no* not quickly enough.

See eyes: black eyes[3]; mankind.

quiet. See ass; birthday: father's birthday; cigar[2]; coat: fur coat; orator[1]; powder: sleeping powder; ring: diamond ring.

quit. Doctors think a lot of patients are cured who have simply quit in disgust.

See police; self-made: self-made man[9].

quotations. They cover a multitude of sins.

See broker; orator[2].

R

R.   The dog's letter-r-r.

rabbit.   1. Hare today and mink tomorrow.   2. A little animal that grows the fur other animals get credit for when it's made into a lady's coat.

See catskin; coat: mink coat.

rabbit's foot.   A poor substitute for horse sense.

race.   Don't race trains to crossings; if it's a tie, you lose.

See bet[2]; coeducation; navy.

horse race.   See horse: horse race.

human race.   The human race seems to have improved everything except people.

See Adam; civilization[1]; horse: horse race[2, 3]; rumor[2].

racketeer.   1. A man with the courage of his non-conviction.   2. You can't expect a racketeer to be respectable so long as he has to do business with people who do business with a racketeer.   3. When a racketeer dies, he usually leaves his family and half a dozen cops without support.

See freedom[1].

radical.   1. Anyone whose opinion differs radically from ours.   2. A conservative out of a job.   3. A person who insists upon convincing us instead of letting us convince him.   4. The radicals of yesterday are the liberals of tomorrow.

See liberal; reactionary[1]; right[3].

radio.   1. A device to teach mankind the blessings of silence.   2. It started in the Garden of Eden when a rib was taken from Adam to make the first loud-speaker.   3. A recent invention to give a person the air without hurting his feelings.   4. If it's out of commission, it's also out of commotion.   5. Radio is still in its infancy, but a lot of its jokes aren't.   6. The radio is within the reach of all, and it's strange more aren't smashed.   7. We have to keep our radio on to drown out others kept on to drown out ours.   8. What you can get on your radio depends on the pawnbroker.

See air[3]; apartment[2]; applaud; broadcasting; Christmas[2]; dust[2]; home: American home; party: life of the party[1]; Rip Van

Winkle; song: popular song[2], Southern songs; soprano; swat; vocabulary; voice[2].

radio announcer. 1. A person on the ether who should be under it. 2. A well-paid person who will not work for the love of mike.

radio commentators. 1. Pollyanalysts. 2. When better predictions are made, radio commentators won't make them.

radio program. It's usually fair to maudlin.

radio serial. Some families have enough troubles to be a radio serial.

rag. The girl who didn't have a rag on her back before marriage, probably has plenty of them now.

See woman[9].

raid. In wartime, it's nice weather if it doesn't raid.

railroad. 1. It has a stake in three kinds of stock: live, rolling, and watered. 2. It's generally built on three gauges: broad gauge, narrow gauge, and mortgage.

See fare; stop: stop, look & listen.

railroad crossing. 1. Some people buy auto parts and others live near railroad crossings. 2. A minute lost at a railroad crossing may save all the rest of your time.

See crash; crossing.

rain. 1. If it looks like rain, it's probably water. 2. When it rains, it bores.

See knee[3]; living: cost of living; poodle; spitz; umbrella[3]; weather: beastly weather.

rainy day. 1. The man who looks out for a rainy day generally makes many a sunny one for his heirs. 2. Some people don't save up money for a rainy day because they never shop when it rains.

See law: blue law; taxi[2]; umbrella[1].

raise. 1. An increase in pay you get just before going a little more into debt. 2. It's far easier to raise a laugh than a loan. 3. Everybody would like to see the underpaid get increases in wages, but the problem is how to raise the raise.

See bee; cabbage; elevate; farm: farm hand; farmer: gentleman farmer; financier; middleman; placenta; price[1]; rent; tax[3]; twins[2]; vice-president[2]; voice[3].

raisin. A grape that worried too much and got wrinkles.

ranch. See nudist: nudist colony.

rank. See cheese: Limburger cheese[1]; perfume: bad perfume.

rap. People who don't believe in ghosts don't give a rap if ghosts give a rap.

rare. See painting.

rat. See reformer[7].

rate. See prayer[1].

rationing. 1. One banned thing after another. 2. It has its good points. 3. Less and less amounts of more and more foods. See war[1].

rattle. The average man detects a rattle in his car more quickly than one in his head.

razor. The argument over shaving with the safety razor or the electric razor is merely a matter of hairsplitting. See shaving: clean-shave; man.

razor blades. See thrift: thrifty man.

reach. The pedestrian views with alarm the fact that a car is now within the reach of every man. See billboard[3]; board: boarding house[1]; club[2]; radio[6]; speech[3].

reactionary. 1. A person who thinks there is something radically wrong with radicals. 2. One who wants the rules enforced so nobody can take his pile away from him the way he got it from others.

read. See book: book ends; bookworm; friend: good friend; journalism: yellow journalism; letter[1]; movie: movie titles; poet[2]; shut: shut up; suppress; tabloid[6].

> **reading.** 1. An ingenious device for avoiding thought. 2. If your life is an open book, don't bore your friends by reading out of it. See browse; literature: current literature; writing: easy writing.

reader. There are two kinds of readers: those who read to remember, and those who read to forget. See story: detective stories[2].

real estate agent. It's not the land that lies; it's the real estate agent. See realtor.

reality. See headless.

realize. When a man begins to realize the truth about himself, it reduces his desire to reform the neighbors.

realtor. One who believes in deeds, not words.

See real estate agent; monologue³.

reap. See gardener.

rear. See paddle.

rear admiral. The official title given to backseat drivers in the navy.

reason. 1. A man always has two reasons for doing something: a good reason and the real reason. 2. Some men dislike women without any reason, while others like them that way.

See action; anger; die; dress³; flowers²; happy: happy people; insane: insane asylum²; skirt: short skirt; suit: bathing suit⁷; twins³.

  good reason. If you haven't got a good reason for doing something, you have a good reason for letting it alone.

  trivial reasons. People wouldn't get divorced for such trivial reasons if they hadn't gotten married for such trivial reasons.

recede. Nothing recedes like success.

receipt. When some people pay you a compliment, they look as though they expected a receipt for it.

receive. See alimentary canal; Christmas: Christmas gift¹; give: give & receive; revenge²; thanks.

receiver. A person appointed by the court to take what's left.

receivership. The man who does nothing but wait for his ship to come in is likely to find it a receivership.

recognize. Some people don't lie; they merely present the truth in such a way that nobody recognizes it.

See temperament.

record. See driving⁴; politician².

recount. The only time a politician can't demand a recount is when his wife gives birth to triplets.

recover. When a doctor doesn't think the patient will recover, to make sure he calls in another physician.

See Thanksgiving²; thought¹.

recreation. The automobile is responsible for changing recreation into wreck-creation.

recruit. See soldier¹.

red. You can't blame a man who sees red every time he looks at a girl's face.

See blackberry; bleed; colorful; fascism²; green; light², traffic light²; reformer⁸; wine.

Red. See communism.

red tape. See America: history of America; bureaucrat.

redistribute. The two agencies that redistribute great fortunes are taxation and offspring.

redress. It is woman and not her wrongs that ought to be redressed.

reducing. 1. A case of the survival of the fattest. 2. When a woman says she's reducing, it's generally some man's account. See diet: dieting; loser; nation: Christian nations; walking[3]; weigh.

reducing exercise. Shaking the head from side to side when offered a second helping.

reducing expert. One who lives on the fat of the land.

reducing machine. It costs so much, you have to starve yourself to keep up the payments.

refer. A woman may consent to forgive and forget, but she will never drop the habit of referring to the matter now and then.

reflect. When a woman finds time for reflecting, she looks in a mirror.
See mirror[2].

reflection. The best light on the subject of marriage.
See eclipse; hair: golden hair; love[14]; maid: old maid[4].

reform. 1. Reforms should begin at home and stay there. 2. You never hear of a man marrying a woman to reform her. 3. Reforms come from below; no man with four aces howls for a new deal.
See realize.

reformer. 1. A person who insists on his conscience being your guide. 2. One whose business is what's none of his business. 3. A person with life, liberty, and the pursuit of other people's happiness. 4. One who thinks there's more wrong with the country than with him. 5. One who wants to reform others, not himself. 6. One who doesn't go to heaven because they have no use for them there. 7. One who, when he smells a rat, is eager to let the cat out of the bag. 8. The average man's idea of a good time is to paint the town red; the reformer's idea is to paint the town blue.
See freedom[1]; Sabbath; satiety.

professional reformer. One who is generally bent on getting the pie out of piety.

refuse. See clever: clever girl.

regain. Some men lose their health getting wealth, and then lose their wealth regaining their health.

regeneration. Every generation needs regeneration.

regular. Regular hours are kept by many people, but most of them are in jail.

See habit[2].

rehearse. Some men drive as if rehearsing for an accident.

reins. The farmer can best be helped by the reins of government.

reject. See editor; novel: great American novel.

relation. The richer the man, the poorer his relations—with other people.

relatives. 1. Inherited critics. 2. What the rich never lack. 3. Persons who live too near and die too seldom. 4. Persons whom we inherit, and who wish to inherit from us. 5. A tedious pack of people who haven't the remotest knowledge of how to live nor the smallest instinct about when to die. 6. The best way to make your relatives think a lot of you is to make a fortune and then drop dead.

See Darwin; dissatisfy; enemy[3]; evolution[2]; forgive[2]; friend[8]; kindred; mother-in-law[5]; philanthropy[2].

distant relative. 1. One who is usually not distant enough. 2. One who can be very distant when he has money.

See husband: second husband[2].

poor relatives. 1. With poor relatives it is usually touch and go. 2. It is only after a man gets rich that he discovers how many poor relatives he has.

See foreign: foreign relations.

rich relatives. 1. The kin we love to touch. 2. The type of persons who live the longest. 3. They are usually distant relatives or close ones.

relativity. Some people don't believe in the theory of relativity because it often breaks up the home.

relax. See office.

relief. See farm: farm relief; toilet[1]; widow[2].

religion. 1. Insurance in this world against fire in the next. 2. A cloak used by some people in this world who will be warm enough without one in the next. 3. The daughter of hope and fear, explaining to ignorance the nature of the unknowable. 4. It teaches a man to spend the best part of his life preparing for the worst. 5. When it is a question of money, everybody is of the same religion.　6. If your religion doesn't change you, you had better change your religion.　7. Religion is caught, not taught.　8. There is more religion in men's science than there is science in their religion.

See church[4, 8]; dyspepsia[2]; fire: fire escape; God[1]; sex[2]; taste[3].

remark. See conversationalist; deliver; lecturer.

remedy. See cure; drug store[1].

remember. If you want to remember, tie a string around your finger; if you want to forget, tie a rope around your neck.

See husband: tactful husband; kiss: first kiss; lady[4]; poor[1]; prophesy; reader; truth: truthful person; witness[2].

remind. 1. Wives of great men all remind us of it.　2. What some girls want for their birthday is—not to be reminded of it.

See souvenir; tombstone[1].

remorse. A sign that it wasn't quite as pleasant as one expected it to be.

See stone: rolling stone[2].

Reno. Where many of the old folks are moving to be near the children.

rent. The landlord often raises a tenant's rent when the tenant himself can't raise it.

See avenue; jail[1]; skin[1]; tailor[2].

repair. The face that's lifted usually falls when it sees the bill for repairs.

See hedge; jury: fix a jury; mind: open mind[3].

repartee. 1. Repartit-for-tat.　2. An insult in a dress suit.　3. Better never than late.　4. Saying on the instant what you didn't say until the next morning.

See majority[1]; repertory.

repeal. Husbands lay down the law but wives usually repeal it.

repeat. 1. You can't believe everything you hear, but you can repeat it.　2. Women and telephones repeat what they hear, but the telephone repeats it exactly.　3. A lot of history isn't fit to repeat itself.　4. Tell a girl a good joke and she'll laugh at it; tell her a bad one and she'll repeat it.　5. Marry in haste, repeat at pleasure.　6. History repeats itself, and so do crooked voters.

See history[8], personal history; inevitable.

repent. Marry in haste, and repent insolvent.

See father-in-law; meal: mealtime; sin: sinning.

repertory. The secret of repartee.

report. The sound made when some men discharge an obligation. See committee: committee-of-five; kiss[5]; obligation; snore[1].

reporter. See inventor.

republic. A form of government in which the majority get at least two guesses as to which minority will rule them next.

Republican. See party[3].

reputation. 1. A personal possession, frequently not discovered until lost. 2. Many people live on the reputation of the reputation they might have made.

See character[4]; confession: open confession[2]; defend.

requirement. Many a college lowers its entrance requirements with a specific end in view—not to mention promising halfbacks and quarterbacks.

research. When you take stuff from one writer, it's plagiarism; when you take it from many writers, it's research.

reserve. See club: night club[1]; home[5].

resist. Woman begins by resisting a man's advances and ends by blocking his retreat.

See temptation[2].

resistance. Girls who offer no resistance lead a very nice existence.

See housewife: popular housewife.

sales resistance. The triumph of mind over patter.

resolution. It proves that the good die young.

good resolution. A useless attempt to interfere with scientific laws.

New Year's resolution. 1. A fragile bit of crockery fashioned on the first day of January and usually broken on the second. 2. The best way to keep it is to have a copy locked up in a drawer.

See swallow; swear.

resort. A place where the natives live on your vacation till next summer.

See cemetery[1].

ideal summer resort. Where the fish bite and the mosquitoes don't.

summer resort. 1. Where they charge you enough to make up for the nine months you are not there. 2. A place that overlooks a lake, and also overlooks comfortable beds, good food, and running water. 3. A place where the men are stuffed

shirts and the women are stuffed shorts.   4. A summer resort
may be crowded but there's always room for one bore.
See bellboy[1].

resources.   See civilization[3].

respect.   The belief that the girl you married is better than the
ones you go out with.
See tie: Christmas ties[1].

respectability.   The offspring of a liaison between a bald head
and a bank account.

respectable.   Age renders men respectable as well as their jokes.
See ashamed; racketeer[2].

responsible.   No man is responsible for his father; that's his
mother's affair.
See success: husband's success.

responsibility.   Some men grow under responsibility, while
others only swell.
See corporation[2]; dodge.

rest.   God created the universe and rested; then God created man
and rested; finally God created woman, and since then neither
God nor man has rested.
See bellboy[1]; club: night club[4]; prescribe[1]; rust; sleep: sleepwalker; vacation[2].

restaurant.   1. An institution for the spread of dyspepsia.   2. A
place where you can exchange your hat and coat but not your
pants.   3. A place where the public pays the proprietor for the
privilege of tipping the waiters for something to eat.   4. An
eating place that doesn't sell drugs.   5. In some restaurants the
music makes you feel like dancing; in others, it's the food.
See club: night club[4]; cover: cover charge[2]; diner; fast: hunger
fast; hash[6]; pie: homemade pies; waiter[3].

restroom.   There's no difference between the restroom and the
grave: when you must go, you must go.

ladies' restroom.   No man's land.

result.   The man who wants results never wants consequences.
See collaboration; hen[1]; obstinacy; present[2]; self-made.

retailer.   It takes nine tailors to make a man but it doesn't take
nine retailers to break him.

retake.   A Hollywood wedding.

retire.   Nowadays the rising generation retires when the retiring
generation rises.

See schoolteacher ; singer.

retreat. See resist.

return. If prosperity will only return, we will ask no questions.
See goods: stolen goods; keep[1]; vomit.

revenge. 1. It's often like biting a dog because the dog bit you.
2. Revenge is sweet, but not when you're on the receiving end.

revolution. That which makes the world go round.
See crank; door: revolving door[2].

revolve. Nowadays the earth revolves on its taxes.

revolving door. See door: revolving door.

revolver. The only instrument lacking in a swing band.

rhetoric. Language in a dress suit.

rheumatism. 1. Nature's first primitive effort to establish a
weather bureau. 2. Misery loves company, but it's better to have
rheumatism in one leg than to have it in both. 3. Even when
only one person has it, rheumatism is a joint affair.
See sick: sick people.

rib. Most married men wish Adam had died with all his ribs in
his body.
See lie: lie detector; radio[2].

rice. A weapon for assaulting the newly-married.

rich. 1. The only ones to whom even second cousins write letters.
2. A girl can always live on love, if he is rich.
See acquaintanceship; appetite[1]; beach; boxer; burglar; church[6];
democracy[2]; doings; feeling[1]; insurance: life insurance[2]; jail[3];
menace; parents: rich parents; philosophy[3]; pretend[1]; relation;
relatives[2], poor relatives[2]; shekels; support[1]; wrong[3].

rich man. See husband: rich husband; laryngitis; scalp.

rich people. The disadvantage of being rich is that you have
to live with rich people.

rid. See chewing gum[4]; cold[3]; discharge; feet[2]; headache[2]; specialist; yield.

ride. Some girls walk home from rides, while others ride home
from walks.
See car: second-hand car[2]; commuter[1]; safe; subway[2].

joy ride. A thing of beauty has joy rides forever.

joy-rider. One who rides when we are walking; a jay-walker
is one who walks when we are riding.

riding habit. The person who has the riding habit usually has
a riding habit.

right. 1. Do right, and fear no man; don't write, and fear no woman. 2. No man has a right to all his rights. 3. If a man is right, he cannot be too radical; if wrong, he cannot be too conservative.

See action; apologize; bet[4]; boast[2]; copyright; direction; divide; endow; fighter; give: give in; gown: low-cut gown; hear[1]; heaven[2]; intuition; lawyer[3]; left; marriage[21]; mistake[2]; nudist[6]; pedestrian[17]; politics[10, 12]; President[2]; prophesy; socks[3]; wrong[1, 2].

divine right. Kings believe in the divine right to govern wrong.

righteousness. Some people spend so much time hunting after righteousness that they haven't any time to practice it.

ring. 1. Opportunity knocks for every man, but a woman gets a ring. 2. Putting a ring on a girl's third finger puts you under her thumb. 3. A girl admires the tone of a bachelor's voice when there's a ring in it.

See bellboy[2]; bracelet; show[1]; telephone[1], telephone operator[1, 4]; wedding[3].

diamond ring. Something to keep the baby quiet.

engagement ring. The only sign of toil on a girl's hand.

See diamond: diamond jubilee.

wedding ring. 1. Jewelers ought to keep up with the times and rent out wedding rings. 2. The modern wedding ring is very thin and narrow; the old-fashioned type was made to last a lifetime.

riot. All's riot with the world.

See wrong[1].

ripe. Never pick a quarrel even when it's ripe.

Rip Van Winkle. The man who was able to sleep for twenty years because his neighbors had no radio.

rise. To avoid getting up with a grouch, rise before him.

See day[1]; early[1]; folly: height of folly; generation: rising generation; head[2]; height; kite; lark[1]; miss[3]; retire; sit: sit down; truth[9]; yeast.

early rising. 1. He who rises early with the sun shouldn't stay up late with the daughter. 2. The benefits of early rising are immediately noticed when a man sits down on a tack.

rival. He who falls in love with himself will have no rivals.

See departure.

river. See Wall Street[1].

road. 1. It's a wrong road that has no turning. 2. It's a short road that has no advertising signs. 3. What makes a chicken cross the road is often a shop window with a mirror in it. 4. Women drivers demand only half the road, but they allow only a quarter of the road on each side.

See billboard[2]; detour[4]; driver: woman driver[4]; hobo; philosophy[2]; pioneer; truck; turn[2].

> **road hog.** 1. It's always the other motorist. 2. If all the road hogs were laid end to end, that would be Utopia.
> See lane.

> **roadhouse.** Man is merely a roadhouse where his ancestors stopped off for a while on their way to becoming his descendants.

roast. The main course at a political banquet.

See toast.

rob. See news[2].

rod. Spoil the rod and spare the fish.

role. See actor[4]; ham.

roll. Never break your bread or roll in your soup.

See bake; dice; score.

romance. 1. Anything which ends in a wedding. 2. It begins by deceiving oneself and ends by deceiving the other person. 3. It often begins by a splashing waterfall and ends over a leaky faucet. 4. It begins with sentiment and ends with a settlement. 5. White lies, like red roses, are very important to romance. 6. A man always wants to be a woman's first love; a woman always wants to be a man's last romance.

See marriage[3].

> **broken romance.** A busted coupling.

> **lifelong romance.** To love oneself is the beginning of a lifelong romance.

romantic. See antique: romantic antique.

Rome. When in Rome, do as the Romeos do.

See Caesar; globetrotter.

room. A new room sweeps clean.

See apartment: modern apartment[1]; hotel: hotel guest; resort: summer resort; restroom; top[1, 3].

> **dressing room.** An undressing room.

waiting room. You can tell how long a dentist has been practicing by the dates on the magazines in his waiting room.

rope. Give a man enough rope and he'll start selling it.

See box: boxing; businessman[2]; criminal[3]; face: face-lifting[3]; generation: younger generation[2]; remember; skip; walk: tightrope walker.

rose. It speaks the language of love but tulips do a much better job.

See romance[5].

rouge. See modern: modern girl[4].

rough. See golfer[2].

round. 1. Never go around with a married woman unless you can go two rounds with her husband. 2. The man who squares his debt will probably be round again.

See dress[2]; earth[2]; indigestion[4].

row. See discover; laugh: laugh last[4].

royalty. People who are not only out of style but also out of luck.

rub. People who are rubbed the wrong way never feel up to scratch.

See itch[1].

rubber band. See bankroll.

rudeness. Wealth doesn't change a man even though his rudeness becomes eccentricity and his vulgarity becomes wit.

rug. It is sold by the yard and worn out by the foot.

See ash tray; breeding: well-bred man; elephant[1].

ruin. See health[3]; moral: morals[1].

rule. Every rule has its exception, including this one.

See exception[1]; pocketbook; reactionary[2]; republic.

golden rule. The rule that proves there are no golden rules.
See health[2].

rum. At a party there's always rum for one more.

ruminant. An animal that chews its cub.

rumor. 1. The only flyer that can speed in all directions at once. 2. The long-distance champion of the human race. 3. A monster with more tales than an octopus.

See gossip[1, 4, 7]; grape: sour grapes.

flying rumor. It never has any trouble in making a landing.

rump. The rumble seat.

run. 1. Any fool can run the universe; the wise man is he who can run his own business. 2. Some horses try so hard to win a race that they run out of wind; others just run out of curiosity. 3. The man who boasts he runs things in his own house, usually does—the lawn mower and the errands. 4. The man who thinks he can win in a walk is usually anxious to run.

See clock[2]; color; creditor[4]; curious[2]; doctor: best doctor; exercise[2]; grab; motorist; nose[6]; politician[8]; stockings: women's stockings; taxi[3], taxi driver[2]; tongue[1], salesman's tongue; water: still water.

run after. Never run after a bus or a woman; another will be along shortly.

run away. The girl who won't elope will let her imagination run away with her.

See kiss[12].

run down. 1. The one thing that sounds worse than a phonograph that's almost run down is a pedestrian who's almost run down. 2. People run down careless drivers and vice versa. 3. Most men who run down women are running down one woman only.

See detective; gossip[7]; hospital[2]; license number.

running. Running is good for the figure, especially when fleeing from danger.

run over. See car: streamlined car.

rung. When a girl is up on a ladder, men get rung ideas.

rust. The man who rests on his laurels usually rusts on them.

rye. See moonshiner.

S

Sabbath. Reformers seem bent on making the Sabbath a day of arrest.

sable. The skin girls love to touch.

sacrifice. See bride[1]; patriotism.

safe. A pedestrian these days is safe only when he is riding.

See kangaroo[1]; tease[1]; tell[3].

safety. There's safety in numbers; that's why poor singers form choruses.

safety zone. Where the car driver can strike you only from the side.

sailor. 1. A man who makes his living on water but never touches it on land. 2. One who complains that there's many a ship 'twixt the cup and the lip. 3. Even the laziest sailor never has grass growing under his feet.

See diet[2]; goblet; schooner; wave: permanent wave[1].

sailor's life. It's simply the knots.

saint. A dead sinner revised and edited.

See sinner[2]; telephone: telephone operator[3].

sainthood. The last refuge of a misfit.

salad. A woman is like a salad: much depends on the dressing.

salary. A man's salary that goes to five figures probably goes to his wife and four children.

See chorine; command; economy[1]; exception[2]; financier; high-brow[6]; love[19]; save; truth: truthful woman; twins[3]; vice-president[2]; wages[2], small wage.

small salary. It isn't so hard to live on it if you don't spend too much money trying to keep it a secret.

sale. See auctioneer[2]; confession: open confession[1]; resistance: sales resistance; salesman[1].

bargain sale. See bargain: bargain sale.

for sale. See California[1].

salesman. 1. An individual who needs to have the wind taken out of his sales. 2. A person with both feet on the ground who takes orders from a person with both feet on the desk. 3. Getting orders from some people is like pulling teeth; salesmen have to give them a lot of gas. 4. A soft answer turneth away wrath, but hath little effect on a door-to-door salesman.

See door; housewife: popular housewife; marry: married man[4]; tongue: salesman's tongue.

same. 1. Man wants but little here below, but the same cannot be said of woman. 2. When a man gets fifty dollars a week, the chances are his wife also gets fifty dollars a week—the same fifty.

See design; extravagant; news[1]; religion[5].

Samson. He had the right idea about advertising: he took two columns and brought down the house.

sand. See beach; gold[2].

sandwich. An unsuccessful attempt to make both ends meet.

See hors d'oeuvres; medicine: medicine cabinet.

garlic sandwich. Two pieces of bread traveling in bad company.

western sandwich. Two slices of bread with wide open spaces in between.

sanitary. If you can't be good, be sanitary.

Santa Claus. He doesn't come through the chimney any more but through a large hole in the pocketbook.

See investor.

sap. 1. What a person discovers himself to be when he pays to have his family tree looked up. 2. In all trees the appearance of the sap is a sign of continued vigor, except in the family tree. 3. Only God can make a tree, but it takes a college to make the sap.

sarcasm. Sourcasm.

sarcastic. Sourcastic or sarcaustic.

satiety. One of the famous reformers.

satisfy. The man who demands very much in others is satisfied with very little in himself.

See marry: married life[5]; obituary; tailor[2]; tennis; wish.

savage. A person whose manners differ from ours.

save. 1. At twenty, he thinks he can save the world; at thirty, he begins to wish he could save part of his own salary. 2. Save a part of your salary each week; enough for lunch and bus fare, anyway. 3. Try to save something while your salary is small; it's impossible to save after you begin earning more.

See budget: balance the budget; daylight; senator[2]; tax: income tax[4]; Thanksgiving[3]; wizard.

savings. Doing without what you need in order to have money for something you can do without.

sawmill. A person should sleep like a log, not like a sawmill.

saxophone. 1. An ill wind which nobody blows good. 2. Not a musical instrument but a weapon. 3. An ill wind that blows nobody good. 4. The evil that men do lives after them; the saxophone was invented a century ago. 5. It's an ill wind that blows most saxophones.

See execution; music: musical instrument.

saxophone player. What he needs is not harmony but hush money.

say. 1. It often shows a fine command of language to say nothing.

2. When there's nothing to be said, you can depend upon some people to say it.

See against; believe[3]; boast[1]; democracy[3]; echo[1]; fascism[1, 3]; favor; flattery[2]; flower[3, 4]; flyer; keep: keep on; least; marriage: marriage ritual; mouth[2], gum chewer's mouth; nose[4]; object; payment: easy payments; persuade; repartee[4]; sing; think[6]; tongue: woman's tongue[2]; wise: wise man[4]; wit[1]; woman[11].

scab. A workman who refuses to strike while the iron is hot.

scald. People who sing in the bath should be scalded or scolded.

scales. 1. Something too often on the eyes of Justice instead of in her hands. 2. When a fat woman steps on the scales, she always experiences a sinking feeling.

See disarmament.

social scale. The one in which money is weighed.

scalp. Woman's crowning glory is a rich man's scalp.

scandal. 1. An ill wind that blows nobody good. 2. One touch of scandal makes the whole world chin.

See busybody; light: dim light; talebearer; wind: ill wind.

scandalmonger. A prattlesnake.

scar. Not every scar on a man's face has been gotten in a barber shop.

See wrinkle[1].

scarce. When everybody attends to his own business, news is scarce.

scare. Some people are scared of ghosts, but more are scared of guests.

See sense: horse sense[7].

scenery. It's a rare person who can enjoy scenery along the detour.

See highway[2].

scent. See flowers[1]; perfume: expensive perfume.

scheme. Some people do more scheming to get by without working than working to get by without scheming.

See faith: faith, hope & charity.

school. See coach; fish[5]; principal; space; weak[1].

schoolboy. The problems of a schoolboy serve to keep the home sires burning.

schoolhouse. The little red schoolhouse is better than the little-read citizen.

schoolteacher. If children had their way, she would be paid so well that she could retire immediately.

See principal.

schooner. When a sailor sights a schooner, he usually drinks it.

science. Science is always wrong; it never solves a problem without creating ten others.

See monkey[2]; religion[8]; sleep[4].

scientist. One who is always trying to prolong life so we can have time to pay for all the gadgets he invents.

score. A rolling football gathers no score.

Scotch. See college: college courses.

scratch. 1. Many a wound starts from scratch. 2. Some people itch for what they want when they should be scratching for it.

See breeding; home[7]; man: marked man; mosquito[7]; rub.

scratch pad. What the person with an itch to write should use.

screech. Too many persons are enjoying the right of free screech.

screen. See mosquito: smart mosquito; newspaper.

fly screen. A device for keeping insects in the house.

screw. The man who's tight probably has a screw loose somewhere.

sculptor. A poor unfortunate who makes faces and busts.

sea. Days at sea are either gorgeous or disgorgeous.

See diet[2]; island[1]; wave: Waves.

seal. See coat: sealskin coat.

seam. See dressmaker.

seamstress. See ahem.

seasickness. 1. Outward bound. 2. You don't need a doctor to tell you what do about it. 3. An illness in which the stomach goes into reverse: whatever goes down must come up. 4. Many a tourist has wondered what to do about seasickness and then given up.

See boat; ocean: ocean liner; sea.

season. The four seasons are pepper, salt, vinegar, and mustard.

See pride[1]; spring; summer[2]; winter.

seat. The only people who always give up their seats in the bus to others are those who walk to work.

See amendment; lazy: lazy people; politeness[3]; spanking[3]; subway[1]; sweets; tax[2].

aisle seats. The most downtrodden class in modern society are those who sit in aisle seats.

See elevator : elevator man.

back seat. 1. When a woman occasionally does take a back seat, she drives the car from it. 2. The wife who drives from the back seat is no worse than the husband who cooks from the dining-room table.

See driver : backseat driver.

rumble seat. A grumble seat.

See duck[2] ; rump.

second. See husband : second husband ; reducing : reducing exercise ; sight, second sight ; undo.

secret. 1. What we give to others to keep for us. 2. Something either not worth keeping or too good to keep. 3. What a woman can keep with telling effect. 4. What three may keep if two of them are dead. 5. A woman can't keep a secret, nor let anybody else keep one. 6. Nothing circulates so rapidly as a secret. 7. The only secret a woman can keep is the one she doesn't know. 8. When a woman is told a secret, she promises to tell everybody not to tell anybody. 9. When somebody asks if you can keep a secret, it's always somebody who can't.

See alcohol[2] ; betray ; entrust ; gland ; gossip[3] ; hush ; moonshine[2] ; onion[5] ; party[3] ; salary : small salary ; share ; success : secret of success[1].

secret treaty. It's hard to keep a secret ; it's harder to keep a treaty ; but it's hardest to keep a secret treaty secret.

secretary. See education : college education[2].

pretty secretary. A girl who can't add but who can certainly distract.

security. One of the most insecure things in the world.

see. 1. See America first if you would see it last. 2. Seeing is believing, which is why men believe in the modern girl. 3. Women see without looking ; their husbands look without seeing. 4. Love may be blind, but people in love always see much more in each other than other people do.

See believe[2] ; blackout ; burlesque : burlesque girl ; champagne ; dress[4] ; fisherman : fisherman's motto ; ghost[1] ; slim : slim girl ; green ; knit[2] ; marriage : before & after[8] ; miracle ; movies[3] ; nose[8] ; obscene ; parents[3] ; pedestrian[4] ; photograph : passport photograph ; platitude ; town : small town[3].

see through. A woman can see through a man by intuition ; a man needs the sun to see through her.

seed. See florist; wallflower.

seem. To seem to be what we are not is easier than not to be what we seem.

select. The wife who selects everything in the home usually picks the quarrels too.

self-defense. Never strike your child except in self-defense. See marriage: before & after[4]; telephone: telephone pole.

self-denial. The only thing the poor can afford.

self-importance. Usually a case of mistaken nonentity.

selfish. See altruism[1].

selfishness. A vice which no one will forgive in others, and which everyone forgives in himself.

self-love. The kind of love that passeth all understanding.

self-made. A complimentary term for uncomplimentary results.

self-made man. 1. A horrible example of unskilled labor. 2. One who can't blame it on his wife. 3. One who's always proud of a poor job. 4. The man who worships his maker. 5. One who always wants to talk shop. 6. One who has no alibi: he has no one to blame but himself. 7. A person who never gets tired of bragging about his job. 8. A person who would have done better by letting out the contract. 9. The trouble with the self-made man is that he quit the job too soon. 10. Everybody respects a self-made man; it is much better to be made that way than not to be made at all. 11. A self-made man always admits it, and thus relieves the conscience of the rest of the world.

See alteration; hero: hero worshipper; humility.

self-possession. With a young lawyer, self-possession is equal to nine points of the law.

self-possessed woman. One who has failed to acquire a husband.

sell. See match: matches[1]; milliner; restaurant[4]; rope; stall; wedding[4].

Senate. As long as it has the Senate, America will always have one form of air mastery.

senator. 1. There's only one person who can speak louder than a senator, and that's another senator. 2. Any boy may become President, but if he wishes to become a senator he had better begin to save early.

See Spain.

sense. 1. Some people live by their wits; the rest have more sense. 2. Many people have horse sense but few have more sense. 3. The woman who marries a man without a dollar also hasn't any sense. 4. Dollars and sense do not always travel together.

See attract; censor[9]; driver: careless drivers; eccentricity; menace; prude[3]; sight: strange sight; wit: half-wit[2].

common sense. The most uncommon thing in the world.

See wisdom[2].

horse sense. 1. A degree of wisdom that keeps one from betting on the races. 2. Just stable thinking. 3. The ability to say *nay*. 4. What a horse has and what a jackass can never acquire. 5. What the auto will always lack no matter how much it is improved. 6. Something a horse has that keeps him from betting on people. 7. When automobiles first came out, horses were scared of them; that's what you call horse sense.

See advantage[1]; co-operation; driving[1]; government: stable government; nag; rabbit: rabbit's foot.

sensible girl. One who is more sensible than she looks because a sensible girl has more sense than to look sensible.

sixth sense. Some people must have a sixth sense because they show no sign of the other five.

sentence. See chair: electric chair; coma; crime; driving: reckless driving; judge[3]; marriage[2]; preposition; prisoner; proposal[2]; stop[2]; suspend.

life sentence. See house[1]; marriage[17].

sentiment. See romance[4].

separate. If the divorce courts didn't separate some couples, the police would have to.

serenade. To press one's suit.

serge. All that shines is not serge.

serious. 1. Youth is always too serious, and just now it is too serious about frivolity. 2. There is so much humor in the world because there are so many people who take themselves seriously.

See comedy; gravity; waiter[2].

sermon. 1. A moralogue. 2. Angel food.

See gospel; sleep[7].

drowsy sermon. A speech that attracts the pillars of the church and the sleepers.

servant. 1. People who keep servants would like to know how to keep them. 2. Servants are white or black, but more often green. See housework[1].

> **servant problem.** It has become so serious that many housewives are now playing Bridget instead of bridge.

serve. 1. Not every man who serves two masters is a bigamist. 2. Youth must be served, especially at cannibal dinners. 3. One way of making ends meet is to serve ox-tail soup and calves' brains at the same dinner.

See advise: advisory capacity[1]; carry: carry out[1]; tavern.

service. See fast: hunger fast; sex[2].

set. It's easier to set an example than a hen.

See creditor[2]; teeth: false teeth[1]; upset.

> **smart set.** Its members never got that way by listening to one another.

settle. 1. Some men marry poor girls to settle down, and others marry rich ones to settle up. 2. When a couple marries, the girl's father often settles something on them—the rest of the family. 3. First you get married and settle down; then you settle up and get divorced.

See conference[2]; dust[3]; strike[2].

settlement. See romance[4].

settler. History shows that many of America's early settlers didn't pay their bills on time.

See sun.

sew. As ye sew, so shall ye rip.

See graveyard; tiny.

sex. 1. All is not sex that appeals. 2. Religion has done sex a great service by making it a sin.

See Hollywood: Hollywood life; masculine: masculine woman; woman[4, 5, 10].

> **fair sex.** 1. The unfair sex. 2. Whoever gave women this name was a poor judge of justice.

sexes. The three sexes are men, women, and insects.

See coeducation.

shade. See awning; blind: Venetian blinds; prude[4].

shadow. 1. A woman is like your shadow: follow her, she flies; fly from her, she follows. 2. The shadow of a girl's skirt would reach below the knees, if the material were heavy enough to cast a shadow.

shake. See dancer: tap dancer; jam; politician[7]; reducing: reducing exercise.

shape. 1. What a bathing suit takes when a girl's in it. 2. A girl in good shape is often the reason why a man is in bad shape. 3. Few girls are as well-shaped as a good horse.

See spread: middle-age spread.

share. Every woman should have at least one husband to share her joys and sorrows, and her friends' secrets.

sharp. If a husband's words are sharp, maybe it's from trying to get them in edgewise.

See temper[5].

shaving. 1. Some men have such long faces, their barbers ought to charge them double for shaving. 2. Barbers always go over a man's face twice in shaving, if there's any left after the first time.

See barber[1]; cut: short cut; razor; thrift: thrifty man.

clean-shaven man. One who stands close to his razor when he shaves.

sheep. Many a man counts sheep at night because he counted calves by day.

See furs[1]; goat[2]; insomnia[4]; Wall Street: Wall Street men; wool[2].

sheepish. How the cotton in an all-wool suit looks.

sheepskin. See college: college graduate[2]; education: college education[4]; experience: school of experience[3]; leather: shoe leather[2]; pigskin[2].

sheet. Some people sleep between sheets; others sleep between midnight and morning.

See farce.

shekels. In time of war the rich get the shekels and the poor get the shackles.

shell. Many a man comes out of his shell when his wife eggs him on.

shellfish. He's not the only one that has a crab for a mate.

shelter. See air: air raid.

shield. Some men never lie except to shield a woman or themselves.

shin. See bridge: bridge player; chair; man[5, 6]; stockings.

shine. The first thing some people would do if they were in other people's shoes would be to get a shine.

See bootblack; moonshine[1]; serge; sunstroke.

shingle. See education: board of education.

ship. 1. It's always called *she* because the rigging costs so much, and she always keeps a man on the lookout. 2. It's always referred to as *she* because it costs so much to keep one in paint and powder.

See dry dock; Mayflower[1]; ocean: ocean liner; promoter; receivership; sailor[2]; shipment; wave: permanent wave.

shipment. When it goes in a car, it's a shipment; but when it goes in a ship, it's a cargo.

shirk. Many a young man shirks his way through college.

shirker. A person who is clock-eyed.

shirt. 1. Man's bosom friend. 2. It's true that a bachelor has no buttons on his shirt, but then a married man has no shirt.

See horse: race horse.

stuffed shirt. It usually goes with an empty head.

See resort: summer resort[3].

shock. See grain.

shoemaker. If you run into debt with your shoemaker, you can't call your sole your own.

shoes. See duck[1]; education: college education[3]; extremist; feet: big feet[1]; fill[1]; home[3]; shine.

low shoes. They are high these days.

new shoes. They squeak for themselves.

tight shoes. If you want to forget all your troubles, wear tight shoes.

shoot. Many a man brags of his hunting experience though it's chiefly confined to shooting pool, craps, and the bull.

See movies[5].

shop. A man may be forced to shut up shop but you can't force a woman to shut up shoptalk.

See fortune; inventory; rain: rainy day[2]; road[3].

closed shop. One that is air-conditioned.

shopping. 1. Women who go shopping bring back everything but prosperity. 2. Many a man loses his balance when his wife goes shopping.

shoplifter. Bright people pick up things fast, and so do shoplifters.

shoptalk. There's more shoptalk among women who don't work than among women who do.

See self-made: self-made man[5]; shop.

shopworn. All things come to him who waits, but they are apt to be shopworn.

shopworn articles. They often get that way from shopworn women.

short. See artist; farmer: good farmer; man: tall man; memory: good memory[2]; socks[1]; speech: good speech[1]; traffic: rotary traffic.

short girl. It's better to have loved a short girl than never to have loved a tall.

shortcoming. The more a girl tolerates a man's shortcomings, the more she tolerates his long stayings.

See marriage: happy marriage[3].

shorten. Kissing shortens life—single life.

shot. A gangster who works his way to the top of the gang becomes a big shot at.

shoulder. Many a man wishes he had a good head on his shoulders; but many another would prefer a pretty one.

show. 1. Women wear rings to show they're married, while men wear last year's clothes. 2. The girl who wears clothes that show everything should be sure she has something worth showing.

See ability[2]; burlesque; censor[4]; clothes[4]; golfer[5]; keyhole[1]; peep; problem: girl's problem; sense: sixth sense; style; vote: straw vote; wear: women's wear[3]; wit[2].

show-off. One who always shows up in a show-down.

showgirl. More show than girl.

shun. Always be ready to speak your mind, and all your friends will shun you.

shut. 1. If you keep your mouth shut, you'll get credit for knowing what you're talking about. 2. Take a tip from nature: your ears aren't made to shut, but your mouth is.

See eyes[2]; mouth[3]; vague.

shut up. The man who can read his wife like a book, wishes he could shut her up like one.

See public speaker[4]; shop.

shy. A woman is always shy about telling her age—several years shy.

Siamese twins. See twins: Siamese twins.

sick. See homesick[1].

sick people. People who usually complain about their health, except those with rheumatism who can't kick.

sickness. Its four stages are: ill, pill, bill, and will.

side. See Creation; divorce: divorce suit; half: better half[3]; inside; majority[2]; marry: married woman; mind: broadminded; mother-in-law[5]; mugwump; optimist[7]; politics[2]; reducing: reducing exercise; safety: safety zone; statistics[3]; vogue.

shady side. The man who boasts about his family tree probably comes from its shady side.

two sides. 1. There are two sides to every question, and a politician usually takes both. 2. There are two sides to every question—the wrong side and our side.
See bottom[1]; question[1].

winning side. There is no such thing as fighting on the winning side; one fights to find out which is the winning side.

sight. When love begins at first sight, it often ends with a second look.
See girl[2].

far-sighted. The man who thinks he's far-sighted is a poor judge of distance.

first sight. See marriage[12]; time: time-saver.

second sight. The cure for love at first sight.

strange sight. A man talking sense and his wife agreeing with him.

sign. When a married man dreams he's a bachelor, it's a sign he's going to be disappointed when he wakes up.
See etc.; highway[2]; itch[2]; language: sign language; paint: fresh paint; ring: engagement ring; road[2]; sense: sixth sense; stop: stop, look & listen; tack; temper[4]; tracks: railroad tracks; voice[3].

signal. Many a traffic jam is caused by a woman driver who signals she is about to make a turn—and does.
See driver: woman driver[3].

silence. 1. The only successful substitute for brains. 2. It may not be golden but it's worth its weight in gold. 3. Something rarely found in men, women or children. 4. It isn't always golden; sometimes it's just plain yellow. 5. Occasional silence is golden, in wives or conversation.
See beat; golden; radio[1].

silent. See female; stammer.

silent man. 1. The one most worth listening to. 2. The still-life of the party.

silhouette. See nudist[5].

silk. A material which was invented so that women could go naked in clothes.

See America[5].

simmer. Some people summer in the country; others simmer in the city.

See summer[1].

simple. See truth[8].

sin. Nowadays the sins of the children are visited upon the fathers.

See collaboration; forsake; golf[6]; guest: unwelcome guest[3]; installment: installment collector[3]; play: modern plays; providence; quotations; saint; society[1]; Sunday; tabloid[3]; writer: woman writer.

original sin. A misnomer because every kind of sin has been practiced before.

sinning. The best part of repentance.

See cynic[3].

sins of omission. Those we ought to have done and haven't.

wages of sin. 1. They vary with the sinner. 2. Nobody ever objects to a reduction in the wages of sin. 3. They depend on how much the confession magazines are paying.

See debt[4]; depression[5].

sing. Nowadays whatever is not worth saying is sung.

See chorus; contralto; musician: true musician; quartet[2]; safety; scald; song: old songs; voice[2].

radio singing. A crooning achievement.

singing. People who go away to study singing should.

singer. Some singers who have rich voices ought to retire them.

See tune[1]; voice[1].

single. Two can live as cheaply as one, but it's worth the difference to stay single.

See champagne; folly; marry: married life[4]; progeny; shorten.

singly. Misfortune and twins rarely come singly.

See misfortune[1]; together.

singular. See maid: old maid[1]; pants[5]; spinster[2]; trousers.

sinister. The sister of a minister.

sinner. 1. A stupid person who gets found out. 2. The only

difference between the saint and the sinner is that every saint has
a past and every sinner has a future.

sip.   There's many a sip 'twixt the cup and the lip.

siren.   A great help in an air raid, but not when it's a woman.

sister.   Every brother is interested in a sister—if she's someone
else's sister.

See sinister.

sit.   See chic; column: spinal column; committee: standing committee; conference[1]; cream; discover; generation: rising generation[1]; hen[2]; hero: movie hero; skiing; thick[1]; tight[2].

   flagpole sitter.   The only person who never lies down on the
   job.

   sit down.   Many can rise to the occasion, but few know when
   to sit down.

   See rise: early rising[2].

situation.   If you want to flatter somebody, just look serious
and ask him what he thinks of the general situation.

   grave situation.   An undertaker's business.

size.   Size isn't the only difference between a flea and an elephant;
an elephant can have fleas but a flea can't have elephants.

See head[2]; heart: big heart; lot[1]; majority[3].

skeleton.   1. A lot of bones with the people scraped off.   2. The
body with the inside out and the outside off.   3. Every house
has a skeleton but boarding houses have half a dozen.

See corset[2].

   skeleton in the closet.   1. It's usually in the shape of a
   whiskey bottle.   2. A skeleton in the closet rarely has enough
   sense to stay there.   3. There's a skeleton in every closet,
   and some people don't make any bones about it.

skeptical.   Nothing makes a woman more skeptical than when
her husband tells the exact truth.

skier.   One who starts at the top and works his way to the
bottom.

skiing.   A sport that people generally learn in several sittings.

skin.   1. The only thing you can occupy without paying rent.
2. The skin men love to touch is the skin girls love to retouch.
3. Today the college student accumulates the horsehide, the
pigskin, the coonskin, and by the time he gets the sheepskin,
father hasn't much hide left either.

See banana[1, 2]; beauty[1]; boy[1]; catskin; cosmetics[2]; experience: school of experience[3]; pigskin; sable.

skinflint. One who wants to become the wealthiest man in the cemetery.

skip. Give a convict enough rope and he'll skip.

See generation: younger generation[2].

skirt. 1. Once a common noun, but now a mere abbreviation. 2. A garment whose initial length doesn't matter; it's the up-creep. 3. The only thing at mother's knees these days. 4. In the old days the girls used to hold up their skirts when they crossed the streets, but now they hold them down.

See shadow[2]; slip.

> **modern skirts.** 1. They are tight, but the women can't kick. 2. It's high time for the modern skirt.

> **mother's skirts.** A child has to be big enough to take care of himself nowadays before he can hang on to his mother's skirts.

> See chair: high chair.

> **short skirt.** 1. It has plenty of legs to stand on. 2. Many a woman has two slim reasons for not liking short skirts.

> See mosquito[2].

> **woman's skirts.** See coward[2]; hide[2]; magician; pants[4].

skunk. 1. A phew-cat. 2. A pungent pussy.

sky. See disguise[2]; walk: walk on air.

skyscraper. See church: skyscraper churches; giraffe[1].

slacker. A woman who wears slacks.

slacks. 1. Another proof that women wear the pants in the family. 2. The trouble with slacks is that they are not slack enough. 3. Women took to slacks when they couldn't wear short dresses any shorter and wouldn't wear long dresses any longer.

See slacker.

slam. The bridge player who is absent from the game gets the most slams.

slang. See language: colloquial language.

> **saloon slang.** It's usually tavernacular.

slap. See chiropractor; mosquito[3].

slave. See liberty[4]; matrimony: state of matrimony.

sleep. 1. A condition in which some people talk, some walk, and others snore. 2. The most wonderful thing in life because it takes you out of life. 3. The person who lies easily ought to sleep well. 4. Science cannot abolish sleep but babies can. 5. Getting the baby to sleep is hardest when she's about eighteen years old. 6. When a fellow can't sleep nights thinking of the girl he loves, her father probably can't sleep either thinking of him. 7. How late a person sleeps on Sunday morning often depends on the length of the sermon.

See college: college boy[3]; dormitory; floor[1]; henpeck; insomnia[2, 4]; janitor[3]; lie[7]; mosquito[9]; powder: sleeping powder; professor[2]; Rip Van Winkle; sawmill; sermon: drowsy sermon; snore[2], snoring[3]; snorer; stage; story: bedtime story; telegram[2].

sleeptalking. If you want your wife to listen to what you say, talk in your sleep.

See begrudge; edgewise; mumble; nerve; preacher[4].

sleepwalker. The only person who gets his rest and exercise at the same time.

sleepwalking. When a man walks in his sleep he leaves his wife; when he talks in his sleep, his wife leaves him.

sound sleep. 1. Soundless sleep, except with snorers. 2. The sleep you're in when it's time to get up.

sleeve. When a diplomat lays his cards on the table, he usually has another deck up his sleeve.

slim. See dress[2]; skirt: short skirt[2].

slim girl. A slim girl must be seen to be appreciated; a fat girl must be lean to be appreciated.

slip. Nowadays when the skirt goes below the knees, something has probably slipped.

See bottle[2]; cup; hiccup; tongue[2]; wave: Waves.

slogan. America for Americans is a wonderful slogan; but not too much of America for too few Americans.

slouch. The fellow who invented money was a genius, but the one who thought up interest was no slouch.

slow. One objection to evolution is that it is too slow for this age.

See light: traffic light[1]; street.

slush. It's snow matter.

See spring[3].

small. See debt[2]; home[4]; package: small package; vocabulary: woman's vocabulary; wish.

smart. 1. Most men would rather say a smart thing than do a good one. 2. Some children are smart because they have been made to smart.

See children: smart children; clothes: smart clothes; expert: efficiency expert[2]; honest: honest man; society: smart society; whip.

smash. See radio[6].

smell. 1. They that smell least smell best. 2. To a dog the whole world is a smell. 3. The best way to keep fish from smelling is to cut their noses off.

See censer; flattery[1]; perfume[1]; prohibitionist[3]; wedding[2].

smile. See camera; miss[2]; value: face value.

smoke. 1. Smoke and the world smokes with you; swear off and you smoke alone. 2. Smoke affects paint, but not the complexion of women smokers.

See cigar[2]; cigarette; coal[1]; coed[3]; graveyard; missionary[1]; problem: Christmas problem; tobacco: tobacco habit; train[1].

smoking. The best way to give up smoking cigarettes is to smoke cigars.

smoker. See fret.

smooth. The course of two loves never runs smooth.

See golf: golf course[1]; tongue: salesman's tongue.

snake. See scandalmonger.

sneeze. See cold: bad cold; fever: hay fever season.

snob. 1. One who was born with his face lifted. 2. A person who talks as if he had begotten his own ancestors. 3. One who lives in public as the rich do, and in private as the poor do. 4. One who thinks it's his duty to be snooty.

See solitary.

snore. 1. An unfavorable report from headquarters. 2. Sleep and the world sleeps with you; snore and you sleep alone. 3. You can never tell a man's real character, and whether he snores, till you marry him.

See sleep: sound sleep[1].

snoring. 1. Zzzz. 2. Sheet music. 3. Just sleeping out loud. 4. A pleasure that is all yours. 5. You can cure your husband's snoring by kindness, patience, and stuffing an old sock in his mouth.

snorer. Just a sound sleeper.

snow. See slush.

soak. See critic[4]; living: cost of living[7]; water[4].

soap. Soap long deferred maketh the dirt stick.

soft soap. The thing to apply when you get a dirty look from your wife.

See flattery[3]; grit; head: hard-headed man.

soar. When prices soar, so are consumers.

sober. Driving a car while drunk may become almost as dangerous as crossing the street while sober.

See line: straight line.

social. See success: social success; tact[1].

social register. Mostly cash register.

socialism. A system which advocates capitalist punishment.

socialist. An individual who is not an individualist.

society. 1. It covers a multitude of sins. 2. Where girls start in by coming out. 3. To get into it you have to feed people, amuse them, or shock them. 4. What some folks are born in, others are taken in, but most folks pay to get in.

See aloud; arrive; class; dish: chafing dish; earn[2]; Hollywood: Hollywood society.

smart society. It's made up of the worldly, the fleshy, and the devilish.

socks. 1. Short stockings usually worn too long. 2. Some socks don't wear well while others stand up—if worn long enough. 3. Some people are as non-political as a pair of socks: neither right nor left.

See circle: sewing circle; darn[2]; snore: snoring[5]; spats[1]; stockings: women's stockings.

sofa. On a sofa, it's often couch as couch can.

soft. See hardship; heart: soft-hearted woman; liquor[6]; luck: hard luck.

soil. Farmers are not the only ones who make their living from it; consider the laundry.

solace. A woman is a man's solace, but if it wasn't for her he wouldn't need any solace.

soldier. 1. An army man who is first drawn and then quartered. 2. Every war makes soldiers change nearly all their ideas, except their opinion of officers.

sole. See depression[2]; shoemaker.

solemn. It's a solemn thing to be married, but it's a good deal more solemn not to be.

solitary. When a snob grows old, he spends his life in solitary refinement.

somebody. See everybody.

something. 1. A woman simply has to love something, even if it is nothing but a man. 2. Man is always trying to make something for himself rather than something of himself.

See education: educated person; fame[2]; gamble: gambling[2]; nothing[1]; statesman[4].

son. One who usually finishes college and his dad at about the same time.

See college[7]; day[1]; farmer[1, 3]; father: average father, self-made father, wise father; habit[1]; heredity[2]; turn: turn out[2]; wealth: wealthy man.

favorite son. A living proof that you can't trust the judgment of parents.

prodigal son. One who leaves home, and nothing else.

song. See music: modern music; sing.

old songs. They are best because nobody sings them any more.

popular song. 1. The best thing about a popular song is that it is not popular very long. 2. The radio wears out popular songs faster than it does tubes. 3. There are two things that kill a popular song: playing it and singing it.

song hit. If we should lock up all the feeble-minded, who would write our song hits?

song writer. 1. One whose host of imitators died before he was born. 2. A person who was calm and composed. 3. One who does not show the genius of Bach and Beethoven, but whose tunes do. 4. One who takes something composed by one of the masters and decomposes it. 5. One who can't carry a tune but can lift a lot of them. 6. A person who devotes a lifetime to his job without becoming well versed in it.

Southern songs. The radio is such a great educator that even the people down South are beginning to learn Southern songs.

sophisticated. A man is drunk when he feels sophisticated and can't pronounce it.

sophistication. The art of admitting that the unexpected is just what you anticipated.

soprano. It took the short-wave radio to teach people that every country in the world is full of sopranos.

sorrow. See irrigate.

sorry. Don't feel sorry for yourself; feel sorry for those who have to live with you.

See make-up[2].

soul. See heel; suit: bathing suit[3].

sound. It is possible to make a sound argument without making a lot of noise.

See argument[2]; business[2]; complaint; convention: political convention; fascist; home: American home; opinion[1]; price: falling price; professor[1]; snorer; soup[1]; violin; Washington, D. C.[3].

musical sounds. None of the anthropoid apes can emit musical sounds; but, on the other hand, none of them tries to.

soup. 1. An appetizing food, or maybe it only sounds that way. 2. Persons who like music with their meals should drink soup. See mustache[1]; roll; water[1].

alphabet soup. A dish made up of silent letters and noisy liquid.

sour. 1. The surest way to keep milk from souring is to leave it in the cow. 2. Milk at least has the decency to go sour when it is no longer fit to drink.

See breakfast: Sunday breakfast; sarcasm; sarcastic.

source. 1. The original source of evil was the apple source. 2. What's sauce for the goose is the source of propaganda.

souse. A teetotaler is afraid to take his first drink; a souse is afraid to take his last.

South. See backside; song: Southern songs; tobacco[1]; winter[6].

souvenir. A far-fetched reminder.

sow. See gardener; wild: wild oats.

space. The only thing some pupils take up in school.

See parking: parking space[1].

wide open spaces. See chewing gum[2]; sandwich: western sandwich.

spade. Always call a spade a spade, especially in a card game. See gardening[1]; hand[2].

spaghetti. This should not be cooked too long, at least not over three feet.

Spain. Spain has her matadors, the United States her senators.

span. Some people would look more spic if they didn't have so much span.

Spanish. The language that many a tourist speaks like a native—like a native American.

spanking. 1. It is inflicted on one end to impress the other. 2. It takes less time than reasoning and penetrates sooner to the seat of memory. 3. Many parents are not on spanking terms with their children. 4. Spank your child every day; if you don't know the reason why, he does.
See child³; grandmother²; temperament.

spare. People who have an hour to spare usually spend it with someone who hasn't.
See mind³; rod.

spare parts. If nature had foreseen the automobile, she would have provided spare parts for pedestrians.

spats. 1. A dignified means by which men hide holes in their socks. 2. A covering for the ankles, sometimes confused with long underwear.

speak. The longer the spoke, the greater the tire.
See ass; Bostonian; eventually; golfer²; insult²; keyhole⁴; mirror²; miserable: miserable woman; orator²; philosophy⁵; shun; Spanish; talk: talk about²; woman⁷,⁸.

speaker. See calendar².

after-dinner speaker. 1. A person who has only a few words to say but who seldom stops when he has said them. 2. After-dinner speakers are always after dinner.

after-dinner speaking. A pastime monopolized by men because women can't wait that long.

halting speaker. One who umphasizes every other word.

loud speaker. 1. There are none so deaf as those who have a loud-speaker. 2. The loudest speaker doesn't always get the best reception.
See radio².

public speaker. See public speaker.

public speaking. See public speaking.

speaking terms. 1. People who are not on speaking terms are usually on spiking terms. 2. Men who think they are on speaking terms with some women are merely on listening terms.

specialist. In the old days a doctor couldn't get rid of a troublesome patient by sending him to a specialist.

nerve specialist. All work and no play makes jack for the nerve specialist.

spectacles. 1. The eyes have it. 2. Nature is wonderful: a million years ago she didn't know we were going to wear spectacles, yet look at the way she placed our ears.

speech. 1. A speech is like a baby: easy to conceive, hard to deliver. 2. The female of the speeches is deadlier than the male. 3. If some men's speeches don't reach down to posterity, it isn't because they aren't long enough.

See bore[5]; chewing gum[1]; filibusterer; wife[5]; wisdom[3].

> after-dinner speeches. 1. Usually a diarrhea of words and a constipation of thought. 2. They may be boring but they give us the low-down on a lot of people we used to think were bright.

> free speech. 1. Women who believe in free speech are certainly free enough with theirs. 2. There's an important distinction between free speech and cheap talk.
> See prudence.

> good speech. 1. A good speech, like a woman's skirt, should be long enough to cover the subject and short enough to create interest. 2. A good speech has a good beginning and a good ending, both of which are kept very close together.

speechless. If stupid people said what they thought, they'd be speechless.

speed. To speed is human; to get caught, a fine.
See haste[1]; light: traffic light[1]; waist.

> speed limit. See cyclone.

> speed up. The reason a driver speeds up when he sees you is so that he can slow down when he gets in front of you.

speeder. If speeders knew they were driving to jail, they wouldn't be in such a hurry.

speedometer. You can't always tell how far a couple has gone in a car merely by looking at the speedometer.

spell. See synonym; tax: income tax[2]; vocabulary: large vocabulary[1].

spend. It's never too late to spend.
See boss[3]; budget[2]; capitalist; chewing gum[5]; economy[3]; evening; extravagant; haste[2]; ideal: ideal man[2]; progress[4]; successful: successful man[2]; vacation[3].

spendthrift. The more checks he has, the faster he goes.

spinach. It's difficult to say anything nice about it except that there are no bones in it.

See gold[2].

spinster. 1. A bachelor's wife. 2. The most singular of women. 3. An unmarried woman who lives longer than a married woman because while there's hope there's life.

spirit. The difference between spirit doctors and doctored spirits is that the latter really show you the next world.

See ghost; hiccough; price[3]; whiskey[6].

spirits. See drink: mixed drink; drunkard[1]; flesh.

spiritual. See priest.

spiritualist. The well-known circulating medium—the medium that most of the spiritualists are really looking for.

spiritualism. Gnome man's land.

spit. 1. Do not spit if you expect to rate as a gentleman. 2. Don't spit; remember the Johnstown flood. 3. If you spit on the floor at home, spit here; we want you to feel at home.

spitz. There's no danger when it rains cats and dogs, but when it's spitz dogs, look out.

spoil. See rod.

spoils. Set a thief to catch a thief, and they'll divide the spoils.

See grandmother[2].

sponge. See friendship[3]; Sunday.

sponger. A person who is either clean or mean.

spoon. 1. The man who is born with a silver spoon in his mouth rarely makes much stir with it. 2. When a politician is born with a silver spoon in his mouth, it has a hotel name on it.

sports. See fight: prize fighting[1]; fishermen[1]; lion; skiing.

See also baseball; fishing; football; golf; etc.

good sport. One who will always let you have your way.

indoor sport. See bridge[1]; love[5].

spot. See hunter: big game hunter[1]; laughter; leopard.

spread. The three quickest ways of spreading news are: telephone, telegram, and tell-a-woman.

See propaganda[1]; restaurant[1].

middle-age spread. The destiny that ends our shapes.

spring. 1. Formerly a delightful season, but now obsolete except in poetry. 2. The season of balls: golf, tennis, base, and moth. 3. A season seldom as slushy as the poetry it inspires. 4. The time of year when farmers and golfers start their plowing.   5. The season when boys begin to feel gallant, and girls buoyant.   6. Spring isn't the only season it's windy in Washington.   7. We all spring from animals, but some people didn't spring far enough.

See fancy; frog; pride[1]; winter[5]; year: leap year[1].

spurn.   When a girl is sure of a man, she usually spurns him on.

spy.   See gossip[6].

squander.   1. It is sad to see people squander money and know you cannot help them.   2. Take care of the pennies and the dollars will be squandered by your heirs.

square.   A nation is not made great by the number of square miles it contains but by the number of square people it contains. See chess; circle: family circle; earth[2]; indigestion[4]; round[2]; telephone: telephone booth[1]; triangle[3].

squeak.   The man who is a big noise in the office is only a little squeak at home.

See oil[1]; shoes: new shoes.

squeal.   The only part of the hog the packers waste, but the consumers supply it.

squeeze.   See friend: close friend; loose: loose woman.

stable.   See etiquette[2]; government: stable government; sense: horse sense.

stage.   It's full of people who became actors because they liked to sleep late.

See ability[2]; center; education[2]; foul: foul play.

stagger.   It's hard to tell some drunkards apart, they stagger so much alike.

stall.   The seller's problem is to keep the stall out of installment.

stammer.   1. To st-st-stutter.   2. The best way to keep from stammering is to remain silent.

stand.   See candidate[1]; careful; drinking[2]; figure[3]; golf[3]; ideal: man's ideal; modern: modern man; newspaper; political: political platform[1, 2]; politician[2]; socks[2]; standpatter; Star-Spangled Banner; straphanger; tree[1].

standpatter.   The most annoying thing about him is not his stand but his patter.

star.   See movies: movie star; press: press agent[2]; producer: movie producer; telescope.

stare.   It isn't the clothes that make the men stare; it's the women in them.

See virtue[1].

Star-Spangled Banner. The only way to get some people to stand on their own feet is to play the Star-Spangled Banner. See American[2].

start. The trouble with many people is that they take so long to start to begin to get ready to commence.

See day[1]; club: glee club; scratch[1]; successful: successful man[1].

starve. See dog[4]; honesty[6]; icebox; moth[3]; nation: Christian nations; reducing: reducing machine; teacher.

state. A woman can get a divorce only in certain States, but a man can get a divorce no matter what state he's in.

See insanity; Kentucky; matrimony: state of matrimony; next; politician: active politician; statement; statesman[7]; tobacco[1]; Utopia.

statement. Their statements show the mental state of statesmen. See narrow.

statesman. 1. A dead politician. 2. One who tries to solve grave problems which wouldn't exist if there were no statesmen. 3. A man who finds out which way the crowd is going, then jumps in front and yells like blazes. 4. One who tries to do something for everybody; a politician tries to do everybody for something. 5. One who tries to arouse the nation, while the politician tries to lull it to sleep. 6. A politician thinks of the next election; a statesman thinks of the next generation. 7. A statesman thinks he belongs to the state but a politician thinks the state belongs to him.

See statement.

statistician. 1. One who can go directly from an unwarranted assumption to a preconceived conclusion. 2. A fact man, and nobody loves a fact man. 3. Give a statistician some facts and he will draw his own confusions. 4. If all the statisticians were placed end to end, they would not reach a conclusion. 5. Statisticians have figured the time lost in every business operation but their own.

statistics. 1. Statistics may be made to prove anything—even the truth. 2. Facts are stubborn things, but statistics are more pliable. 3. Statistics are like witnesses: they will testify for either side. 4. Statistics prove that fifty percent of the married people in the United States are women.

See birth[1]; lie[4].

traffic statistics. Doctors say Americans are living too fast and traffic statistics show they are dying the same way.

statue. See disarmament; statute.

status quo. A Latin phrase to describe the mess we're in.

statute. The only things more amusing than some of our statues are some of our statutes.

stay. 1. Some people can stay longer in an hour than others can in a week. 2. When company stays too long, just treat them like members of the family and they'll soon leave.

See height; installment: installment buying[5]; mother-in-law[2, 3]; parking[3]; reform[1]; shortcoming; skeleton: skeleton in the closet.

steak. See painting; waitress[2].

steal. See goods: stolen goods; moral: morals[2]; nervous; vote.

steam. Water gone crazy with the heat.

steer. Bulls and bears aren't responsible for as many stock losses as bum steers.

stenographer. The sudden entrance of a wife has forced many a stenographer to change her position.

See ability: executive ability; dictation; efficient; office[2].

fast stenographer. The kind a businessman prefers.

step. See steps; suicide[3].

goose step. See descend; Nazi: Nazi youth.

stepfather. A father who steps out.

step-ins. Watch your step-ins.

See instep.

steps. They should be taken to make lazy people walk.

See gas; stepfather.

stew. The man who is always in a stew generally goes to pot.

stick. See collector[2]; courtship[3]; dough[2]; perseverance.

stigma. Any stigma will do to beat a dogma.

still. The product of the still makes most men noisy.

See husband: peaceful husband; moonshine[2]; parents: well-behaved parents; water: still water.

sting. The *b* in debt is silent, but it supplies the sting.

stink. See guest[2].

stitch. A stitch in time saves embarrassing exposure.

stock. An unreliable commodity bought and sold by gamblers: if you win, it's an investment; if you lose, it's speculation.

See railroad[1]; steer; Wall Street: Wall Street men; water[4, 6].

stock market. 1. People who play it are often led astray by false profits. 2. People who play it are either bulls or bears, but more often asses. 3. You can make money out of the stock market—if you stay out of it. 4. You can't fool with the stock market without the stock market fooling you. 5. Many a man who plays the stock market soon finds out that Wall Street is a one-way street.

See gentleman[9].

stockbroker. The more you visit your stockbroker today, the more you'll visit your pawnbroker tomorrow.

stockings. They cover a multitude of shins.

See darn[1]; feet: big feet.

stocking run. It's on its last leg.

women's stockings. They may not be more durable than men's socks but they have a longer run.

stomach. 1. An infernal organ of the body. 2. It's a strong stomach that has no turning. 3. The way to a man's heart is through his stomach, but who wants to go through his stomach? See burlesque: burlesque dancers; child[1]; cocktail; desert; dyspepsia[1]; seasickness[3]; success[2]; surgery; wrestler.

stone. See diamond[2]; house[2]; throw.

rolling stone. 1. A rolling stone gathers no boss. 2. A rolling stone gathers no moss, but very often remorse.

Stone Age. The period in history when people were petrified.

stop. 1. It's a wise answer that knows when to stop. 2. Some wives can't even send a telegram without saying *stop* after every sentence.

See bachelor[3]; clock[2]; club: glee club; crossing: grade crossing; drinking[1]; driver: woman driver[2]; will: will power[2].

stop, look & listen. Marriage is like a railroad sign: when you see a pretty girl, you stop; then you look; and after you're married, you listen.

See bus[1]; censorship; crash; motor.

sudden stop. It's never the fall that injures; it's the sudden stop.

storage. The only logical explanation for the price of coal is that the earth has begun to charge storage.

store. See inventory.

general store. A store that has everything in it but a general.

stork. 1. The bird with the big bill. 2. The only thing that discriminates in favor of the poor. 3. Most folks could manage

the wolf at the door if only the stork wouldn't fly in at the
window.   4. Many a mother should have thrown away the baby
and kept the stork.

See bird[1]; obstetrician; pregnant.

storm.   See engagement[1]; peace[3].

story.   Some writers do a story every month and think nothing
of it; their readers think likewise.

See bore[4]; laugh: laugh last[8]; man: second-story man; match[2];
truth[2]; writer: pulp writer.

> **bedtime story.**   The kind of tale that keeps one awake at night,
> or that puts one to sleep.

> **detective stories.**   1. Pure fiction, which is more than can be
> said for lots of other stories.   2. They have gone so far that
> the only murder suspect left now is the reader.

> **off-color story.**   If the truth were told about some blondes, it
> would be an off-color story.

> **radio story.**   You can always give it a happy ending by turn-
> ing the dial.

> **risqué storyteller.**   The low-life of the party.

straddle.   No politician ever builds his fences so high that they
can't be comfortably straddled.

straight.   1. Nowadays a woman looks in the mirror to be sure
that her hat isn't on straight.   2. A girl may be bent on
matrimony and still be perfectly straight.   3. It's better to go
straight than to move in the best circles.

See crooked; heaven[2]; liquor[6]; pedestrian[12].

strain.   The reason polygamy would never work in this country
is because the divorce courts couldn't stand the strain.

See fortune-teller.

strange.   See chivalry; publicity[5]; sight: strange sight.

stranger.   See philanthropy[2]; telephone[2]; thought[2]; truth[2, 4, 6].

straphanger.   His complaint is one of long standing.

straw.   Something a drowning man will clutch at; so will a
thirsty one.

See wind[2].

streamline.   It usually goes with extreme lines.

See car: streamlined car.

street.   Something torn up by fast drivers and slow contractors.
See avenue; driver: bad driver[2]; fill[2]; wear[1].

Main Street.   See Main Street.

one-way street. 1. The nice thing about a one-way street is that you can be bumped only in the rear. 2. The advantage of a one-way street is that the pedestrian knows from which direction he's going to be knocked down.

See stock: stock market[5].

street cleaner. 1. The only man who disagrees that it's a one-horse town. 2. The only man who is sure to get something from following the horses.

strength. See chorus; onion[1].

stretch. See check: rubber check.

stretching. An aid to health, but it doesn't seem to help truth any.

strike. 1. It's never a hit. 2. The best way to settle a strike is to strike a settlement. 3. Even in baseball a man is entitled to more than one strike.

See baseball; gentleman[1, 5]; labor; lightning; maid: old maid[3]; safety: safety zone; scab; self-defense; telephone: telephone pole; typewriter.

string. See fishnet; remember; violin.

strip-tease. See burlesque.

stripper. The only girl who feels overdressed in a bathing suit.

strip-tease dancer. A girl who never worries about getting ahead because she doesn't need one.

stripe. See career: checkered career; college: college boy[1].

strong. 1. Man wants but little here below but wants that little strong. 2. If seven days make one week, how many days will make one strong?

See cheese: cheese business; conscience: international conscience; eyes: black eyes[1]; eyesight; housework[4]; obstinacy; weak[2]; wink[1].

stubborn. See fact; firmness; quack; statistics[2]; wrinkle[1].

student. Most students major in alibiology.

See college[6]; honor: honor system; lecture; liquor[5]; professor[2].

study. See postgraduate.

stuff. See doctrine; research; resort: summer resort[3]; snore: snoring[5]; taxidermist[1]; wood.

stupid. Some people are born this way and constantly increase their birthright.

See chastity[2]; dumb; movie: movie titles; peer[1]; speechless; understand[1].

stupidity. It's not the heat, it's the stupidity.

- See limit.

stutter. The only way to get a word in now and then after you're married is to marry a woman who stutters.

See minister: stuttering minister; stammer.

style. Many a woman shows a lot of style, and many a style shows a lot of woman.

See brassiere[5]; brevity; design; fashion[2]; opinion[3]; royalty.

out of style. Time was when a girl who had nothing to wear was out of style.

stylist. One who knows all the latest wrinkles in clothes that won't wrinkle.

subject. 1. Your knowledge of love depends on the way you grasp the subject. 2. The best fools the world has ever produced had nothing to say on the subject.

See expert[2]; fanatic[3]; ignorant[1]; reflection.

subscription. If you want to make sure that what you write will be accepted by a magazine, write a check for a year's subscription.

substitute. See beauty[3]; lie[1]; rabbit: rabbit's foot; silence[1].

subway. 1. A place so crowded that even the men can't all get seats. 2. People who ride in it are always in a hole.

See travel[3].

subway contractor. One who begins at the bottom and works his way sideways.

succeed. See cry[1]; excess; manufacturer; trombonist.

success. 1. The end of hope. 2. It gives a man a big head, and also a big stomach. 3. The reward of everyone who looks for trouble. 4. It is determined by determination. 5. Thoroughly planning your work and then thoroughly working your plan.

See diamond[2]; get[2]; pluck; public speaking[2]; recede.

howling success. Marriage turns out to be a howling success only after a baby is born.

husband's success. A woman is usually responsible for her husband's success because of the money she makes it necessary for him to make.

ladder of success. 1. Many a girl climbs it wrong by wrong. 2. Many a girl climbs it lad by lad.

road to success. It's paved with good inventions.

secret of success. 1. A secret to many people. 2. It's known only to those who have not succeeded.

social success. The infinite capacity for being bored.

successful. See conceit[4]; publicity[1]; writer[1].

successful man. 1. One who starts at the bottom and wakes up. 2. One who can earn more than his wife can spend. 3. One who gathers a fortune he doesn't need to leave to people who don't deserve it.

successful people. Those who didn't have the advantages others had.

sucker. 1. Little girls want an all-day sucker; big girls want one just for the evening. 2. There's still one sucker born every minute, but the trouble is he hasn't got anything you can take.

See swindler.

sue. See gold: gold digger[6]; promise: breach of promise[1].

suffer. See charity[2].

sufficient. A word to the wife is rarely sufficient.

See yes[3].

sugar. 1. If you don't like granulated sugar, you can lump it. 2. If you swallow hard sugar, you get a lump in your throat.

See uncanny.

suggestion. 1. A hintimation. 2. An ounce of suggestion is worth a pound of lure.

See tax: tax suggestions.

suicide. 1. The last thing a person should do. 2. Suicide is despise of life. 3. The easiest way to commit suicide is to take gas or step on it.

See pessimist[11]; preventive.

suit. Some women wear the pants in the family, but others wear the whole suit.

See career: checkered career; college: college boy[1]; frankness; serenade; sheepish; sheet; try: try on[1].

bathing suit. 1. A garment with no hooks but plenty of eyes on it. 2. Merely a fragment of decency. 3. Brevity is the soul of it. 4. A garment that holds fast going around the curves. 5. Brevity is the soul of wit, and the sole charm of a woman's bathing suit. 6. A bathing suit may let the water in, but it doesn't let the dirt out. 7. Those who censor the modern bathing suit have scant reason for doing so. 8. A bathing suit, like a barbed-wire fence, is designed to protect the property without obstructing the view.

See bait[2]; brawn; shape[1]; strip-tease: stripper; thigh.

dress suit. See repartee[2]; rhetoric.

two-pants suit. 1. The best costume for a chess player. 2. Because a man buys a two-pants suit, it doesn't mean he intends to lead a double life.

sum. If you can't get a sum of money, get some.

summer. 1. The good old simmer time. 2. An oppressive season invented by summer resort owners and by railroad and steamship companies. 3. The advantage of summer is that if you don't pay your bills, your creditors think it's because you are away.

See air[3]; baseball: baseball season; climate: temperate climate; drawers[2]; fall; fly: horse flies; furs[2]; hotel[2]; resort; simmer; swallow; thermometer[3]; winter[2].

summer resort. See resort: summer resort.

sun. The oldest settler in the west.

See doctor[4]; eclipse; family: family tree[5]; moonshine[1]; rise: early rising[1]; see: see through; sunstroke.

Sunday. A sponge to wipe out all the sins of the week.

See accident: auto accidents[4]; Decoration Day; golf[6]; pray; sleep[7]; town: small town[2].

Sunday afternoon. If all the autos in the world were laid end to end, it would be Sunday afternoon.

sunrise. See day[1].

sunshine. See nose: red nose.

sunspot. See freckle.

sunstroke. What you get if you make hay while the sun shines.

superfluous. A word to the wise is superfluous.

superstition. A premature explanation overstaying its time.

See tracks: railroad tracks.

supply. See price[1]; squeal.

supply & demand. 1. The trouble with the law of supply and demand is that those who have the supply do the demanding. 2. The law of supply and demand determines the price of everything: you supply what the profiteers demand.

See amend; talk[3]; trouble[4].

support. 1. Only the brave deserve the fair but only the rich can support them. 2. Another bar to marriage nowadays is that a man can't support the government and a wife on one income. 3. A father can support a dozen children, but a dozen children cannot support a father.

See atheist[1]; hold: hold up; modern: modern girl[3]; prejudice[2]; racketeer[3]; suspenders.

suppress. When better books are suppressed, more people will read them.

See Bible[2].

Supreme Court. See court: Supreme Court.

sure. You can't be sure of certain things.

See crossing; friendship[4]; golf[8]; prophet; recover; spurn; train[2].

surgeon. One who bleeds for his fellowmen.

See corn[1]; inside: inside information.

plastic surgeon. One who maims to please.

surgery. In surgery also, the way to a man's heart is through his stomach.

surrender. See engagement[2].

suspect. See husband: conceited husband, educated husband; story: detective stories[2].

suspend. In the past, prisoners were suspended; now only sentences are.

suspenders. Some men won't wear suspenders to support their pants because their pants never did anything to support them. See pessimist[2].

suspense. See lawsuit[1, 3].

swallow. 1. One swallow doesn't make a summer, but too many swallows make a fall. 2. One swallow doesn't make a summer, but it breaks a New Year's resolution.

See defeat; flattery[1]; frog; heartburn[2]; insult[1]; lark[2]; pride[2].

swamp. A man who sits in a swamp all day waiting to shoot a duck, will kick if his wife has dinner ten minutes late.

swat. The radio will never take the place of the newspaper because you can't swat flies with it.

swear. 1. We swear off on New Year's and after that we swear off—and on. 2. About the time a man is cured of swearing, another income tax is due. 3. Women who swear they've never been kissed, can't be blamed for swearing. 4. It's always swear weather when good fellows golf together.

See angry[2]; liar[4]; marriage: before & after[9].

sweat. See frau; lawyer[7].

sweep. See room.

sweet. See sweets.

sweetheart. A sweet tart.

See letter: love letter[2]; make up[2]; place[2].

sweets. Girls who eat a lot of sweets will soon develop bigger seats.

See advertisement; courtship[2]; eat[2]; revenge[2]; sweetheart.

swell. See celebrity; congressman[1]; responsibility.

swift. See navy.

swim. The girl who loves to swim always complains that washing dishes spoils her hands.

swimming instructor. A holdup man.

swimming pool. A crowd of people with water in it.

swimmer. Many a swimmer has been killed in a low dive.

See diva.

swindler. Usually a mere sucker can locate a swindler even when the most skilled detectives are baffled.

swindler's son. A gyp off the old block.

swine. See fat.

swing. The musician who invented swing ought to.

swing band. A group of musicians who are paid for playing static.

See band; revolver.

Swiss cheese. See cheese.

switch. That which regulates everything in the modern home except the children.

sword. See pen; pension; pun[4].

sycophant. One who hopes to lift himself up by his bootlicks.

syllable. See magistrate; politician[15].

sympathizer. A fellow that's for you as long as it doesn't cost anything.

sympathy. What one girl offers another in exchange for details.

syndicate. The way of the transgressor is syndicated.

See writer: woman writer.

synonym. The word you use when you can't spell the word you want.

See gift[1].

syntax. It has nothing to do with paying for your fun.

system. See Adam: Adam & Eve[1]; dancer: fan dancer[1].

table 275 **talebearer**

T

table. See club: night club; cover: cover charge[2]; hungry; thirteen[2].

tabloid. 1. A screamlined newspaper. 2. A newspaper with a permanent crime wave. 3. It covers a multitude of sins. 4. The course of true love never runs in the tabloids. 5. The voice of the tabloids is the vice of the people. 6. Tabloids are based upon the principle that a little child shall read them. 7. A tabloid's idea of heaven is a murder in a divorce court. 8. Tabloids have contributed much to crime, and vice versa.
See woman: woman's place.

tabloid reader. One who just scums through the tabloids.

tack. It's a sure sign somebody has been thinking of you when you find a tack in your chair.
See rise: early rising.

tact. 1. Social lying. 2. A man's ability to convince his wife that a woman looks stout in a fur coat. 3. What some people have, whereas others tell the truth.
See age[4]; far.

social tact. The ability to make your company feel at home even though you wish they were.

tactless people. They suffer from chronic indiscretion.

tail. See dachshund[3]; enthusiasm[2].

tailor. 1. The man who cuts everybody. 2. The only one who is satisfied with an increase in rents. 3. One who takes your measure on first sight, gives you a fit, sews you up, and follows suit until paid. 4. It takes nine tailors to make a man, and one-third of them get paid for doing it.
See retailer.

take. See dictator[1]; generous: generous men; gold: gold digger[8]; guest: unwelcome guest[1]; headache[1]; kiss[17]; leave[3]; philanthropist[2]; philanthropy[1]; politician[3]; receiver; sucker[2]; worse[2].

take-off. See burlesque.

tale. See medium; rumor[3]; widow[3].

talebearer. A person who puts two and two together and makes a scandal out of it.

talent. See genius[1]; writer[1].

talk. 1. Talk is cheap except when you hire a lawyer. 2. When some women talk, no one can get a word in sledgewise. 3. Talk is cheap, because the supply always exceeds the demand. 4. The man who talks to himself never knows it; he thinks someone is listening.

See back[1]; barber[4]; bore[1, 3]; catalogue; child[3]; Congress[4]; films; knit: knitting; libelous; marriage[29]; money[6]; mouth[2]; pantomime; parents: well-behaved parent; quarrel[1]; speech: free speech[2]; tongue: mother tongue; voice[2]; windbag.

back talk. It's more honest than behind-back talk.
See writer[2].

talk about. 1. The only thing worse than being talked about is not being talked about. 2 Even when a woman doesn't know another well enough to speak to, she knows her well enough to talk about. 3. Once there were things people couldn't talk about, but now they can't talk about anything else.

See clergyman; ether; ghost[1]; gossip[2]; hear[3]; lover[2]; marriage: before & after[2]; party: hen party; plenty; preacher[2]; public speaker[2]; weather[1].

talkative woman. One who is always chatterboxing.

talking machine. God make the first one, but Edison made the first one that could be cut off.

talker. See public speaker.

dry talker. One who is usually all wet.

women talkers. There are two types of women talkers: the inimitable and the illimitable.

tan. Girls used to hide their tans; now they tan their hides.
See tourist[2].

tantrum. A bicycle built for two.

tapeworm. Another mouth to feed.
See bureaucrat.

tariff. When our country enacts it, it's a protective tariff; when a foreign country adopts it, it's a tariff war.

permanent tariff. One intended to last till the next election.

tariff supporter. One who believes a thing of duty is a joy forever.

taste. 1. There's no accounting for taste, unless it's the taste of lipstick. 2. Do not do unto others as you would that they should do unto you; their tastes may not be the same. 3. It is only when a missionary is captured and eaten by cannibals that they get their first taste of religion.

See food; power: water power.

bad taste. See lipstick[2].

good taste. See keyhole[1]; wear: women's wear[3].

tavern. Some taverns don't serve women at the bar; you have to bring your own.

See slang: saloon slang.

tax. 1. The only thing that defies the law of gravitation. 2. That which makes the seat of government uncomfortable. 3. If it were only as easy for people to raise taxes as it is for Congress.

See certain; congressman[3]; conservative; death; dodge; inevitable; inherit; painless; pax; revolve; taxi[3].

amusement tax. It's no laughing matter.

income tax. 1. It may cost you a lot of money, but think how it develops your brains. 2. The months during which we feel free from income tax worries are those that have an x in their spelling. 3. The only thing that's worse than having to pay an income tax is not having to pay one. 4. The person who saves his money to pay his income tax will have to borrow some to live on.

See patriot: patriotic people; poorhouse; swear[2].

income tax return. 1. The most imaginative fiction being written today. 2. When a person has untold wealth, it doesn't appear on his income tax return.

See exemption.

tax cut. The kindest cut of all.

tax suggestions. A tax on tax suggestions ought to fill the treasury.

taxation. See alimony[1]; redistribute.

taxi. 1. Where all sorts of things are lost, including the lives of the passengers. 2. Everything comes to him who waits for taxis on rainy days, except taxis.

See aviation[3].

taxi driver. 1. A man who drives away customers. 2. One who runs into so many interesting people. 3. The man who knows most about love. 4. One who goes through life just missing everything.

taxi fare. It's worth the taxi fare to feel you don't care what happens to the fenders.

taxidermist. 1. A man who knows his stuff. 2. One who can mount any animal except a horse.

taxpayer. A person who resents that death and taxes don't come in that order.

tea. See tease[2].

afternoon tea. Giggle, gabble, gobble, git.

teach. See teaching.

teacher. A person who swore he would starve before teaching and has been doing both ever since.
See experience[6]; honor: honor system; whip.

kindergarten teacher. One who knows how to make the little things count.

teaching. 1. What a person takes to when he is incapable of learning. 2. He who can, does; he who can't, teaches.
See religion[7].

secret of teaching. Pretending that you have known all your life what you learned this afternoon.

teacup. See fortune-teller.

tears. The refuge of plain women but the ruin of pretty ones.
woman's tears. The greatest water power known to man.

tease. 1. It is safer to tease a dog than a woman. 2. The attractive clothes that women wear to teas are worn to tease.
See appetizer; travel: travel folder.

tee. When a golfer misses his drive, he expresses himself to a tee.

teeth. Be true to your teeth or they will be false to you.
See age: middle age[2]; dentist[3]; Elks[1]; fall: fall out; fingernails[2]; life[1]; platitude; salesman[3]; tooth.

false teeth. 1. More women than men have them because women wear out the original sets with their tongues. 2. Nothing that is false ever does anybody any good—except false teeth.

teethe. Adam and Eve had many advantages, but the principal one was that they escaped teething.

teetotaler. 1. One who refuses to have his portrait done except in water colors. 2. Among teetotalers water flows like wine.
See bar: behind the bars; souse.

telegram. 1. The only place where words, not deeds, count.

2. A form of correspondence sent by a man in a hurry and carried by a boy in his sleep.

See love[7]; spread; stop[2].

telephone. 1. An object which rings when the only person at home is taking a bath. 2. A wonderful instrument; it connects you with so many strangers. 3. A device which makes it easy to distinguish voices and hard to extinguish them. 4. An invention which takes away some of the advantages of making a disagreeable person keep his distance. 5. One man's telephone is another man's wrong number.

See convenience; guess[2]; housewife: typical housewife; impossible; inform: best-informed woman; nickel[1, 3]; repeat[2]; spread.

telephone booth. 1. A good place to square yourself. 2. A vertical coffin where sweet dispositions are buried. 3. It's no fun to kiss a girl over the phone unless you are in the same booth with her. 4. If a woman stays more than ten minutes in a telephone booth while others are waiting, she deserves the wrong number she gets. 5. If you want privacy, go to a telephone booth, put in a nickel, and you'll find yourself cut off from the world.

telephone directory. See Bible[3].

telephone operator. 1. The girl who always has rings in her ears. 2. One whose job is neither a trade nor a profession; it's a calling. 3. She's like a saint: there's a continual hello around her head. 4. A man should be careful about marrying one for she seldom rings true. 5. Sometimes it seems that anyone can get your number better than the telephone operator can.

telephone pole. It never strikes an automobile except in self-defense.

telescope. It will magnify a star, but it has nothing on a Hollywood press agent.

tell. 1. The man who tells his wife everything, knows nothing. 2. You can tell a married woman, but you can't tell her much. 3. It is safest to tell your wife everything, but tell her before someone else does. 4. Everything you tell a woman goes in one ear and out over the back fence. 5. Parents embarrassed by small children know it is the little things that tell.

See bore[2, 6]; egotist[1]; expert: military expert: golfer[1]; half:

better half[1]; miracle; newlywed; secret[3, 8]; spread; time: good time; word: few words[3].

temper. 1. The only thing you can lose and still have. 2. A thing that improves the longer you keep it. 3. What you lose but always find again. 4. To lose it is the sign of a weak mind; to keep it is the sign of a weak backbone. 5. That quality which, when lost, makes a knife blade dull and a woman's tongue sharp. 6. Keep your temper—nobody wants it. 7. When a husband loses his temper, he usually finds his wife's.

See temperamental: temperamental person.

even-tempered person. One who is always mad.

temperament. An artistic temperament is seldom recognized until it is too late to spank.

temperamental. See girl[6].

temperamental person. One who is ninety percent temper and ten percent mental.

temperance. It takes some people's breath away.

temptation. 1. If you resist it, it may never come again. 2. Something which, when resisted, gives happiness and which, when yielded to, gives greater happiness. 3. One can resist everything but temptation.

See bachelor[8]; chastity[1]; yield.

Ten Commandments. 1. Wonderful laws in more ways than one. 2. Man is an able creature who has made millions of laws, but he hasn't yet improved on the Ten Commandments.

See commandment.

tenderfoot. A person who gets that way by always being in hot water.

tennis. Tennis professionals are usually satisfied with net profits.

term. See poetry[3]; self-made; spanking[2]; speaker: speaking terms.

termite. People who live in wooden houses shouldn't throw termites.

terrible. It is a terrible thing for a man to find out suddenly that all his life he has been speaking nothing but the truth.

See album: family album[1]; conscience[7].

test. See examination; fame: test of fame; mosquito: smart mosquito; friendship[4].

mental test. Most of our troubles would have been averted if the Constitution had provided for mental tests for congressional candidates.

Texas. Miles and miles of miles and miles.

text. See minister.

thanks. Some writers receive payment for their work; others receive thanks.

See producer: movie producer.

Thanksgiving. 1. It would often be much more enjoyed if it came before election. 2. Thanksgiving is fine; it's the recovering afterwards that's painful. 3. The Puritans celebrated it because they were saved from the Indians, and we celebrate it because we are saved from the Puritans.

theater. 1. Nothing risqué, nothing gained. 2. Those who want the theater purer never patronize it.

See critic: drama critic; encore[1]; man: man higher up; usher.

theory. A funny little thing that doesn't work unless you do.

See idea: theoretical ideas; relativity.

  beautiful theory. It's no crime to murder a beautiful theory by a gang of brutal facts.

thermometer. 1. A short glass tube that regulates the weather, and usually does a poor job. 2. The trouble with it is that it can't read the weather forecasts. 3. It should be bought in winter because it is much higher in summer.

See degree[2].

thick. 1. There is nothing more boring than sitting up with a thick friend. 2. Autos are becoming thicker, and so are drivers.

See conversation: thin conversation; dimension; molasses; mud.

thief. It takes a thief to catch a thief, and a jury to let him go.

See congressman: crooked congressmen; honor; policeman; spoils.

  car thieves. They have put many a man on his feet.

thigh. In bathing suits, the thigh's the limit.

thin. See fast[2]; molasses.

thing. See good[1]; hash[2]; prosperity[1]; shopworn; talk: talk about[3].

  little things. See teacher: kindergarten teacher; tell[5]; theory.

think. 1. As a man thinketh, so is she. 2. You are what you think, and not what you think you are. 3. The more you think of some people, the less you think of them. 4. Husbands and wives usually think alike, but the wife always has the first think.

5. If you can't make a man think as you do, make him do as you think.   6. When you think little of some person, say as little as you think.   7. The best way to think fast on your feet is to be a pedestrian.

See breeding: good breeding; college[4]; Congress[6]; egotist[4]; knit: knitting; love[11]; pipe; prude[2]; public opinion[1]; sleep[6]; story; tack; wise[1], wise man[4]; world[1].

thinking people.   They are never herd thinking.

thirsty.   See drinking[3]; girl[5]; straw.

thirteen.   1. An unlucky number if you only have dinner enough for twelve.   2. It's bad luck to have thirteen people seated at the table, especially if you're paying for the drinks.

thirty.   1. A nice age for a woman, especially if she happens to be forty.   2. The woman who declares she won't marry till she's thirty, usually remains thirty till she's married.

See save[1]; time[5]; women[4].

thought.   1. When some people are not engaged in thought, they are employed in recovering from its effects.   2. Most people who are lost in thought are lost because they are strangers there.

See coma; conclusion; forty-five; language[1]; marry: married couple; read: reading[1]; speech: after-dinner speeches[1]; wit[1].

second thoughts.   Second thoughts are best only when they arrive on time.

See afterthought.

train of thought.   Usually a string of empties.

threaten.   When a woman threatens to leave her husband, it's pretty tough for him, unless he gets it in writing.

three.   The man who wants a girl who is good, clever and beautiful, doesn't want one; he wants three.

See bridge[3]; chowder; company[1]; kiss[8].

thrift.   A wonderful virtue, especially in an ancestor.

See installment[3].

thrifty man.   One who makes good use of old razor blades; he shaves with them.

thrill.   See miss[1].

throat.   Many a man, when offered a drink, turns it down—his throat.

See gag; sugar[2]; tongue: fool's tongue.

throw.   Let him among us who runs the fastest throw the first stone.

See apartment[1]; ground; house: glass houses[2]; wastebasket.
throw away. See boy[7]; file.

thumb. See hand[1]; hitchhiker; ring[2].

sore thumb. Many a man with a sore thumb hit the wrong nail.

ticket. The reason more people enjoy baseball than football is
that they don't need a college education to get tickets.

See green.

tickle. Many a girl is more than tickled when her boyfriend
calls.

See pet: petting[1].

tide. See driver: woman driver[5]; moon; time[5]; wait[3, 4].

tie. See bald; censor[6]; college: college boy[1]; hitch; matrimony[4],
matrimonial bureau; moon; race; remember.

Christmas ties. 1. Nowadays the marriage ties are given about
as much respect as the Christmas ties. 2. When a man starts
wearing his Christmas ties, business must be really bad.

home ties. When a person becomes a nudist, he has to discard
everything, even home ties.

tiger. A tiger eating man must be a man-eating tiger.

tight. 1. The tighter a man, the looser his tongue. 2. It's easier
to sit tight than to walk tight.

See accident: auto accidents[1]; censor[8]; circulation; fiddle;
friend: close friend; habit: loose habits; intoxicate: intoxicated
woman; loose; screw; skirt: modern skirts[2]; tippler.

timber. See wood; tree.

presidential timber. 1. Mostly bark. 2. About the only thing
a man needs in order to become presidential timber is the
ability to plank down.

time. 1. The only money that cannot be counterfeited. 2. The
champion flyer of them all. 3. Time wounds all heels. 4. If
you want to kill time, try working it to death. 5. Time and tide
wait for no man, but time always stands still for a woman of
thirty.

See currency: confederate currency; curve[1]; dear; deposit[2]; depression[2]; driver: woman driver[5]; hearse[1]; humor: radio
humor; pass; punctuality[1]; railroad: railroad crossing[2]; statistician[5]; thought: second thoughts; wait[3, 4]; waste[1]; wrinkle[1];
young[2].

flight of time. It is urged on by the spur of the moment.

good time. Time tells on a woman, especially a good time.

See age: middle age[4]; cork; depression[3]; reformer[8].

on time. 1. If you're there before it's over, you're on time. 2. The man who is always on time wastes a lot of time waiting for other people. 3. The person who never does anything on time will buy that way.

See installment: installment plan; calendar[3]; wait[1].

times. These trying times are the good old days we'll be longing for a few years from now.

See collection: collection plate; compliment[3]; prosperous; ring: wedding ring[1].

time-saver. Love at first sight.

tiny. When the modern girl sews tiny garments, they're her own.

tip. The wages we pay other people's hired help.

See restaurant[3].

tippler. One who would rather be tight than President.

tire. See accident: auto accidents[1]; people: tiresome people; puncture; speak.

old tire. One that's treadbare.

tired. See mouth[1]; vacation[1].

title. See movie: movie titles; Mrs.; rear admiral; vice-president[2].

toast. The kind of girl men toast is the kind of girl women roast.

See zwieback.

tobacco. 1. A plant found in many Southern states and in some cigarettes. 2. A nauseating plant consumed by only two creatures: a large green worm and man; the worm doesn't know any better.

See ash tray; grasshopper.

tobacco habit. If you really want to cure yourself of this, marry a woman who objects to smoking.

today. 1. Today is the tomorrow you worried about yesterday. 2. Never put off till tomorrow what you can do today; there may be a law against it by that time.

See doctor[1]; expert: military expert; hair[1]; radical[4]; work[6].

toes. The man who waits for things to turn up, usually finds that his toes do it first.

See dancer: toe dancer.

together. Misfortunes never come singly; marriages and deaths are always printed together.

See talebearer.

toil. See ring: engagement ring.

toilet. 1. A relief station. 2. A famous watering place.

tombstone. 1. A reminder of one who has been forgotten.
2. That which speaks well of a man when he is down.
See date[1]; Latin.

tomorrow. The best day to get married.
See collector[3]; doctor[1]; expert: military expert; hair[1]; radical[4];
today; work[6].

tone. See ring[3].

tongue. 1. It runs fastest when the brain is in neutral. 2. Remember it's in a wet place and likely to slip. 3. One tongue is
enough for two women.
See beard; chatterbox; muscle; teeth: false teeth[1]; temper[5];
tight[1]; tooth: tooth cavity.

fool's tongue. It's always long enough to cut his own throat.

mother tongue. Money talks, and in most homes it speaks
the mother tongue.

salesman's tongue. The smoothest running thing about a car.

tongue-twister. A group of words and phrases which get your
tang tongueled up.

woman's tongue. 1. It never takes a holiday. 2. Some things
go without saying, but not a woman's tongue.

tonic. See love: Platonic love.

tonsils. If a man still has his appendix and his tonsils, the
chances are that he is a doctor.
See will: will power[1].

tooth. Uneasy is the tooth that wears a crown.
See dentist[2]; teeth; teethe.

infected tooth. Something that drives you to extraction.

tooth cavity. It always seems larger than it is, but then it's
natural for the tongue to exaggerate.

top. 1. There's always plenty of room at the top—for prices.
2. The only men who are sure of coming out on top are those
whose hair is falling out. 3. There's plenty of room at the top
because we all want to get in on the ground floor.
See aviation: aviation industry[2]; boost; bottom[2]; fight: prize
fighting[1, 2]; haircut: hair cutter; heart[2]; ladder; North Pole;
shot; skier; trousers; wig.

toper. The higher he is in the evening, the lower he feels in the morning.

tortoise. See light: traffic light[3].

touch. Everything some men touch turns to gold; everything others touch, they are forced to put back.

See miser[3]; pigskin[1]; relatives: poor relatives[1], rich relatives[1]; sable; scandal[2]; skin[2]; winter[4].

sense of touch. Love is blind; that's why lovers have a marvellous sense of touch.

tour. Travel makes a traveler, but a tour makes a raconteur.

all-expense tour. Perfectly named.

tourist. 1. Usually a motourist. 2. A person with a heavy tan on the left forearm.

See California: California climate; seasickness[4]; weather[2].

towel. The dirtier it is, the cleaner the face.

See wash.

guest towel. Something you look at and never use.

paper towel. Water, water everywhere and nothing but paper towels to dry your hands on.

town. See agriculturist; city; farmer[3]; reformer[8]; street: street cleaner[1]; tune[2].

small town. 1. Where everyone knows whose check is good. 2. A place where the Sunday newspaper can be lifted with one hand. 3. There isn't much to be seen in a small town but what you hear makes up for it.

See big.

trace. See genealogist; genealogy.

tracks. The fact that you see its tracks doesn't mean that a train has just passed.

See direction.

railroad tracks. You don't have to be superstitious to know that, when you are crossing railroad tracks, it's a bad sign to see a train coming.

trade. See competition[1, 2]; dollar[1]; gift[1]; telephone: telephone operator[2].

traffic. See pull-over; wing[2].

rotary traffic. The longest way round is the shortest way home.

traffic jam. Fewer accidents are caused by traffic jams than by pickled drivers.

See signal; whiz.

traffic light. See light: traffic light.

tragedy. There are two tragedies in life: one is not to get your heart's desire; the other is to get it.
See world[1].

train. 1. It smokes a lot and also choos. 2. The only sure way of catching a train is to miss the previous one.
See advantage[1]; air: air-condition; bus[1]; catch[3]; conscious[9]; race; tracks, railroad tracks.

train announcer. The most misunderstood man.

train pass. A form of transportation issued free to those most able to pay.

tramp. See exposure; oboe.

transfusion. See blood[1, 2].

transgressor. See find: find out[2]; getaway; syndicate.

translation. Everything suffers by translation except a bishop.

transplanting. Widows who cry easily are the first to marry again; there is nothing like wet weather for transplanting.

transportation. See train: train pass.

travel. 1. Travel broadens people and also flattens them. 2. When travel doesn't broaden the mind, it lengthens the conversation. 3. Travel broadens people, but not during the subway rush hours.
See Washington, D. C.[3]; tour.

ocean travel. Travel brings out all that is in one, especially ocean travel.

travel folder. A trip tease.

traveler. One who usually returns with brag and baggage.

tread. See tire: old tire; waffle; widow[5].

treasure. See marriage: model marriage.

treasury. See marriage: model marriage; tax: tax suggestions.

treat. See home[2]; stay[2].

treatment. See osteopath[2].

tree. 1. It will stand in the same place for a hundred years and then suddenly jump in front of a car. 2. It takes about five years for a tree to produce nuts; but this doesn't apply to a family tree.
See diamond[6]; sap[2, 3].

dogwood tree. You can always tell a dogwood tree by its bark.

family tree. See family: family tree.

petrified tree. The wind makes it rock.

trial. The legal expression for courting a second wife is moving for a new trial.

See acquit; living[2]; witness[1].

triangle. 1. It was invented by Euclid, tested by Don Juan, and perfected by scenario writers. 2. It often makes or breaks a marriage: it depends on whether the third member is a baby or another woman. 3. A triangle occurs in social circles when some of the members are not on the square.

See circle: family circle; Hollywood: Hollywood society; unfaithful.

domestic triangle. One part of the domestic triangle is generally a curved leg.

love triangle. It usually ends in a wrecktangle.

trick. See card: good card trick; purse[2].

trifle. Trifles light as air don't include cyclones.

See perfection.

trim. There's nobody like a barber when it comes to trimming people.

trip. See misstep; travel: travel folder.

triplets. The man whose wife presents him with triplets can hardly believe his own census.

See production; recount.

trite. Many a magazine has been trite and found wanted.

triumphant. Every bride who is married isn't happy—just triumphant.

trombonist. The only way he can succeed is by letting things slide.

trouble. 1. The easiest thing in the world to borrow. 2. Something that many people are looking for but no one wants. 3. The one thing you can borrow without references. 4. One of the things in which the supply always exceeds the demand. 5. There's no place like home, especially when you're looking for trouble. 6. No trouble is as bad as no trouble. 7. Troubles come in doubles; that's why marriage requires two people. 8. The trouble with most women is their trouble with most men. See brood[2]; chase[2]; clear; dark; drunkard[2]; marriage[6, 24]; miserable: miserable woman; ocean[1]; plenty; quick; radio: radio serial; shoes: tight shoes; success[3]; whiskey[1]; worry[1].

troublesome. The wife who dreams that she is married to a

millionaire is not nearly so troublesome as the wife who thinks
so when she's awake.

trousers. An outer garment, singular at the top and plural at
the bottom.

See example: shining example; molasses; nudist[2]; pants[1].

man's trousers. They are more important than his wife because there are a lot of places he can go without his wife.

trousseau. An outfit that covers a bride's torso.

See bride[2].

truck. You don't need road manners if you are driving a five-
ton truck.

truckdriver. One who believes in the principle that might
makes right of way.

true. Some married men are tried and true, and some are tried
because they are untrue.

See faithful; teeth; telephone: telephone operator[4]; wake:
wake up[1]; whisper[1]; witness: witness stand[1].

trumpet. It wouldn't do Gabriel much good to blow his trumpet
today unless he could get a national hookup.

trust. 1. Put not your trust in money but put your money in
trust. 2. A woman will trust her body and soul to a man whose
own mother wouldn't trust him with a nickel. 3. Men think
women cannot be trusted too far; women think men cannot
be trusted too near.

See age[8]; bust; everywhere; know[5].

trustee. See church[6].

truth. 1. It's merely a lazy expedient of the imagination.
2. Something even stranger than fish stories. 3. A commodity
so precious that we should economize in its use. 4. It's stranger
than fiction, but not so popular. 5. The truth will ouch.
6. Truth is a stranger to fiction. 7. Some people don't mind
the lies told about them; what worries them is the truth.
8. The pure and simple truth is rarely pure and never simple.
9. Truth crushed to earth will rise again, but so will a lie.

See album: family album[1]; ambiguity; cigar[1]; conference[3];
decent; diary; doctrine; doubt; exaggerate[2]; fiction[2]; friction;
history[7]; lawsuit[6]; liability; liar[4]; lie[1, 3, 8, 9]; popularity; publicity[5]; realize; recognize; skeptical; statistics[1]; story: off-color
story; stretch: stretching; tact[3]; terrible; unless; useless; well;
witness[1], witness stand[2].

naked truth. See compliment[2]; fact: bare facts.

truthful person. One who doesn't have to remember what he said.

truthful woman. One who never lies about anything except her age, her weight, and her husband's salary.

try. In this country we are willing to try anything once, except the crooked politicians.

See failure; prostitute; punishment: capital punishment[4]; true.

try on. 1. Men have less courage than women: imagine a man with ten cents in his pocket trying on ten suits of clothes. 2. After trying on a few dresses and a dozen hats, a woman begins to wish she had brought some money along.

tune. 1. Singers who can carry a tune generally carry it too far. 2. When a musician plays out of tune, he should play out of town.

See carry: carry out[2]; song: song writer[3, 5].

turkey. The bird that goes to the chopping block three weeks after the politicians.

See Greece.

turkey gobbler. An animal that would strut less if he could see into the future.

turn. 1. One good turn deserves applause. 2. A person learning how to drive has made considerable progress when the road begins to turn when he does.

See driver: woman driver[2, 6]; eventually; justice: wheels of justice; nurse[1]; page; pay: pay envelope; road[1]; signal; stomach[2]; story: radio story; touch; water[3].

turn in. See parents[2].

turn out. 1. Another thing that doesn't turn out as it should is the automobile just ahead of you. 2. Nowadays one never knows how a son is going to turn out, or when a daughter is going to turn in.

See family: large family; minority; nightmare; parents[2]; success: howling success; Wall Street[2].

turn up. See grindstone; toes; vegetarian.

turnover. See automobile: automobile industry; vocabulary: woman's vocabulary.

twenty. See save[1]; women[4]; youth[2].

twenty-five. The proper age for a woman; if she is not proper by that time, she never will be.

twice. See lightning; mathematics.

twins. 1. Insult added to injury. 2. The greatest incentive to industry, enterprise, and thrift. 3. The two best reasons for wanting a raise in salary. 4. What a man feels like when he's beside himself. 5. There are two things in the world for which we are never fully prepared, and they are—twins.

See apart; singly.

Siamese twins. The only persons who never have any trouble making both ends meet.

two. It takes two to make a quarrel, and the same number to get married.

See alimony[4]; bridge[3]; cheap[1]; chowder; company[1]; drum[2]; expensive[1]; golf[5]; hangover[1]; kiss[1, 3, 8, 18]; manufacturer: hat manufacturer; marriage[11, 13, 23]; talebearer; wrong.

typewriter. The secret of successful writing lies in striking the right keys on the typewriter.

noiseless typewriter. One who doesn't chew gum.

U

ugly. See fashion[4]; photographer.

ukulele. The missing link between music and noise.

See music: musical instrument.

umbrella. 1. The only thing some people put away for a rainy day. 2. Like medicine, it is usually taken after meals. 3. It rains alike on the just and unjust; on the just especially because the unjust have borrowed their umbrellas.

See bank[2]; loss.

umpire. 1. What a baseball player becomes after he loses his eyesight. 2. A man who is no jeweler, but a high authority on diamonds.

unattractive. See homely: homely girl.

unattractive woman. A woman to whom virtue comes easily.

uncanny. Those who want to can fruit find sugar prices uncanny.

Uncle Sam. The reason Uncle Sam wears a tall hat is that he can pass it around.

uncomfortable. Clothes make the man—uncomfortable.
See moral.

underhand. In running the government it's not the overhead that matters, it's the underhand.

understand. 1. The clever man tells a woman he understands her; the stupid one tries to prove it. 2. Men never love women whom they don't understand, and women never love men whom they do.
See argue[1]; critic[6]; egotist[3]; husband: misunderstood husband; level: level-headed man; movies[2]; originate; psychology; self-love; women[2, 6].

undertaker. 1. A man to whom health is not wealth. 2. No matter how busy he is, he can never bury himself in his work. 3. One whose price is stiffer than his customers.
See fighter: prize fighter; inter; mortician; politeness[2]; situation: grave situation.

underwear. Something that creeps up on you.
See lady[3]; lingerie; spats[2]; unmentionables.

undo. It takes only a second to wink the eye, but often a lifetime to undo it.

undress. See feet: big feet; house: glass houses; room: dressing room.

uneasy. Uneasy lies the head that tells a good many of them.
See tooth.

unexpected. The unexpected always happens when you least expect it.
See house[4]; sophistication.

unfaithful. When a woman's unfaithful, it's usually a triangle; when a man's unfaithful, it's usually a hexagon.

union. See chorus.

United States. See American: loyal American; dense; mortgage[1]; Spain; statistics[4]; Washington, D. C.[2].

universal. See fashion[1].

universe. See run[1].

unless. It's always the best policy to tell the truth, unless of course you're an exceptionally good liar.

unlucky. 1. It's unlucky to postpone a wedding, but not if you keep on doing it. 2. It's unlucky to walk under a ladder, unless there's a pretty girl on it.
See thirteen.

unmarried. Some men are men of few words; the rest are un-married.

  unmarried woman. She is not an old maid until she is in the prim of life.

  See maid: old maid; spinster.

unmelodious. Melodorous.

unmentionables. Ladies' underwear, most of which are no longer worn and the rest of which are mentioned everywhere. See mention.

unnecessary. When two men in a business always agree, one of them is unnecessary.

unpopular. See girl: unpopular girl.

unreasonable. God made woman beautiful that man might love her, and unreasonable that she might love man.

unselfish. See altruism[1].

unsettled. A term that covers a multitude of weather conditions.

untouchable. He who tries to borrow money soon discovers that all the untouchables don't live in India.

up. See aviation: aviation industry[1]; prejudice.

  up & down. 1. Only a person who is down can be up against it. 2. Many a man is down on something he is not up on. 3. A person is never down as long as he is up to something. See elevator: elevator man; living: cost of living[5]; seasickness[3].

  upside down. See depth.

upkeep. In brassieres, it's not the cost but the upkeep.

  See air: castles in the air[1]; downfall; outcome.

uplift. Too much of the uplift in this country is confined to noses.

  uplift movement. The most common one in America is that which is done with the automobile jack.

upset. Things that used to upset the old-fashioned girl, simply set up the modern one.

use. Married couples often have words, but only the wife uses them.

  See excuse; friend[4]; hanging; leisure; reformer[6]; towel: guest towel; truth[3].

useless. The truth and the news are never the same: one is useless if not whole, the other is useless if not broken.

  See pin[1]; resolution: good resolution; wrong[3].

usher. One who takes a leading part in the theater.

Utopia. A perfect state where every man has a dog but no dog has a flea.

See camper; road: road hog[2].

V

vacant. See mind: open mind[5].

vacation. 1. A system whereby the tired become more tired. 2. A long-awaited rest, except for the pocketbook. 3. The best place to spend your vacation is just inside your income. 4. Most people use this year's vacation to find out where to stay away from next year.

See Congress[3]; fall; fish[1]; oyster[2]; pleasure[2]; resort.

vacuum. See head: swelled head.

vacuum cleaner. See elephant[1].

vagabond. An irredeemable bond.

vague. Dreams are vague because you see them only when your eyes are shut.

See vogue.

value. If you want to know the value of money, try and borrow some.

See alimony[1]; antique[3]; college: college career; cynic[5]; fortune hunter; love[25]; price[4].

  face value. Everybody accepts a smile at its face value.

vanity. Our admiration of the wisdom of those who come to us for advice.

See fashion[3].

  extreme vanity. A parent trying year after year to make his child just like himself.

varnish. See culture.

vaseline. See millennium.

vegetable. An onion can make people cry, but there is no vegetable that can make them laugh.

See diet[2]; hash[1]; lettuce; meat[1]; peanut; weeds[2].

vegetarian. A man with carroty hair, reddish mustache, and a turn-up nose.

See diet[2]; widow: grass widow[1].

vegetarianism. A harmless practice, though it is apt to fill a man with wind and self-righteousness.

velocity. What a person puts a hot plate down with.

veneer. Some people have a veneer that comes off easily with a little alcohol.

ventilation. See cheese.

Venus. 1. She must have been beautiful but dumb because she wasn't all there. 2. She must have been an ideal wife; she had no hands to go through her husband's pockets.

verse. See poet[1]; poetry; prose; song: song writer[6].

free verse. 1. The triumph of mind over meter. 2. A publisher's conception of all kinds of poetry.

vice. 1. It's hard sometimes to choose between vice and advice. 2. There's no vice as bad as advice.

See cultivate; fishing[2]; maintain; tabloid[5]; vice versa[2].

vice-president. 1. Any good golf player. 2. The title given to a bank officer in place of a raise in salary.

See bank[8].

vice versa. 1. Versa vice. 2. He who hesitates is probably torn between vice and versa.

See car[8]; preventive; run: run down[2]; tabloid[8]; wink[2].

victim. When a man makes a mistake in his first marriage, the victim is his second wife.

view. The only sure way to change a woman's views is to agree with her.

See album: photograph album; interview; prison[2]; suit: bathing suit[8].

violation. See graft.

violator. A man who plays the viola.

violin. Many a violin sounds as though its strings were still in the cat.

violinist. One who is always up to his chin in music.

virtue. 1. It is praised and starves. 2. It has more admirers than followers. 3. A quality often associated with intelligence, but rarely with beauty.

See Broadway[4]; defend; friend[2]; thrift; unattractive: unattractive woman.

old virtues. The only antiques that are not highly prized.

virtuous. The reason the poor are so virtuous is because money is the root of all evil.

See eccentric[2]; goodness.

virtuous man. There are nine hundred and ninety-nine patrons of virtue to one virtuous man.

vision. What people think you have when you guess correctly.

See girl[2]; visionary.

visionary. We call loudly for a man of vision, and when we get one we call him a visionary.

visit. Visit, that ye be not visited.

See commuter[2]; mother-in-law[3]; stockbroker.

vitamin. Some day man may be wise enough to get the vitamins that wild animals get by eating what they like.

See conceit: conceited man.

vocabulary. The radio has added thousands of words to our vocabulary, not counting those used when it gets out of order.

See proposal[1]; public speaking[1].

large vocabulary. 1. Its advantage is that you can reject the big word and choose one you can spell. 2. Many a man has acquired a large vocabulary by marrying it.

woman's vocabulary. It may be small, but think of the turn-over.

vogue. The woman who is vogue on the outside is usually vague on the inside.

voice. 1. Singers make up in noise what they lack in voice. 2. Radio proves that you can't talk without a voice but you can sing without one. 3. When a woman lowers her voice, it's a sign she wants something; when she raises it, it's a sign she didn't get it.

See adolescence[2]; money: hush money[2]; positive; ring[3]; singer; tabloid[5]; telephone[3].

volume. See bankbook; orator[2].

vomit. Happy returns.

vote. It's sometimes stolen but more often paid for in cash.

See congressman[3]; minority; politics[8]; polls[1].

straw vote. It only shows which way the hot air blows.

voter. 1. Only half the voters vote, and generally the wrong half. 2. There are two kinds of voters: those who will vote for your candidate. and a lot of prejudiced fools.

See repeat[6].

vulgarity. The conduct of others.
See rudeness.

W

waffle. A batter cake with a non-skid tread.

wages. 1. Something that never meets high prices even when they are both going in the same direction. 2. The difference between wages and salary is that there is more money in wages. 3. Many girls are getting men's wages today, but then, they always have.
See depression[5]; labor: labor union; laborer; philanthropist[4]; raise[3]; tip.

> **living wage.** 1. Its definition depends on whether you are getting it or giving it. 2. It's easy to figure out a living wage for the other fellow to live on.

> **small wage.** Usually a weekly salary.

> **wage slave.** One who is lucky enough to have a job.

wagon. See harness[1].

waist. The more waist, the less speed.
See hug[1]; diet: reducing diet[1]; obesity; pound.

wait. 1. A woman's promise to be on time carries a lot of wait. 2. A woman is known by the company she keeps waiting. 3. Time and tide wait for no man, but a woman will. 4. Time and tide wait for no man, but a woman expects all three to wait for her. 5. Some wives don't wait for their husbands when they come home late; they go for them.
See driver: woman driver[5]; hearse[2]; marriage: before & after[5]; receivership; shopworn; speaker: after-dinner speaking; swamp; taxi[2]; time[5], on time[2]; toes; waiter[1].

waiter. 1. What finally comes to him who waits. 2. It's a good thing that life is not as serious as it seems to a waiter. 3. The only difference between the waiters in a restaurant is that some work there.
See restaurant[3].

waitress. 1. A man is old when he watches the food instead of the waitress. 2. The man who flirts with a waitress is probably playing for big steaks.

wake. See awake; dreams³; rise.

wake up. 1. If a man wants his dreams to come true, he must wake up. 2. Babies usually wake up in the wee wee hours of the morning. 3. Some people wake up and find themselves famous; others wake up and find themselves late.

See boxer; college: college graduate¹; famous; successful: successful man¹.

walk. See walking.

tightrope walker. He doesn't get that way from a balanced diet.

walk on air. With the skies full of planes these days, there's no advantage in walking on air.

walking. 1. A primitive method of locomotion achieved by putting one foot in front of the other. 2. It isn't a lost art: one must, by some means, get to the garage. 3. Some people walk to reduce; others are reduced to walking. 4. The man who never thought anything of walking ten miles a day now has a grandson who never thinks of it either.

See drug store³; duck²; ride: joy-rider; run⁴; seat; steps; tight².

wallet. No man is a hero to his wallet.

wallflower. One that usually goes to seed without being picked.

Wall Street. 1. A thoroughfare that begins in a graveyard and ends in a river. 2. A lot of good buys in Wall Street turn out to be farewells.

See goat¹; investor; janitor⁴; stock: stock market⁵.

Wall Street men. They make good farmers because they know how to water the stock and shear the sheep.

want. 1. What man wants: all he can get; what woman wants: all she can't get. 2. If you can't marry the girl you want, take the girl who wants you. 3. Some people don't know what they want, and won't rest till they get it. 4. When a woman really loves a man he can make her do anything she wants to do. 5. Some people would be happy if they had all the money they want; others would be happy if they had all the money their creditors want.

See advertise: advertising; feeling¹; get¹, ²; less¹; modern: modern girl²; prohibition: Prohibition Era²; remind²; result;

same[1]; scratch[2]; strong[1]; three; trite; voice[3]; wish: woman's wish; woman: woman's influence.

war. 1. Preparations, rations, reparations. 2. The worst thing about it is that it ruins conversation. 3. If war is hell, earth is no place for it. 4. War doesn't pay, but it makes everybody else pay.

See bleed; doldrums; hell: road to hell; pay: pay off; raid; shekels.

warden. 1. The most anxious man in a prison. 2. One who makes his living by his pen.

warm. See cash: cold cash[1, 2]; coat: fur coat; hell[3]; house[3]; religion[2].

wash. The best way to find out if your face is clean after washing, is to look at the towel.

See bald: bald-headed man[1]; love: puppy love[2]; water[3].

Washington, D. C. 1. The City Bureauful. 2. A territory hounded on all sides by the United States of America. 3. The only place where sound travels faster than light.

See air: hot air[1]; spring[6].

waste. 1. Money may be all right but you can certainly waste a lot of time making it. 2. Although four years at college are usually wasted, there are few better ways for a father to receive an education.

See time: on time[2].

wastebasket. Many a writer who throws his work into the wastebasket would save time by throwing himself into the wastebasket.

watch. The car to watch is the car behind the car in front of you.
See calendar[2]; clock[1]; conscience[6]; golf[8]; step-ins; waitress[1].

water. 1. Dog soup. 2. What some people drink—when they run out of beer. 3. A clear, colorless liquid which turns dark when you wash in it. 4. A thin substance applied to stocks with which to soak buyers. 5. The only way heavy drinkers can keep above water is by not drinking anything else. 6. There's no water in a permanent wave, nor in watered stock, but both of them have sunk many a man.

See beer; drunk; dry[1]; hotel[2]; island[1]; liquidate; liquor[4]; matrimony: sea of matrimony; meal: hearty meal; milk: spilt milk[1]; ocean[1]; opportunist[2]; rain[1]; sailor[1]; steam; suit: bathing suit[6]; swim: swimming pool; teetotaler[2]; tenderfoot; toilet[2]; towel: paper towel; Wall Street: Wall Street men.

still water. Still water runs deep, but how can it run if it's still?

water wagon. Most men on the water wagon feel better off.

waterfall. A drop of water.

See romance[3].

wave. See flag.

   crime wave. The only permanent wave that's permanent.

   See tabloid[4].

   permanent wave. 1. What many a sailor's ship of peace has been wrecked on. 2. Marriage is often the result of a wave of enthusiasm, but it is not a permanent wave.

   See crime; permanent; water[6].

Waves. The girls who go down to the sea in slips.

way. 1. Man has his will but woman has her way. 2. The girl who has a way with her generally has a man with her. 3. The only way to avoid quarreling with your wife is to let her go her way and you go hers.

See agree[1]; clever: clever woman; diplomacy[2]; divorce[9]; explorer: modern explorer; gangster; getaway; go: going concern; harmony: domestic harmony[2]; health[2]; invest; lawyer[9]; mule[6]; path: primrose path; pedestrian[14, 21]; recognize; rub; sports: good sport; stomach[3]; subway: subway contractor; Ten Commandments[1]; traffic: rotary traffic; will.

   one-way. A woman is generally a one-way person—her way.

   See pennypincher.

   right of way. The pedestrian always has the right of way—in an ambulance.

   See driver: woman driver[7]; provision; truck: truckdriver.

weak. 1. Five days of school make one weak. 2. A man is never so weak as when a pretty girl is telling him how strong he is.

See eyes: black eyes[1]; eyesight; flesh; housework[4]; temper[4]; whiskey[2]; wink[1].

wealth. 1. A burden on those who have it and a greater burden on those who haven't it. 2. Wealth is a curse—when the neighbors have it. 3. Wealth often brings with it the more abundant wife.

See happiness[3]; health[2]; philanthropist[3]; regain; rudeness; skin-flint; tax: income tax returns[2]; undertaker[1].

wealthy man. One who has so much money, he doesn't even know his son is in college.

wealthy people. Those who appreciate the blessings of poverty.

weapon. See rice; saxophone.

wear. 1. Modern girls wear less on the street than their grandmothers did in bed. 2. The woman who complains that she has nothing to wear usually needs several closets to keep it in.

See bargain[4]; clothes[1]; dress: house dress; mention; furs[2, 3, 4]; glass; laundress; line; mention; night: nightcap[2]; old: old fashioned girl[1]; show[1]; style: out of style; suit; tie: Christmas ties[2].

women's wear. 1. The thing women's wear leaves to the imagination is what makes it so expensive. 2. Women's wear was never funnier, if brevity is the soul of wit. 3. Women's wear shows a girl's good taste nowadays, and that isn't all.

See album: family album[3]; alligator.

weather. 1. Everybody talks about the weather but nobody does anything about it. 2. When the tourist says the weather is rotten, the native says it's unusual.

See eat[1]; miser[4]; molasses; raid; swear[4]; thermometer[1, 2]; transplanting; unsettled.

bad weather. The only thing it's good for is conversation.

beastly weather. When it rains cats and dogs.

fair weather. It's always fair weather when Floridians get together.

unusual weather. It's the usual thing.

weather bureau. About the only person who can make a living out of the guessing contests is the man in the weather bureau.

See rheumatism[1].

zero weather. So-called because it's so cold.

wedding. 1. About all that is necessary for divorce nowadays. 2. A funeral where you smell your own flowers. 3. A ceremony in which a ring is put on the finger of the woman and through the nose of the man. 4. A trade in which the bride is generally given away and the groom is often sold. 5. A public confession of a strictly private intention.

See bride: beautiful bride; bridegroom[1, 4]; divorce[4]; house-warming[1]; morning; proof; retake; romance; unlucky[1].

wedding-dress. The mother who saved her wedding-dress for her daughter now has a daughter who saves her own wedding-dress for her next wedding.

wedding march. See marriage[22].

wedding ring. See ring: wedding ring.

weeds. 1. The quickest way to destroy them is to marry a widow. 2. The best way to tell them from the vegetables is to watch your neighbor's chickens. 3. The best way to distinguish between weeds and flowers is to cut them all down; those that come up again are weeds.

See widow: grass widow[2].

week. See pray; stay[1]; strong[2]; Sunday; wage: small wage.

weekend. It's easy to make both weekends meet.

See accident: auto accidents[4]; beauty: beauty parlor[1]; forecast; loaf[2].

weep. Laugh and the world laughs with you; weep and you spoil your make-up.

weigh. When a girl reduces, she's going out of her weigh to please some man.

See diet: reducing diet[3]; power: balance of power; scale: social scale; wish: woman's wish; word[2].

weight. 1. When a woman refuses to tell her weight, she probably weighs a hundred and plenty. 2. When a fat woman loses a lot of weight off her hips, it certainly is a weight off her mind.

See butcher; enlarge; silence[2]; truth: truthful woman.

weight control. Girth control.

welcome. 1. The only thing that can't be reconditioned. 2. The early bird catches the worm, and he is welcome to it.

well. Truth lies—at the bottom of a well.

See dermatology; end[1]; tombstone[2].

well-to-do. When a person is well-to-do he is usually hard to do.

West. 1. Where men are men and the women love it. 2. Where men are men and the plumbing is outside.

See sun.

wet. See talk: dry talker; tongue[2]; transplanting.

whale. Jonah's experience with it proves that you can't keep a good man down.

baby whale. Just a young squirt.

wheel. The part of the car which causes the most accidents is the nut that holds the wheel.

See accident: auto accidents[2]; driver: backseat driver[2]; driving[5].

when. Most of us know how to say nothing but few of us know when.

where. To get anywhere, strike out for somewhere, or you'll get nowhere.

whip. Teachers should not whip their pupils to make them smart.

whiskey. 1. Trouble put up in liquid form. 2. A great drink if you don't weaken—it. 3. The only enemy man has succeeded in really loving. 4. It kills more people than bullets—because bullets don't drink. 5. It kills germs, but how can you get them to drink it? 6. The thing that best exemplifies the Bourbon spirit.

See headache[1]; skeleton: skeleton in the closet[1].

whisper. 1. Many a true word is spoken in jest—a whisper. 2. The whisper of a beautiful woman can be heard further than the loudest call of duty.

See aloud; heart: faint heart; price: high prices.

whistle. See cop: traffic cop.

white. 1. In the hands of the painter or lawyer, white becomes black. 2. Less than a third of the world's population is white, and less than a third of these act that way.

See blackmail; bleed; colorful; optimist[1]; servant[2]; yellow.

Whittier, John Greenleaf. Many a wit is not a whit wittier than Whittier.

whiz. You know you're in a traffic jam when you sit in your car and watch the pedestrians whiz by.

whole. See bread; loafer; partial; useless.

whoopee. All jack and no work makes whoopee.

wicked. If epitaphs were to be believed, no wicked person ever dies.

wide. See fat: fat man; will: willful woman.

widow. 1. A dangerous animal to be at large. 2. There are two types: the bereaved and the relieved. 3. One who finds it easy to marry again because dead men tell no tales. 4. A widow and her money are soon married. 5. Widows rush in where old maids fear to tread. 6. Some are born widows, some achieve widows, while others have widows thrust upon them.

See amiss; husband: second husband[1]; insurance: life insurance[1]; marriage[25]; property; transplanting; weeds[1].

grass widow. 1. The wife of a dead vegetarian. 2. One who is often in clover but seldom in weeds.

little widow. A little widow is a dangerous thing.

wealthy widows. The only second-hand goods that sell at first-rate prices.

widower. The only man who has an angel for a wife.

See freethinker.

wife. 1. The bitter half. 2. Sometimes spelled "yph." 3. A man's booin' companion. 4. A continual buzzing in a man's ear. 5. The most common impediment in a man's speech. 6. Merely another kind of disease: easy to get, and hard to get rid of. 7. A young man's mistress, a companion for middle age, and an old man's nurse. 8. Every man should have one, preferably his own. 9. What every wife wants to know: how the other half lives. 10. People say you mustn't love your friend's wife, but how are you to love your enemy's wife?

NOTE: This word has not been cross-referenced because it occurs very often in this dictionary.

clever wife. One who gets around her husband by hugging him.

See find: find out[1].

first wife. See deserve.

indulgent wife. One who lets her husband indulge.

modern wife. One who tries to love, honor, and display.

See back[2]; darn[2]; homemaker.

obedient wife. One who obeys her husband when he tells her to do as she pleases.

old-fashioned wife. See back[2]; darn[2].

peevish wife. One who whines her husband around her little finger.

second wife. See laziness[2]; marry: unhappy married man; trial; victim.

small wives. Wise men marry small wives; of all evils, choose the least.

wig. A convertible top.

wild. See life: wild life; vitamin; zoo, zoological garden.

wild oats. The man who sows his wild oats should pray for a crop failure.

will. 1. A dead giveaway. 2. Where there's a will, there's a lawsuit. 3. Where there's a will, there's a way—for the lawyer. 4. Where there's a will, there's a way to break it. 5. Where there's a will, there's a way; but where there are many wills, there's no way.

See dissatisfy; executor; lawyer[9], persistent lawyer; legacy; obstinacy; way[1].

willful woman. One who is all will and a yard wide.

will power. 1. The continued possession of your tonsils. 2. The ability to stop after eating one salted peanut. 3. A man with will power is no match for a woman with wile power. 4. Children have plenty of will power, but even more won't power.

See conscience: conscience-stricken people; diet: reducing diet[1].

willing. A woman forgives the man who kisses without consent, but never the man who lacks the courage to kiss when she is willing.

See flesh.

willing people. The world is full of willing people: some willing to work, the rest willing to let them.

win. See run[4]; side: winning side; stock.

wind. 1. Air in a hurry. 2. Straws show which way the wind blows, and knees show when the wind blows.

See cyclone; kite; run[2]; salesman[1]; spring[6]; vegetarianism; winter[1].

ill wind. The breath of scandal.

See saxophone[1, 3, 5]; knee[2]; scandal[1].

windbag. A person who talks so much, you get hoarse listening to him.

window. See glacier; road[3]; stork[3].

bay window. Not every man with a bay window has an outstanding personality.

Pullman window. See Pullman: Pullman window.

window demonstrator. People who live in glass houses have children who turn out to be window demonstrators.

wine. Look not at the wine when it is red; get busy and drink it.

See grape; teetotaler[2].

wing. 1. Birds on the wing are possible only because of the wings on the birds. 2. What pedestrians need more than traffic rules are wings, and sometimes they get them.

See angel[4]; pedestrian[20].

wink. 1. A girl is as strong as her weakest wink. 2. It's better for a man to get something in his eye first and then wink, then vice versa.

See undo.

winter. 1. The season that's so cold that even the wind howls about it. 2. The season when you keep the house as hot as it was in the summer when you complained about it. 3. People who go to Florida for the winter will find no winter there. 4. The first real touch of winter is the coal dealer's. 5. If you wish to have a short winter, have your note come due in the spring. 6. Why go South for the winter when you have lots of winter where you are?

See climate: temperate climate; drawers[2]; fancy; furs[4]; hotel[2]; pride[3]; thermometer[3].

wire. See electrician; professor[1].

live wire. A person or thing that's never down long.

See connection.

wisdom. 1. Knowing when to appear ignorant. 2. Common sense in an uncommon degree. 3. Knowing when to speak your mind and when to mind your speech. 4. Knowing how to keep folks from finding out what a fool you are.

See dumb; vanity.

wise. Some men wish they were as wise as they think their wives think they are.

See advice[4]; college[5]; father: wise father; fatherland; give: give in; otherwise; stop[1]; superfluous.

wise man. 1. One who has an open mind and a closed mouth. 2. One who noes a lot. 3. A person who, when he has nothing to say, says it. 4. A wise man thinks all he says, while a fool says all he thinks.

See manners; run[1].

worldly-wise man. One who philosophizes about pretty women, but never in their presence.

wisecrack. See crack; wit: half-wit[1].

wish. The modern woman doesn't want a man who will satisfy her smallest wish; what she wants is a man who will satisfy her biggest ones.

woman's wish. To be weighed and found wanting.

wishbone. A man will sometimes devote all his life to the development of his wishbone.

See ambition[2].

wit. 1. The man who says what you would have said if you had thought of it. 2. If you have wit, show it. 3. The fellow who thinks he's a wit is usually half right.

See clever: clever man; levity; rudeness; sense[1]; wear: women's wear[2]; Whittier.

> **half-wit.** 1. A person who spends half his time thinking up wisecracks. 2. If some people had a little more sense they'd be half-wits.
>
> See half: better half[2]; humor: wholesome humor.

witness. 1. Witnesses who testify at trials are full of the truth because they let none of it out. 2. You never know how much a man can't remember until he is called as a witness.

See circumstance; statistics[3].

> **witness stand.** 1. Half the lies told on the witness stand are not true. 2. People on the witness stand have a great reverence for truth, for they always keep a respectful distance from it.

wizard. The man who saves money nowadays isn't a miser; he's a wizard.

wolf. See mink; opportunist[1]; stork[3].

woman. 1. The animal that's most attached to man. 2. Something a man can't get along with or without. 3. A person who hates the person who gets the man she discarded. 4. The female sex and the nuder gender. 5. The contrary sex. 6. A woman is like a gun; don't fool with it. 7. Woman, generally speaking, is generally speaking. 8. Woman needs no eulogy; she speaks for herself. 9. A woman is still a bone and a hank of hair but the rag is fast disappearing. 10. Woman may not be much, but she is the best other sex we have. 11. Woman may be taken for granted, but she never goes without saying. 12. Woman would be more charming if one could fall into her arms without falling into her hands.

See under different entries according to type. For example, see cat: catty woman; chastity: chaste woman; etc.

woman's influence. Woman's influence is powerful, especially when she wants something.

woman's place. Woman's place is in the tabloids.

woman's sphere. It's this one on which we live.

women. 1. Noted for untold ages. 2. Women are made to be loved, not to be understood. 3. Women are like money; keep them busy or they lose interest. 4. Women are attractive at twenty, attentive at thirty, and adhesive at forty. 5. Women love men not because they are men but because they are not women. 6. No man really understands women, no matter how young he is.

NOTE: This word has not been cross-referenced because it occurs very often in this dictionary.

women's wear. See wear: women's wear.

wonder. See hussy.

wonderful. See conscience[7].

woo. The man who woos a woman woos woe.

wood. Some antique hunters seek the real stuff in aged wood; others seek the real stuff aged in wood.

See athlete; bury: burial ground; termite.

wool. 1. When the wool is pulled over his eyes, a man is usually fleeced afterwards. 2. Many a man, who has cast sheep's eyes at a pretty girl, has had the wool pulled over them afterwards. See cotton[1]; sheepish.

word. 1. Something you must keep after giving it to another. 2. Words should be weighed, not counted.

See barber[3]; bond; businessman: ethical businessman; coolness; crossword puzzle; definition; dictionary; economist[5]; edgewise; flail; guess[1]; hardship; homer[2]; lawyer[2]; oration; preposition; prude[3]; realtor; sharp; speaker: halting speaker; speech: after-dinner speeches[1]; stutter; sufficient; superfluous; synonym; talk[2]; telegram[1]; tongue: tongue-twister; use; vocabulary, large vocabulary[1]; whisper[1]; writer[2]; yes[3].

appropriate words. Appropriate words are usually appropriated.

few words. 1. The man of few words generally keeps them mighty busy. 2. The man of few words is probably married to the woman of a few million. 3. The man of few words usually takes several hours to tell you he is a man of few words.

See begrudge; husband[1]; mumble; object; often[2]; speaker:
after-dinner speaker[1]; unmarried.

last word. See apologize; dictionary; echo[2]; love[7]; yes[2].

work. 1. An unpopular way of earning money. 2. The curse of
the drinking classes. 3. All work and no play makes Jack a
dead one. 4. Many hands make light of work. 5. Some people
like work so much, they can sit and look at it for hours. 6. Some
men do their best work today and forget about it, while others
promise to do their best work tomorrow and forget about it.
NOTE: This word has not been cross-referenced because it occurs
very often in this dictionary.

worker. See laborer.

fellow worker. Girls who are neither fellows nor workers may
still be fellow workers.

steady worker. He should not be too steady or he'll become
motionless.

workman. See laborer; scab.

world. 1. A comedy to those who think and a tragedy to those
who feel. 2. It is hard to tell what or when the world is coming
to. 3. The world which took only six days to make will probably take six thousand years to make out.
See alcohol[1]; bad[1]; bunk; cemetery[2]; divide; expression; gigolo;
gossip[5]; grouch[1]; half; installment[2]; living[1]; North Pole; people; pessimist[14]; pocketbook; religion[1, 2]; revolution; riot; save[1];
smell[2].

next world. See next; spirit.

worm. 1. The early worm gets caught by the bird. 2. Finding a
worm in your apple is not so bad as finding only half a worm.
See bird: early bird[2, 3]; bookworm; catch[2]; caterpillar; fishing[3, 4];
man[10]; pay: pay envelope; tobacco[2]; welcome[2].

worry. 1. Interest we pay on trouble before it is due. 2. It's a
funny thing that when a man hasn't anything on earth to worry
about, he goes off and gets married.
See budget[2]; expression; generation, next generation; kill; level:
level-headed man; lose; raisin.

worse. 1. Everyone is as God made him, and often a good deal
worse. 2. When a woman takes a man for better or for worse,
she may find him much worse than she took him for.
See divorcee; family: family tree[1]; less[2]; life[4]; worry[2]; more:
more or less; talk: talk about[1]; tax: income tax[3].

worst. If a woman wants to hold a man, she has only to appeal to what is worst in him.

See half: better half[3]; optimist[4]; pessimist[12]; prude; religion[4].

worst people. The ones who give the best advice.

See free[1].

worth. Some people think they are worth a lot of money just because they have it.

See gold: gold digger[3]; lend[1]; liver; living: cost of living[4]; silence[2]; taxi: taxi fare.

wound. See scratch[1].

wrap. See girl: up-to-date girl.

    wrap up. See cellophane; clothes[5]; nudist[4]; package: small package.

wreck. There were fewer wrecks in the horse-and-buggy days because the driver didn't depend wholly on his own intelligence.

See wave: permanent wave[1].

wrestler. One who, like an army, appears to live mostly on his stomach.

wrinkle. 1. Time heals our scars but our wrinkles are more stubborn. 2. A woman is always interested in the latest wrinkle in cosmetics provided it isn't on her own face.

See complexion; raisin; stylist.

write. See check[1]; college: college student[1]; critic[2]; forger; history[5]; letter[2]; novel: great American novel; novelist; pen: fountain pen; right[1]; scratch: scratch pad; song: song hit; subscription; writing.

writer. 1. By the time a writer discovers he has no talent for literature, he is too successful to give it up. 2. The only way some writers can get a dollar a word is to talk back to the judge.

See anonymous; crazy; novel; philosopher[3]; plagiarist; research; story; thanks; wastebasket.

    pulp writer. One who can turn out a story every day on his tripewriter.

    woman writer. A person who used to be ashamed of her sin, but now she has it syndicated.

    writer's cramp. The most common diseases among writers are writer's cramp and swelled head.

writing. 1. There's money in writing, but it all depends on how generous are those to whom you write. 2. A man doesn't mind telling a girl he loves her so long as she doesn't ask him to put it in writing.

See agreement: gentleman's agreement; check: bad check; threaten; typewriter.

easy writing. It makes hard reading.

wrong. 1. Two wrongs don't make a right but they often make a riot. 2. Two wrongs don't make a right but they make a fight. 3. What's wrong with the poor is poverty; what's wrong with the rich is uselessness.

See apologize; bet[4]; conscience: liberty of conscience; forger; give: give in; go: going concern; human; king[3]; people; politics[12]; prophesy; puritan; redress; reformer[4]; right[3], divine right; science; side: two sides; success: ladder of success[1]; thumb: sore thumb; voter[1].

Y

Yank. See dentist[1].

yard. See rug; will: willful woman.

yawn. 1. One yawn makes two yawners. 2. It is always dullest before the yawn. 3. The only time a married man ever gets a chance to open his mouth is when he yawns.

See gadabout: tired gadabout.

year. 1. A period of three hundred and sixty-five disappointments. 2. Twenty years from now the modern girl will be five years older.

See calendar[3]; Christmas[6]; coal[2]; cold[4]; count[2]; installment: installment buying[4]; marriage: long marriage; Rip Van Winkle; vacation[4]; world[3].

formative years. Youth consists of the formative years; old age of the informative years.

lean years. A man hopes that his lean years are behind him; a woman hopes that hers are ahead.

leap year. 1. It takes four springs to make one. 2. Every year recently has been leap year for prices.

light-years. What a woman reckons her age by.

yearn. 1. A woman is never too old to yearn. 2. Before marriage a man yearns for a woman; after marriage the *y* is silent. See capacity.

yeast. If an alarm clock won't make you rise, try yeast.

yell. See baby[6]; birth: births, marriages, deaths[2]; college: college yell; debt: government debt; experience: school of experience[1]; statesman[3].

yellow. What white lies usually are.
See colorful; heart: heart of gold; silence[4].

yes. 1. The answer to any question the boss asks. 2. When a married man has the last word, it's usually *yes*. 3. A word to the wife is sufficient, when it's *yes*.
See acquiesce; diplomat[5]; lady[5]; quarrel[3]; quick.

yes man. 1. One who always stoops to concur. 2. A fellow who hangs around the man nobody noes.
See Hollywood[1].

yesterday. See radical[4]; today[1].

yield. The only way to get rid of temptation is to yield to it.
See temptation[2].

young. 1. The young are always ready to give to those who are older than themselves the full benefit of their inexperience. 2. Some women grow old before their time trying to look young after their time.
See bleach; die; enthusiasm; everything[1]; forty; longevity; old[3]; resolution; women[6].

young girl. Just a pretty baby who loves to go buy, buy.
See better; marriage[30].

young man. A sylph-conscious youth.
See advice: good advice; daughter[1, 2]; faithless; fancy; girl[1].

youth. 1. When youth calls to youth, it often gets the wrong number. 2. The first forty years of your life, but the first twenty of everybody else's. 3. A woman should hold on to her youth, but not when he's driving.
See billiards; carry: carry out[1]; nature: possessive nature; serious[1]; serve[2]; year: formative years; young: young man.

modern youth. A new gineration.

Z

zeal. A woman cherishes the memory of her first love-affair with the same zeal with which a man forgets his.

zebra. 1. A horse behind the bars. 2. A Sing Sing mule.

zero. It's nothing at all.

See weather : zero weather.

zoo. A place where people go but where wild animals are barred.

zoological garden. A place where wild animals grow.

zwieback. 1. Bready-made toast. 2. A toast that's never drunk.